The Structure of Urban Reform

The Structure of Urban Reform

Community Decision
Organizations in Stability
and Change

Roland L. Warren
Brandeis University

Stephen M. Rose
State University of New
York at Stony Brook

Ann F. Bergunder
Legal Aid Society of New York

Lexington Books
D.C. Heath and Company
Lexington, Massachusetts
Toronto   London

Library of Congress Cataloging in Publication Data

Warren, Roland Leslie, 1915-
    The structure of urban reform.

    1. Community development—United States—Case studies. 2. Communi-
ty power—Case studies. 3. Community development—Research—United
States. I. Rose, Stephen M., joint author. II. Bergunder, Ann F., joint
author. III. Title.
HN90.C6W35   309.2'62'0973   73-22155
ISBN 0-669-92809-7
ISBN 0-669-92817-8 (pbk.)

International Standard Book Number: 0-669-92809-7

Library of Congress Catalog Card Number: 73-22155

Contents

List of Figures

List of Tables

Preface

The research project from which this book emerges was a fairly large one, involving fifty-four organizations in nine cities. It was financed by a research grant from the National Institute of Mental Health. It could not have been carried forward without the assent of the leadership of the fifty-four organizations, who were asked to give large amounts of time and effort to supplying information and who had little to gain, personally, in exchange. At all times, the officials of the Model Cities Administration were helpful in response to requests for information, requests which fell especially heavily on Bernard Russell.

The original nine field research associates—and their successors, in some instances—constituted the channel through which most of the data were obtained. Our debt to the following people is especially great. Victor Carlson, Walter Cogswell, Frank Fitzgerald, Selma Goode, Thomas Hagerty, Patricia Hill, Andrew Lea, Martin Lowenthal, Barbara Marshall, Robert Macdonald, Jane Patterson, Margaret Sebastian, Sara Snelling, Charles Stinson, Lucy Thoma, Marymal Williams, and Robert Wintersmith.

In addition to the present authors, the professional research staff at the Heller School of Brandeis University included Joan Levin Ecklein and Richard H. Uhlig for part of the project period and J. Wayne Newton for all of it. Newton's contribution to the entire project was especially great.

Eleanor Fraser, Anne Freeman, Catherine Nicotera and Gertrude Rogers provided steady, patient, and at times heroic help in the secretarial work involved.

The project employed a number of research assistants, including several Brandeis University undergraduates, in data-processing tasks—a most felicitous benefit for the project and we hope for them. We are especially grateful to Deanna Brown, Duane Dale, David Epstein, Carl Frenning, Lee Friedman, Hilary Sue Green, Julie Gustafson, Sally Hines, David Horowitz, Benjamin Kerner, Nathan Kolodner, Carl Milofsky, Barbara Sproat, Daniel Zavin, and William Zumeta.

In addition, Gerald M. Eggert provided most of the statistical analysis, and Duane Dale and Julie Gustafson were especially helpful in organizing parts of the data.

Community Decision Organizations and Urban Reform

There is at the present time a fairly universal disenchantment with the results of the liberal reform efforts directed at the social problems of American cities in the 1960s and early 1970s. These largely discredited efforts are now being supplanted by numerous proposals for different methods of attacking urban problems. Suggestions for new directions of progress are voiced by different factions in the population with varying degrees of confidence: strengthen the power of local city government; develop greater power at the metropolitan regional level; provide computerized systems-analytical methods of simulating urban conditions and proposed changes in them; abolish the federal categorical grants system; eliminate the distracting role of citizen participation by the poor (or, variously, expand its role and make it more meaningful); develop further methods of comprehensive rational planning and of integrated service delivery—and so on through a long and growing list.

Is there no basis on which such proposals can be assessed in advance and their potentialities or lack of potentialities judged—at least in their major outlines? Or will the history of the past fifteen or so years be repeated, with only minor modifications to what has already been tried and found wanting?

This book, based on extensive research, describes some major aspects of the warp and woof of the structures and processes that urban reform attempts must acknowledge and somehow overcome if they are to be effective. These structures and processes are especially visible in connection with the development of the recent effort, through the Model Cities programs, to "rebuild or revitalize large slum and blighted areas" and "to improve the quality of urban life."

The book reveals the patterns of organizational response to this challenge. It seeks to provide the basis for an assessment not only of the Model Cities effort but of its underlying strategy of collaborative liberal reform as a means of addressing the social problems of the city. Thus, this book constitutes a wide-ranging analysis of the structure of urban reform, with important implications for future strategies of social change. It is based on extensive, systematic research, whose findings are integrated with the theoretical and policy-oriented development of the discourse. It focuses on the role played by community decision organizations.

In the current period of turmoil surrounding urban poverty and its associated social problems, two crucial sets of circumstances have been largely ignored. One is the key role played by community decision organizations in what is done or left undone about the social problems of the inner cities, and the striking

1

similarity of these organizations in city after city across the broad expanse of the American continent.

A limited number of the same key organizations in each city have extraordinary degrees of control over what goes on in their broad purviews. The dramatis personae of organizations playing these key roles is surprisingly similar as one moves from city to city. If anything is to be accomplished locally about the social problems of the cities, it must be done in, through, or around these key organizations. They are at the center of the dynamic confrontation between reform efforts and the strong forces that serve to maintain existing structures and procedures and thus to defeat reform.

The second circumstance is ignored largely because of unawareness of the key roles played by these community decision organizations. It is the fact—both surprising and perplexing—that we have very little systematic knowledge about these different types of community decision organizations. If such organizations were merely peripheral to the processes through which cities address their social problems, such lack of both sustained interest and systematic knowledge would be more understandable. But they are not peripheral to these processes. On the contrary, they dominate these processes and hence largely determine what the cities do, and how they do it, and what they do not do, in responding to the social problems that constitute the "urban crisis."

This book reports a study made of six such organizations in nine cities widely distributed geographically in the United States. It sheds light, we believe, on how these community decision organizations (CDOs) operate as individual organizations in their interaction with each other and with still other organizations. The data and analysis are focused on the way their action and interaction are related to efforts to improve the lot of low-income residents of the inner cities.

In this connection, special attention is given to the Model Cities program in these cities. It represented the culmination of a series of efforts, each building upon the previous one, to address the social problems of the inner city in a comprehensive way. As such, it pulled all of the CDOs of the study into its orbit in one way or another and thus provided an excellent context in which to study the behavior of these organizations in urban social reform efforts.

The CDOs studied intensively were the public school system administration, the urban renewal agency, the health and welfare council, the community action agency (poverty program), the Model Cities agency, and the mental health planning agency. The cities in which these organizations were studied were: Oakland, Denver, San Antonio, Detroit, Columbus, Atlanta, Newark, Boston, and Manchester, New Hampshire.

The Interorganizational Study Project, as it was called, was planned in 1965-66, funded in 1967, and continued through 1972. At its core were twenty-six months of intensive field work by nine half-time field researchers, one in each of the nine cities. The study concentrated on the interaction of the six community decision organizations in each city in connection with the developing Model Cities program in those cities but did not confine itself exclusively to Model Cities interaction. Data were gathered systematically using schedules and questionnaires of various types for different purposes. Less structured data were also gathered, through interviews, attendance at meetings, printed documents, etc. The primary units of analysis were the fifty-four community decision organizations, six in each of the nine cities. A second, subsidiary unit of analysis was comprised of 141 action episodes, in which one or another of the study's community decision organizations was engaged, and which were studied using a carefully conceived outline of variables. (The research methods employed are described in the Appendix.)

The Crucial Role of Community Decision Organizations

Community decision organizations (CDOs) are organizations legitimated for making decisions and/or taking action on behalf of the community in specific sectors of concern. Although the six CDOs singled out for intensive study differ from each other in several respects, they all conform to this definition. These six are not the only types of community decision organizations. Others such as the health department, the welfare department, even the chamber of commerce, might have been chosen for special study, since they also meet the criteria for CDOs.

In the above definition, *legitimation* refers to the acknowledgment by all pertinent actors of the right of these organizations to engage in such activity on behalf of the community. As we shall note, this right has come under challenge by disaffected citizens groups in recent years, but seldom has this challenge to legitimacy been such as to endanger the viability of any of the fifty-four community decision organizations of the present study. In two instances, such organizations have lost their viability and have ceased to exist; but in only one case was this attributable to a challenge to the organization's legitimacy, and that challenge came not from disaffected citizens groups but from the established agencies of government. This important question of legitimacy will receive extensive treatment later.

The central importance of community decision organizations in determining what does and does not take place within their respective fields of activity makes them, in a definite sense, gatekeepers for social change efforts in the direction of reform. In their legitimated decision making, they are expected to perform two principal functions: to develop and maintain some degree of order and coordination among the various organizations working within their respective fields; and to be instrumental in initiating desired changes in their fields and in adapting to changes encroaching on their fields from other sectors of activity. Our study in nine cities supports the assertion that insofar as people in communities are able deliberately to guide, alter, or modify the course of events at the community level, they do so largely in and through and at times "around" such community decision organizations.

Their importance can, of course, be challenged. It can be maintained that community decision organizations are merely epiphenomena, as it were—always acted upon by other forces, never a force in themselves. They may thus be thought to serve only the function of legitimating decisions already made elsewhere by members of various power hierarchies through whatever negotiating process may be involved. They do, indeed, serve this function of legitimating decisions, and in their own decision making they are influenced both directly and indirectly by informal networks of individuals with inordinate power. But they are more than merely agencies for rubber-stamping decisions made by others or simply providing an arena where such decision making by other parties may occur.

Their importance can also be challenged from the standpoint that purposive community-level decision making has little effect on the shape and course of events, that most community change stems rather from forces that are largely uncontrolled at the community level—whether they are uncontrollable or not. Examples are demographic changes such as the influx of blacks and Puerto Ricans into the centers of many large cities, the process of suburbanization, the changing structure of industrial location, the effects of state and federal programs. We agree that such developments far outweigh in importance those developments that occur through deliberate centralized community-level decision making, either by such bodies as the city council or the community decision organizations under consideration here. But if the magnitude of uncontrolled change has been neglected, so has that small but important area in which deliberate intent and influence are exercised; at least, there does not exist anything like an adequate understanding of the scope of possibility here or of the actual dynamics of what occurs—and what does not occur—in the various sectors of interest for which individual community decision organizations are legitimated to make decisions.

A third challenge comes from the dynamic of citizen action movements, particularly the growth of programs by or on behalf of various disadvantaged groups in recent years. A case can be made that insofar as deliberate change takes place, it does so largely as a result of pressure exerted on existing organizations of various types by such groups. We largely agree with this assertion, and there is considerable data from our own observations to confirm it. Yet, here again, to acknowledge that community decision organizations are influenced by various actors in their environment is not to deny their own autonomous status as powerful determiners of activities in their respective fields.

The community decision organizations in the present study have been subject to considerable pressure from citizens groups in recent years. Our findings suggest that much of the thrust of local citizen action programs must of necessity have one or another community decision organization as its target. But insofar as these CDOs have been the direct target of social action programs, their behavior has hardly been consistent with the notion that they are powerless vis-à-vis citizens organizations, or changeable with every pressure from citizens groups. If anything, their ability to resist such pressures or to absorb them with a minimum of change has been noted by many students of the community scene in recent years and is confirmed by our own observations.

Until comparatively recently, it was possible for community decision organizations to plan in relative disregard of each other. And it is still possible to hear an occasional community health and welfare council official make the truly presumptuous assertion that his organization is "the social planning arm" of the community—as though there were not at least a half dozen other CDOs with a function in the social planning field at the community level in cities of any but the smallest size. Today's conditions are characterized by the presence of many CDOs which engage in various amounts and kinds of interaction with each other.

One practical problem for such CDOs as they seek to fulfill their respective functions and come into interaction with each other is that the planning theory that presumably guides their behavior is all too frequently still based on the implicit assumption that there is a single "community interest" and that they represent it, and that there are no other competing CDOs that seek the "community interest" in a different way, for a different set of goals and priorities. An acknowledgment of this prevalent situation is much more apparent in the professional literature of city planners and of social work community organizers than it is in the literature of the studies made by social scientists either from the standpoint of community decision organizations or from the standpoint of interorganizational behavior. The present study seeks to remedy this deficiency.

In the analysis of this study's findings, great weight is placed upon the "institutionalized thought structure" which underlies prevalent approaches to the problems of urban poverty, and how it operates to shape reform efforts. But even at this early stage it is pertinent to indicate, if only parenthetically, one salient aspect of this patterned approach to reform. We refer to the simple circumstance that American cities are so structured that different sectors of interest and activity are fairly well demarcated, that they are demarcated in largely similar manner from city to city, and that these various sectors are "presided over," as it were, by remarkably similar organizations from city to city.

Thus, in the nine cities of the study, the field research associates who gathered data for the project had little difficulty delineating and locating the school system administration, the health and welfare council, the urban renewal agency, and so on. Such CDOs appear in substantially the same form—with minor variations, of course—in virtually all cities above a certain minimum size. Such regularity of appearance documents the essential similarity of the formal organizational structure of American communities, sector by sector. An exception to such patterned ubiquity was the mental health planning agencies. They represent a type of CDO that is gradually becoming more widespread, but is as yet far from universal. The Model Cities agencies were likewise somewhat short of universal, being limited as a matter of federal policy to approximately 150 cities of various sizes.

An outstanding trend in recent years, especially the past decade, has been the proliferation of such community decision organizations, many of which have arisen in accordance with federal legislation establishing grant-in-aid programs. Examples are urban renewal agencies, comprehensive health planning agencies, community action programs, housing authorities, Model Cities agencies, and so on.

As the community field has become more crowded with such CDOs, the overlapping nature of their domains has become increasingly apparent. Indeed, there appears to have been not only the addition of a number of new CDOs, but an expansion in the interests and activities of some of the older ones, so that urban renewal agencies, health and welfare councils, school systems, and other of the older type CDOs have expanded their functions to enter fields of activity in which they were not earlier active. In doing so, they have found that other CDOs as well have had an interest in a part of their field of operation. Hence, in carrying out their usual functions, community decision organizations are increasingly likely to encounter and interact with each other. They do so in ways that appear important both for their own respective operations and in terms of the aggregate "mix" of these endeavors as they mutually reinforce each other or conceivably cancel each other out.

Much recent literature on community-level decision making has dealt not with such formal organizations in this process, but rather with the role of community "power structures." The theoretical position that guided the present study has been that insofar as inordinately influential individuals are able to shape the course of community-level decision making, their decisions and wishes must usually be legitimated by the appropriate CDOs. The power exercised by such individuals is hence understandable in part or in whole in relation to their special access to, or influence on, the behavior of community decision organizations. The emphasis on CDOs instead of power structures, as a principal unit of analysis, does not imply a rejection of the findings and conclusions of community power structure studies, but simply a different—and we believe at least equally important—focus of investigation.

Special Characteristics of Community Decision Organizations

It may be helpful at this point to "locate" community decision organizations within the universe of possible types of organizations. In doing so, it is well to consider their characteristics as nonprofit organizations.

That community decision organizations are all of the nonprofit type does not stem from purely definitional considerations. Although the functions they are legitimated to perform are customarily given over to organizations not in the profit sector, it might conceivably be otherwise. But we can think of no examples of CDOs in the profit sector. A limiting case would be the commercial consulting firm brought in to plan a course of action in some sector of community interest. But this circumstance does not completely meet our definitional criterion, since such an organization is not legitimated to plan or act on behalf of the community in its own right, but rather only by being especially commissioned on an ad hoc basis to do so, either at the behest of the city council or more likely at the behest of one of the existing CDOs that does have such legitimation. Such CDOs, to repeat, appear invariably to be nonprofit organizations.

Nonprofit organizations may be either governmental or nongovernmental. Either type may meet the definitional criterion of a community decision organization. The selection of CDOs in the present study purposely included both types.

A number of important characteristics stem from the nonprofit nature of CDOs. It may seem tautological to observe that one of these is that such organizations are not constrained to "show a profit." Considerable literature points out that in many so-called profit organizations other motives in addition to that of maximizing profits are frequently operative and in some circumstances more powerful. Nevertheless, for most profit organizations the annual profit and loss statement is a constant reminder of a constraint that does not operate in the same way on nonprofit organizations. The parallel constraint in the nonprofit sector might be considered the norm of operating within one's budget, but even this norm is less directly applicable to many nonprofit organizations, including many types of community decision organizations. The "success" or failure of the operations of CDOs is generally judged on the basis of other considerations, in terms of some presumed net benefit to the community. One might say of them that they are expected to fulfill some of the requirements that Thorstein Veblen sought to impose on profit organizations as well: the consideration of success or failure in terms of net effects on society, rather than profit, a point that underlies his *Engineers and the Price System.*

When profit is not considered relevant and hence the profit criterion cannot be applied, it becomes more difficult to define precisely what an organization is seeking to accomplish and how well it is doing it, and for whom.[1] While this circumstance applies to all nonprofit organizations, it applies especially to CDOs in their functions as CDOs as distinguished from the functions of direct service agencies. A CDO may or may not be engaged in administering direct service to a population of clients, consumers, patients, etc. We have purposely included in our sample CDO types that do so and CDO types that do not. Where a CDO provides direct services, these services may be "counted" or otherwise assessed in various ways, more or less tangible. Although this is often difficult, it is still more difficult to assess the indirect planning and decision making and developmental functions performed by CDOs. This largely indeterminate aspect of community decision organizations, along with other indeterminate aspects that we shall consider explicitly, constitutes a two-sided coin. It may contribute to the CDO's adaptability and hence its viability. Its very diffuseness may constitute a spongelike buffer making it more difficult to deal it lethal impacts or even impacts that will necessitate major reorientation. Like Hamlet's father's ghost, it is, as the air, invulnerable.

To say that we have little systematic knowledge about the various types of community decision organizations and how they interact with each other is not to deny the existence or value of a long list of studies of what are here called community decision organizations. There are numerous intensive case studies of individual CDOs.[2] Likewise, many works treat a number of CDOs of a specific type, either by way of a group of case studies, an analytic design, or a more general treatment of the nature and problems of the CDO type.[3]

So far as we know, there is no report of a study of a number of CDOs of different types in their interaction in a specific city, or across a number of cities, and indeed it is only recently that such organizations have all been seen to be but subtypes of a particular kind of organization and given the name community decision organizations.[4]

The present study therefore explores systematically some of the similarities and differences within and between CDO types and also the modes of interaction in which CDOs engage each other at the local level. Our concern has been more than academic, in the antiseptic sense of detached scholarly curiosity. The primary concern has been with how the actions and interactions of community decision organizations are related to the pressing task of ameliorating living conditions in poverty areas of the nation's cities and in a long overdue improvement in distributive justice, especially as this affects ethnic minorities and the poor. The community decision organizations of the present study have a crucial role in this issue. They do not have the only role, nor can they of themselves induce and totally control the corresponding change processes. Many other actors on the local scene are also involved. Moreover, one can question—as we do in the final chapter—the extent to which locally based efforts, even though federally sponsored, can effectively cope with unemployment, chronic poverty, racial discrimination, and other related outputs from a national macrosystem that generally does fairly well by the majority of its population.

Granted all this, there still remains the question of what these key organizations, each assigned a sector of the community's concerns, are actually doing or not doing about addressing the poverty problem, both as individual organizations and in their aggregate interaction. This question is the central orientation of the present book.

The Model Cities Program

By a fortunate coincidence, at the very time these underlying considerations for the project were being thought through, a new federal program was being talked about in its prelegislation stages, a program that itself represented a deliberate attempt to seek coordination and through this make more effective the operations of a number of local agencies in relation to the general goal of improving the conditions of living in urban slum areas. This program later came to be called the "Model Cities" program. We had earlier considered whether it was advisable to study "interorganizational relationships" among CDOs as a sort of stable state, or whether and how they might better be studied in connection with interaction around specific kinds of development. The emerging Model Cities program presented the option of studying a similar type of deliberate and sustained effort across a number of cities, an effort much in line with the considerations outlined in the preceding pages, and one that by its very nature would be likely to occasion considerable tangible interaction among CDOs such as those we were proposing to study.

The Model Cities legislation was enacted in November 1966, being referred to at the time as Demonstration Cities. The decision to use the development of each city's Model Cities efforts as a focus for the study of CDO behavior had an influence on the specific formulation of the study design. It therefore is advisable to describe at this point the salient characteristics of the Model Cities program. The program is best introduced by quoting in full a statement of purpose from an early paragraph in the legislation, which is officially entitled "Demonstration Cities and Metropolitan Development Act of 1966":

The purposes of this title are to provide additional financial and technical assistance to enable cities of all sizes (with equal regard to the problems of small as well as large cities) to plan, develop, and carry out locally prepared and scheduled comprehensive city demonstration programs containing new and imaginative proposals to rebuild or revitalize large slum and blighted areas; to expand housing, job, and income opportunities; to reduce dependence on welfare payments; to improve educational facilities and programs; to combat disease and ill health; to reduce the incidence of crime and delinquency; to enhance recreational and cultural opportunities; to establish better access between home and jobs; and generally to improve living conditions for the people who live in such areas, and to accomplish these objectives through the most effective and economical concentration and coordination of Federal, State and local public and private efforts to improve the quality of urban life.

The inducement offered cities to apply competitively for admission to the program (a total of 150 localities were eventually admitted, a small proportion of the total of U.S. cities, and a small proportion even of the total number of applicants) was the availability of special federal funds and the likelihood that cities admitted to the program would enjoy certain other advantages—in terms of possible prior claims to certain federal grant-in-aid programs and similar desirable emoluments. The financial inducement took the form of funds for an initial period of planning of approximately a year, 80 percent of the cost of which was to be paid by the Model Cities Administration (part of the Department of Housing and Urban Development), and funds to pay 80 percent of the costs of administering the program, once approved, in addition to a complex system of supplemental funding.

In other words, cities would put together a package of programs. The local share that they would normally contribute to these programs, otherwise subsidized heavily by federal funds, would be reimbursed to the city in the form of supplemental funds. These supplemental funds in turn were to be incorporated into the Model Cities plan. Cities thus received funds that they otherwise would not have received, and these funds were not contingent on any particular grant-in-aid program, but could be used for tailor-made programs, especially appropriate for those local conditions for which federal funds were not specifically available.

The granting of such funds to the cities was premised on numerous standards, which covered a wide range of requirements. Among these, some were especially pertinent to the current study. Two such features are already apparent in the long paragraph quoted above. The programs were to be innovative, involving "new and imaginative proposals." Second, the fields of endeavor to be included were many, cutting across a broad spectrum of sectors of city life and including, incidentally, the domains of all of the community decision organizations of the present study. The program in each city must be "of sufficient magnitude to make a substantial impact on the physical and social problems." Hence, to *comprehensiveness* was added *concentration*, the notion not only that the approach to the city's problems must be broad and inclusive, but also that it must be sufficiently concentrated to make a substantial impact.

Another important requirement was "widespread citizen participation in the program." Likewise, there was explicit stipulation that "administrative machinery is available at the local level for carrying out the program on a consolidated and coordinated basis." And the paragraph quoted earlier sets as its purpose "to accomplish these objectives through the most effective and economical concentration and coordination of Federal, State, and local public and private efforts." Thus, the program was to be *comprehensive, concentrated*, and *coordinated*. With *citizen participation* added, these requirements constitute what we have come to designate in the tribal jargon of this study's project staff as "the four Cs."

With each additional requirement, the task before the Model Cities planners appears to be made more complex. To mention only a few of the many other requirements, the various projects and activities in the programs were to be "scheduled to be initiated within a reasonably short period of time." Fullest possible utilization should be made "of private initiative and enterprise." The program must be "consistent with comprehensive planning for the entire urban or metropolitan area." City demonstration agencies (as the local units for administering the program were officially called) were to be encouraged to apply high standards of design in their enhancement of neighborhoods, and to "make maximum possible use of new and improved technology and design, including cost reduction techniques." The planning should likewise make maximum possible use of costs-benefits analysis and should establish "programming systems designed to assure effective use of such analyses by city demonstration agencies and by other government bodies." In addition, there must be "maximum opportunities for employing residents of the area in all phases of the program, and enlarged opportunities for work and training."

While the antipoverty program of the Office of Economic Opportunity had made possible the designation of nongovernmental organizations as the local "community action agencies" of the program, the Model Cities program required that the local city demonstration agency be officially designated by the local governing body and that applications for financial assistance by the local demonstration agency be officially approved by the local governing body, a control that could not be fully delegated to any other body.

In order to implement the objective of concentration, the Model Cities Administration required that the demonstration area be limited to one that included no more than 10 percent of a city's population, except in the smaller cities.

A word of explanation is appropriate at this point regarding the terms *demonstration cities* and *model cities*. The legislation used the former designation exclusively. Later, however, the Johnson administration decided to employ "model cities" in all administrative implementation of the legislation. As the program expanded (for largely understandable political reasons) from one that would involve demonstration programs in a very small number of cities to one that eventually included 150 localities, the term *demonstration* became less appropriate. At that same time, during a period characterized by riots, protests, and "demonstrations" in a quite different sense of the word, it seemed highly desirable to utilize a different term. Since this is the current term (although the local agency is still referred to officially by the term used in the legislation—"city demonstration agency") we shall use the term *model cities* henceforth, rather than *demonstration cities*.

The procedure for cities was first to prepare a complex application for a "planning grant," which, if approved, would impel the city into the Model Cities program and provide it with funds to engage in an extended planning process, out of which would then come a five-year plan and a first-year action program based on a "Problem Analysis, Goals and Program Strategy Statement."

A first round of cities was chosen from those that had applied for a planning grant by the May 1, 1967 deadline. From these, sixty-three were approved, after months of delay, in November 1967. Their number eventually reached seventy-five. A second round of cities was approved in 1968. This second round likewise included seventy-five cities. Actually, the total of 150 included 140 cities, nine counties, and one Indian reservation. By the spring of 1971, three localities had dropped out of the program, leaving a total of 147.[5]

An extremely complex process of program review was set up at the regional and the federal level, and the planning procedure was subjected to standards regarding not only program content, but also the characteristics of the process, e.g., were all appropriate agencies consulted, were citizen participation requirements met? etc.

From this brief summary of the Model Cities program, it is apparent that it quite predictably involved all of the study's community decision organizations in one way or another. It represented an incremental attempt to improve the allocation of resources within and between the various sectors of community interest corresponding to different types of CDOs. It also provided additional resources that constituted a stimulus for a degree of coordination that might not otherwise have been expected to take place. There was in this stimulus not only the attraction of new financial resources for program development, but also a set of requirements for specific types of coordinative effort. And the overriding objective was stated clearly in the preamble: improving the quality of urban life.

This stimulus, coming down the vertical ladder, as it were, from Washington, was supplemented by a stimulus coming up the vertical ladder from the neighborhood which each city delineated as its model cities neighborhood (model neighborhood, demonstration cities neighborhood, demonstration neighborhood). The people of this neighborhood—which was required to be largely residential, and largely disadvantaged—were to have a share in the planning of the program, presumably in order that the program would be more effective, but also in relation to the *cui bono?* question: For whose benefit was this? For the city as a whole? For the model neighborhood residents? Did the two benefits always coincide? If not, how much weight would be given to the presumed interests of the entire city and how much to those of the model neighborhood residents?

Rather than leaving this problem to some central decision-making hierarchy to work out, the program was set up so that this particular kind of "mixing" would be worked out in a process of negotiation. The mix, in other words, was to be accomplished less through some abstract "rational planning" process than through an essentially political process of tug-and-haul between actors whose interests, (at least at times) could be expected to differ.

How this circumstance could be reconciled with a full utilization of costs-benefits analysis and "programming systems designed to assure effective use of such analyses" is but one of the many questions implicit in the multiplicity of goals and standards involved in the legislation itself, in its formal administrative implementation, and in the dramas it occasioned in 150 localities.

Interaction, Coordination, Innovation, Responsiveness

The perceptive reader will recognize the great, indeed somewhat presumptuous scope of the research reported here. Against the backdrop of the emerging Model Cities program, the objective has been to study six different types of CDOs in nine cities, observing their similarities and differences within any given CDO type as well as between CDO types. The intent has been to relate these similarities and differences to the problem of reform of social conditions in the poverty areas of American cities.

This ambitious objective required clarification in terms of just exactly what it was that was to be observed, recorded, analyzed, and reported; it also required rigorous delimitation, lest in trying to study everything at once, the investigation might produce a great mass of data of little use in systematic analysis.

Hence, the project staff did not study "everything," but rather focused on certain key topics and developed systematic analytical strategies for exploring those topics. These topics constitute separate chapters in the bulk of this book. Here, a brief introduction to them is given, with the reasons why they were chosen as the important foci of investigation.

Once the organizational structure of American cities is analyzed and the existence is noted of different fields or sectors of interest and activity, each "headed" by a community decision organization, the question naturally arises as to how these sectors are related to each other. Many observers have alluded to the alleged chaos in which such organizations as those of our study go their own individual ways more or less autonomously and without any overall coordination. Indeed, the Model Cities program was an attempt to encourage them to coordinate their efforts for a common purpose.

This study, therefore, reports the extent and kinds of *interaction* that takes place between and among the six CDOs chosen for study. So as to systematize the data on interaction, it has focused on the extent to which such interaction represented cooperation or conflict or an intermediate stage, which we call contest. Thus, we have developed a systematic way of finding the answer to such questions as these, presented here in the vernacular rather than in our own stilted research terms: To what extent do these community decision organizations cooperate with each other? On the other hand, to what extent are they at each other's throats? What do they cooperate and fight about? Under what circumstances do they cooperate? Or fight? What effect does their fighting or cooperating appear to have on what gets done by way of "improving the quality of urban life?"

The answers given here to such questions in part take the form of relatively general, matter-of-fact statements. In part they also take the form of the more careful and more stilted language and modes of analysis of social science, namely, the reporting of the relationship between variables, in the form of carefully worded, relatively abstract, but more or less rigorously tested hypotheses, or propositions. The findings regarding the extent and nature of interaction are given in Chapter 3.

In the area of urban affairs, a special kind of interaction is the object of considerable interest and activity: *coordination*. We have therefore abstracted out of the interaction data as much information as we could on the question of coordination. The importance of the subject needs no underlining from us. If anything, we feel that its importance is exaggerated in the current dialogue concerning urban reform, and unrealistic expectations are being built around it which will lead to disappointment and disillusion. Our findings, as well as our own interpretations, are reported in Chapter 4. The "problem" underlying the importance of coordination is a familiar one. Organizations often are found to be working at cross-purposes; they often do not pool their efforts. Yet urban problems are multifaceted. The problem of poverty and slum conditions calls for concerted efforts in fields such as those of the six CDOs of this study. To what extent are the efforts of these CDOs coordinated? How? What seems to "work" and what does not? To what extent did Model Cities, one of whose requirements was coordination, bring about increased coordination? In what sense? Indeed, what do we *mean* by coordination, and how do we recognize it when we see it? Is it always good? For whom?

Here again, the answers that can be given to such broad questions in a single study must be limited and sometimes given in the highly constrained confines of the relationship between two or more somewhat abstract variables. But Chapter 4 contains findings from the study that are at least relevant to the answers to all of these questions—some of them directly, others more indirectly.

The sixties and early seventies saw a growing disillusionment with the impact of programs that earlier were thought to have more potential effectiveness than they did. Consider, for example, the reaction to urban renewal, or to the quality of public education in poverty areas, or to the traditional social service agencies in the health and welfare field. Hence there has been growing interest in the need for *innovation*, in the need to find new ways of dealing with urban social problems, to develop programs, in the language of the Model Cities legislation of 1966, "containing new and imaginative proposals to rebuild or revitalize large slum and blighted areas." The Model Cities Administration required that cities that applied for grants should summarize explicitly the "innovative characteristics of the proposal."

The present study therefore sought to explore the extent to which *innovation* actually occurred in the fifty-four community decision organizations under study. To what extent did anything really new emerge in or from the activities of these CDOs during the twenty-six-month intensive study period? What kinds of innovation were developed? Which kinds of CDOs developed the most innovations? What was the response to these innovations? What seemed to be the reasons why some CDOs produced more innovations than others? How important were the innovations? And what potentiality did they have for making a tangible impact on urban poverty and slum living conditions? Chapter 5 reports the study's findings and our interpretation of these findings.

One other topic appeared to demand extended attention in a project studying the relation of community decision organizations to urban reform. This is the whole question of responsiveness to the needs and wishes of low-income citizens. The period studied was one in which the *responsiveness* issue loomed large and engendered extensive controversy, usually under the rubric of "citizen participation" or "neighborhood control," and in which extensive developments were taking place. How important were these developments? How did different types of CDOs behave in connection with the question of increasing their responsiveness to the needs and wishes of low-income people? Which CDOs showed the greatest responsiveness? Why? How important was such responsiveness, really? Did it really "make a difference?" in what respects?

Again, these questions had to be translated into researchable variables. Indeed, as in the case of innovation as well, the very notion of responsiveness had to be broken down into a number of types, in order that analysis would be meaningful and would address the important issues involved. But again, the findings, presented in Chapter 6, include partial answers, at least, to all of the above questions, as well as still others.

In considering interaction and coordination primarily from the standpoint of pairs of organizations, and in considering innovation and responsiveness primarily from the standpoint of individual organizations and CDO types, the methods of analysis employed may be such as to ignore or minimize the importance of the aggregate interaction of these organizations. One may neglect the major configurations of the forest by studying only individual trees.

In the case of the present study, we have found the general characteristics of the interorganizational field within which these CDOs act and interact to be of overriding importance in determining the nature of that individual interaction. Putting this another way, one does not understand adequately the nature of the cooperation and contest, or of the innovation and responsiveness, of these individual organizations unless one has an adequate understanding of the interorganizational context in which their behavior takes place.

It had originally been anticipated that questions regarding this more inclusive context would be treated after a consideration of the behavior of the individual organizations—and as a sort of aggregate treatment of this behavior in terms of the larger patterns it suggests. But the experience of the study and the data analysis have indicated to us that the reverse process is preferable. In this question of which comes first, the hen or the egg, we have concluded that it is more meaningful to delineate the interorganizational context and to consider and interpret the behavior of individual CDOs within it and as formulated by it, rather than to present a fragmented account of individual behaviors and try from these to "construct" a description of the interorganizational field.

All of this will become completely understandable only after both the nature of the interorganizational field and the specific behaviors of the CDOs are reported.

We begin, then, with the interorganizational field. As indicated in the Appendix, the characteristics and importance of the interorganizational field emerged from the extensive narrative data rather than from the numerous schedules and questionnaires employed. The narrative data helped provide some sense of what was actually going on in the flow of events, most of which was lost in the necessarily selective, limited, and fragmented data that went into the quantitative analysis. To repeat, these more quantitative findings appear to be either misleading or meaningless unless they are considered within the context of the nature and operation of the interorganizational field. It is therefore the logical place to begin the exposition.

2

The Interorganizational Field

By far the most important outcome of the research project reported here is the emergence of the interorganizational field as a crucial, indeed, an indispensable framework for understanding the behavior of individual community decision organizations. Whether or not the interorganizational field is of similar importance in the interaction of other types of organizations it is difficult to say, though we suspect that this may well be the case.

In this chapter, we describe the nature of the interorganizational field in the nine cities in which the interaction of these CDOs was studied. Since an important conclusion from the study is the overriding significance of this aggregate field in which the individual CDOs interact, we first address the distinction between the individual organizational level and the interorganizational field level in the analysis of data on the interaction of these CDOs.

The choice between the individual organizational level and the interorganizational field level as a focus for analysis constitutes a choice between alternative paradigms. As in other instances of paradigm selection or development, the choice of paradigm influences not only the theoretical context within which data are related to each other, but even the nature of what is to be considered data and what is not, what is to be considered important and what is to be considered peripheral. Scientific paradigms represent logically consistent ways of relating certain bodies of data to each other for purposes of explanation or prediction, but they are selective and do not accommodate equally well all of the data available. Hence, choice between paradigms is ultimately a question of judgment as to which alternative ways of selecting and analyzing and interpreting data appear most pertinent to the questions being addressed and most helpful in answering these questions.[1]

It is an oversimplification to think of the interorganizational field paradigm to be presented here as simply an "adding up" of the findings from the specific analytic propositions that were systematically tested. For although it helps explain these specific findings, it did not arise solely from them, but rather from the continued effort throughout the course of the project to grapple with the substance of the narrative data as well as the more quantified distributions of these organizations on the variables singled out for special attention. Without the narrative data, it is doubtful that it would have been possible to adduce a theoretical understanding of the interorganizational field as an explanatory framework, and many of the findings that are quite meaningful and understandable and important within this explanatory paradigm would have appeared quite

17

adventitious as well as unimportant in adding to an understanding of organizational interaction. We shall have more to say about this question in later chapters.

Alternative Paradigms of Interaction

The alternative is quite simple, although its implications are important and complex: Does one take as a primary basis for interpreting interorganizational behavior the individual organizations as units, adducing the nature of the interactional field from their aggregate characteristics and behavior? Or does one take as a point of explanatory departure the context of the interactional field, adducing the nature of the individual organizations and their characteristics and behavior from it?

Although both would seem equally appropriate, the overwhelming body of interorganizational studies has tended to take the former alternative, taking the individual organizations as the basic foundation for research, and either ignoring the structure of the interactional field or dealing with it superficially in terms of the presumed desirability of coordination. This was the analytic posture of the present study at its outset, even though some serious reservations accompanied this choice. But during the course of the study, the importance of the field itself pressed itself upon us as we tried to interpret the data we were gathering, and particularly as the narrative data gave us a sense of "what was actually going on" as the dynamics behind statistical findings.

Quite abstractly, each alternative paradigm has its own logical justification. Thus, the question naturally occurs: Can not both alternative paradigms be explored? The answer is yes, and that is precisely what we did. But are not both alternative paradigms equally valid? This question is more difficult to answer, since with Kuhn, we maintain that assertions can be validated only *within* a paradigm, and therefore: "When paradigms enter, as they must, into a debate about paradigm choice, their role is necessarily circular. Each group uses its own paradigm to argue in that paradigm's defense. . . . As in political revolutions, so in paradigm choice—there is no standard higher than the assent of the relevant community."[2]

Since our specific findings have more meaning, more intelligibility, when viewed and interpreted from the interorganizational field paradigm, we shall use it as the basis for the subsequent exposition. We remind the reader that we are alluding to the field in which the community decision organizations of this study interact with each other as well as with other actors. Their interaction with each other is characterized in some instances by cooperation, in others by varying degrees of contest.

Our data suggest that three characteristics of this interaction are important components of the interorganizational field situation in all the nine cities studied.

The first is that over a period of time, these CDOs have reached more or less routinized and mutually agreed upon notions of their respective *domains*. Their interaction takes the form of mutual individual adjustment to the new situations that arise. The mutual adjustments define and redefine the respective domains of these organizations. They are usually of a marginal nature in that insofar as they involve disputes, the disputes seldom strike at the core of the organizations' viability, nor do they pose a basic challenge to the legitimated claim of these organizations to endure and to carry out activities within their allotted functions, activities legitimated by the pertinent groups in the community.

The second is that *norms* have developed which govern the range of acceptable behavior by the respective CDOs in their interaction with each other and with other actors, norms not only of cooperative interaction where similar issue outcomes are sought, but also norms that govern those situations in which different and incompatible outcomes are desired by the respective organizations interacting on an issue. These norms in turn are supported by an underlying norm of "live and let live." As one CDO director put it: "We get into scraps with these other organizations, but we know that after the scrap, we are all still going to be around and are going to have to get along with each other and will need each other in certain situations."

Third, these norms are grounded in a basic consensus, a common *institutionalized thought structure*, to be described presently. The CDOs have their episodes of contest or cooperation, in other words, within a general consensus that what they are all trying to do, respectively, is important and desirable, and fits into a common frame of reference regarding the nature of social reality, of American society, of social problems, and of efforts at social change and human betterment. As a consequence, the interaction norms based on "live-and-let-live" reciprocity and on a common institutionalized thought structure set limits to any possible contest among them and at the same time virtually assure that their viability as organizations will not be impaired.

The Institutionalized Thought Structure

A consideration of the interorganizational field indicates the inadequacy of attempting to explain or understand organizational interaction simply as interaction among fragmented autonomous units which can be understood by examining a set of intraorganizational variables. Organizations, in other words, are not sui generis, but exist and take their form within an interorganizational context. By the same token the interorganizational fields that exist in these nine cities cannot be completely understood or even adequately understood solely in terms of the local social dynamics existing in each of the nine cities of the study. For these local interorganizational fields show remarkable similarity as one moves from city to city, among nine cities widely distributed on a number of important demographic characteristics, as these cities are. The similarities exist because these local contexts are all embodiments of an institutionalized thought structure characteristic of American society, a combination of ways of thinking about social problems and social change and ways of structuring local institutions.

Obviously, we are not the first to discover that institutional forms prevalent in the larger society find their respective embodiments in localities. But the relevance of this circumstance to the CDO interorganizational field level is important, and so we pursue it here.

The concept of institutionalized thought structure has roots both in the sociology of knowledge and in the sociological concept of social institutions, as these are applied to our data. The sociology of knowledge is primarily concerned with the relationship between the structure and content of knowledge and the existing social structure. Institutional analysis emphasizes the structuring of such major social functions as nurture, governance, socialization, and domestic activities, along with the social values that support these structures. What we are concerned with in the concept of institutionalized thought structure is the intricate interweaving or mutual reinforcement of what is known or believed or conceptualized, on the one hand, about urban problems such as those confronted by these six types of CDOs, and the actual configuration of specific organizations and procedures employed in addressing them.

We do not in any way claim that the institutionalized thought structure to be described is characteristic only of these nine cities. Quite the contrary, we consider it to be the dominant combination of thought, structure, and social organization to confront local problems in American society. Our data from the nine cities give credibility to this formulation. Although the dominant institutionalized thought structure is a characteristic of the larger American society, it functions locally as a patterned set of beliefs, structures, and behaviors in which the problems of the cities are defined and addressed. We shall have occasion to refer to the "interorganizational consensus," denoting the interorganizational field level on which basic agreement and essentially cooperative relationships exist among the CDOs of this study (as well as other CDOs and other types of agencies not specifically treated in this study). The institutionalized thought structure constitutes the substance of that interorganizational consensus, the framework of thought and social structure through which the behavior of these organizations takes place and within which it is interpreted.

Some of the more important aspects of this institutionalized thought structure are: (1) its belief-value system, (2) the strategy for addressing social problems, (3) the organizational rationale of organizations in the social sector, (4) the authority structure of these organizations, and (5) their legitimation and power, each of which will be summarized here.[3]

1. Certain components of the belief-value system dominant in American society are basic to the institutionalized thought structure underlying the interorganizational field of community decision organizations. First among these

is that American society, though hardly perfect, is *essentially sound in its institutional composition.* The social problems that attend it, including slums and poverty, are caused either by temporary periods of malfunctioning which are only transitory (business depressions or readjustments), by wickedness (dishonest politicians, occasional fraud and malfeasance by politicians, industrial leaders, or organized criminals), and by a residual problem population comprising individuals who will not or cannot cope with the demands made for norm-abiding performance in various segments of the institutional structure.

Although such problems are serious, progress in solving them is being achieved. The two most important dynamics in such progress are democratic pluralism and science.

Democratic pluralism is a political and governmental system in which an equitable structure of governmental decision making, administration, and adjudication prevails and in which these governmental channels are appropriately responsive to the needs, wishes, and rights of the electorate. This appropriate responsiveness of government is effected through the dynamics of interest group activity. Any group of people who share the same interests and concerns can organize and bring their interests to the attention of appropriate governmental bodies. Since all governmental processes are responsible, in the last analysis, to the voters, it will be to the advantage of legislators and administrators to be mindful of the legitimate interests of different organized groups. If a group is unorganized it is its own fault, for all citizens have the right to organize and press their interests.

The second major dynamic of progress is *science.* As science advances, not only is a basis provided for improved physical well-being, but various professions are able to draw on scientific advance to help solve the so-called human problems.

Another dynamic of progress, perhaps less basic than the first two, is *organizational reform.* Problems of bureaucracy and unresponsiveness must be acknowledged, but there is a constant process of organizational reform taking place which inevitably improves organizational performance. This reform dynamic is based partly on the value commitments of professionals, their professional ethics of personal unselfishness and service to others. It is supported by agency accountability, in that the human services agencies are responsible either to donors or to taxpayers and must constantly render an account of what they are doing and why. And it is supported by pressure from outside the agencies to perform more effectively. Such pressures come from legislators, taxpayers, superior governmental licensing or reviewing authorities, voluntary standard-setting agencies, and pressure groups of various sorts. The constant clamor for organizational improvement is reflected in almost any professional journal in the various social service fields.

A fourth aspect of the belief-value system can be called the *principle of inducements.* It is based on the acknowledgment that in many situations there may be good and sufficient reason why an agency does not care to engage in a particular activity even though it may be in the public interest. The agency may have other, higher priorities and may be constrained by a limited resource base or by other organizational factors. It will hence not always voluntarily do what is "needed."

In such cases, which are frequent, the principle of inducement is employed in one form or another. The economists call it a "side payment." The agency is given enough to "make it worth its while" to take on this new responsibility, function, program, clientele group, or whatever. The most prevalent form of organized inducement to alter agency programs is the financial grant: "We wish you would do thus-and-so, and we will make it worth your while to do it."

2. These major beliefs and practices are closely interwoven with the other aspects of the institutionalized thought structure. From them are derived the rationale for the *strategy for addressing urban problems*, a strategy that consists of two major parts: services and coordinated planning.

Since a large proportion of the problems inheres in groups of people more or less at the margins of an otherwise healthy and sound social order, it follows quite naturally that they must be helped if they are hungry or in misery, and above all they must be helped, if possible, to join the mainstream, from which personal circumstances or inadequacies now exclude them. If this cannot be done—as in the case of the aged and persons with major physical or mental handicaps—then they need services to help them adjust as best they can to their existing conditions.

The community decision organizations of the present study are all involved in one way or another with the social problems of the inner city in general and of so-called disadvantaged populations in particular. They are also confronted with the widely acknowledged realization that despite their own efforts and those of other agencies within their respective service fields, the people who are put in positions of disadvantage or misery apparently grow in number, rather than diminish, and the social problems they hope to impact likewise grow. Obviously, some explanation must be given for this anomalous situation, and some additional strategy is necessary in order to cope with what appears to be a persistent failure of efforts in these respective service fields.

That strategy lies right at hand. It fits in neatly with other aspects of the institutionalized thought structure and converts a potential source of threat to community decision organizations and other agencies operating in the area of urban problems into an increased resource: *comprehensive planning and coordination.* This supplement to the services strategy provides both an implicit diagnosis for its past failures and a promise for its future success. Lack of effectiveness in improving social conditions is attributed to the circumstance that organizations—whether governmental or nongovernmental—are working independently of each other or, worse yet, at cross purposes, and so their combined efforts do not achieve their full potential.

This deficiency can be seen at two levels, and can be corrected at two levels. First, the individuals or groups in need receive fragmented help or perhaps miss out on the help they need and which is available to them, though perhaps not properly allotted to them under present inadequate service delivery systems. Second, since the social problems of the cities are many-sided, they must be attacked simultaneously from many angles—housing, education, health, employment, leisure time facilities, etc.—and consequently require coordinated program planning on the part of the agencies themselves.

The remedy is implicit in the diagnosis: comprehensive planning and coordination. But since organizations usually act only so as to preserve or enhance their own viability, they coordinate their efforts willingly and without additional inducement only in those limited areas and activities and time periods in which they see a benefit to be derived from such effort, or at least not a detriment. Since these areas are not ample to afford the necessary concerting of efforts on a purely voluntary basis, the principle of inducements is brought into the coordinated planning strategy in the form of special grants of governmental or foundation funds. It is quite pertinent that the antipoverty program strategy as it eventually developed embraced this concept of a multiagency approach to poverty, and the Model Cities program likewise embraced this multiagency approach to a wide range of problems of the inner cities. Their local embodiment constituted two of the CDOs of this study, both multifield CDOs. Similar activities can likewise be found in the four other CDOs of this study, which operate in more circumscribed fields.

Hence, the interaction of community decision organizations must be understood against this background of commitment to the services strategy and the supplementary commitment to coordinated planning.

3. By the *organizational rationale* component of the institutionalized thought structure, we mean simply the actual organizational forms and professional and administrative procedures through which services are provided and coordinated. These structures are far from random. The presence of the same CDOs in each of the nine cities indicates the patterned way in which efforts at service delivery and coordination are organized. In the case of the CDOs of the present study, four of them are legitimated as decision-making rubrics for a more or less single, unified service system: the health and welfare councils, the school system administrations, the urban renewal agencies, and the mental health planning agencies. Each is characteristically dominated by a single profession: social workers, professional educators, city planners, and psychiatrists, respectively. The remaining two community decision organizations are much more professionally diverse, reflecting their multifield rather than single-field character, which makes them different in many ways from the other four. Likewise, each CDO is organized along lines that separate out administrators from professional personnel, although the individual CDO types vary from each other on the extent of this separation.

Each CDO has to various degrees its own technical and administrative rationale, and its own legitimation within the organizational structure of the community. Much the same is true of other service agencies that are not community decision organizations and are not the direct focus of the present study.

The point of central importance here is that there is in American society—and specifically in these cities—a structured, institutionalized manner of responding to what are conceived as social problems, including those with which the CDOs of the present study respectively concern themselves. Certain of these problems, or certain aspects of these problems, are broadly acknowledged as coming within the dominant purview of these specific CDOs. The CDOs and the organizations within their respective purviews are the legitimated embodiment of the collective response to the problems. By the same token, they are able to influence and largely control the manner in which the problems will be defined, the methods of intervention to be employed, and who will be able to operate in their problem areas.

But the ability to define the nature of the response to the social problem implies also the ability to preclude other possible responses that do not fit into the community decision organizations' organizational rationales and for this or other reasons might pose threats to their viability. Lowi makes a similar statement regarding all established organizations: "Regardless of its commitment to particular goals, the established organization will resist other organizational forms or approaches to attain these same goals," and he illustrates it with the building trades unions, which "are specifically organized to prevent alternate ways of approaching construction and alternate modes of recruiting and training skilled persons."[4] The manner in which this influence and control over problem definition and intervention strategy operates will be documented in subsequent chapters of this study.

4. An important aspect of the *authority structure* in the functional fields of these CDOs is the hierarchical nature of the decision-making structure and its relative insulation from direct influence from their output constituencies. To take two examples, the school system administrations are employed by boards of education which in many, though not all, instances are directly elected. But the ballot is singularly unfocused as a means of influencing school administration policy, and when it is so used, it is usually confined to a single, fragmented issue. The staggering of terms of office makes any popular effort to change policy ineffective unless it is sustained over a period of years. As an alternative, about the only thing disgruntled taxpayers and parents can do is to vote down school bond plebiscites or school tax increases, which they have done in recent years with increasing regularity, notably in Oakland and Detroit, among the study's nine cities, where they occasioned particular furor. In Detroit, an illustration of the single-issue vote took place around the heated controversy over decentralization. Nevertheless, the educational systems remain singularly immune from

direct attack. Likewise, the health and welfare councils are governed by nongovernmental "volunteer" boards, which are self-perpetuating and which have only remote accountability to any specific constituency other than the agencies within their purview. A corresponding degree of remoteness from popular control characterizes the other four CDOs as well.

5. A final aspect of the institutionalized thought structure of special pertinence to the interorganizational field within which CDOs interact is their *legitimation and power.* Legitimation here means the acknowledgment on the part of all pertinent parties of an organization's right to act in its claimed domain. In the case of community decision organizations, their legitimation is not sui generis, one at a time, as it were, as though each organization achieves its own legitimation as a unique event. The important thing is the rootedness of this legitimation in the local interorganizational field, which in turn is supported by, or an embodiment of, the institutionalized thought structure.

What this means in practical terms is that a community decision organization that remains within the institutionalized thought structure will find its domain legitimated and supported, including those aspects of its domain that give it great power in determining issues, strategies, and actors in its own functional field and in resisting new actors or strategies that are seen as threatening its viability. But by the same token, it places in jeopardy the legitimation of any community decision organization that departs from the major outlines of the institutionalized thought structure or which violates the "live-and-let-live" nature of the interaction that takes place among CDOs as they cooperate or contest with each other over one issue or another.

Likewise, the power these organizations are able to exercise in influencing or controlling activities within their functional fields is not simply a product of the power positions of their boards, the backing of the mayor, the financial and personnel resources at their command, and the support of their respective input and output constituencies, important as these components are. For these components of power, as well as others, are in turn rooted in the legitimation of the individual community decision organizations within the interorganizational field, their sanctioned right to control a large part of what goes on in their respective functional areas, based on their being an accepted part of the institutionalized thought structure and based on the presumption that of course they themselves accept this thought structure, will operate within it, and will oppose alternatives to it, either in their own organizations or in others. Within these easy confines, the professional expertise of these organizations constitutes an important source and fulcrum of power.

Organizational Domain

The salient characteristics of the interorganizational field just enumerated have important implications for the question of organizational domain and of the interaction that takes place on domain issues among these CDOs. The implication of this analysis is that organizational domain cannot validly be conceived solely or even primarily as an individual organizational characteristic. In a very important sense, the domain is "prior" to the organization, in that there exists in the institutionalized thought structure not only an area of concern and activity that the organization comes to claim, but also a whole definition of social reality which indicates this area as one for which activities are appropriate and which also provides the basic outline of the manner in which the individual community decision organization will carry on activities within its functional field.

In this context it is important to note that the definition given by Levine and White, in their widely cited paper on organizational exchange, considered interaction from the standpoint of the individual organizations as discrete units, rather than from the inclusive-level paradigm.

The domain of an organization consists of the specific goals it wishes to pursue and the functions it undertakes in order to implement its goals. In operational terms, organizational domain in the health field refers to the claims that an organization stakes out for itself in terms of (1) disease covered, (2) population served, and (3) services rendered.[5]

The sector in the interorganizational field which comprises an organization's domain may be relatively clearly defined, as in the case of a school system administration, or it may be rather vague in the delineation of specific appropriate activities and support, as in the case of a community action agency. But however vague or specific the prescription of activities, the domain presumes not only a set of live-and-let-live relationships with other organizations established in closely related fields, but also an acceptable manner in which social reality is to be interpreted and what kinds of change efforts, if any, will be acceptable. The domain also includes the kind of legitimation and support that sustain the organization's claim to special prerogatives within its own field of activities, including access to federal, state, and private foundation funding, and afford it a substantial degree of protection from both competitors and attackers. Hence, the domains of these individual organizations are mutually related within a common local interorganizational field, which in turn embodies the pertinent parts of the institutionalized thought structure of American society.

The situation is especially interesting with respect to the community action agencies and Model Cities agencies, both of which were relatively new and both of which, in their turn, were concerned with "establishing a domain." Although their domain did not preexist as a fixed "slot" to be filled, the existing interorganizational field presented both a set of possibilities and constraints within which, under the strong impetus of a funded national program, domains for them were gradually developed. Each of them had to nudge its way into an already highly organized field, and each of them posed a possible threat to the domain position of other CDOs. While through the "microscope" this process appears studded with highly spontaneous activity and impressive controversy, the impact of these organizations on the interorganizational field appears from our data to have been remarkably small, the potential threat to viability of other community decision organizations highly overemphasized, and the general configurations of the field to have shown impressive resiliency. There was room for one more, and even two more, within the interorganizational field without jeopardizing other apparently competing CDOs. The position of these new CDOs became gradually established, acknowledged, legitimated, and routinized in a process that also involved the lopping off of all those proposed or actual activities or programs that challenged the institutionalized thought structure or threatened other community decision organizations at the core of their rationality, rather than merely at the margins of their activities.

In this respect, an early project staff decision to define domain in relation to the interorganizational field appears to have been a felicitous one: *Domain is here defined as the organization's locus in the interorganizational field, including its manifest goals and its channels of access to task and maintenance resources.* For our CDOs, this includes the sector of community interest covered, the type of activity performed within that sector, the population or actors to be served, the geographic area of operations, and the degree of autonomy that they exercise. A threat to any of these is a threat to the organization's domain, and an opportunity to enhance any of these is an opportunity to enhance the organization's domain.

But a threat seldom arises to the institutionalized thought structure that constitutes the legitimating fundament of the domains of these community decision organizations. Such domain threats, our data indicate, are of a quite different nature than those domain threats that simply involve matters of service field, geographic jurisdiction, and so on, as these are worked out in live-and-let-live mutual adjustment with other organizations. Potential threats to a CDO's core rationality can, as we shall show, usually be contained and transformed to be made consonant both with the institutionalized thought structure and with the individual CDO's organizational rationale and its continued viability. At the same time, important controls operate to similarly blunt or transform any possible tendencies on the part of one of the CDOs to attack another CDO at the core of its organizational rationale (to challenge its legitimacy to carry on its allotted functions) or to carry on activities that do not accord with important components of the institutionalized thought structure.

But the social controls operating here, like most effective social controls, are largely internalized and self-imposed. Operation outside of the institutionalized thought structure is abhorrent to the leadership echelons of almost all of these CDOs. In the one or two instances where this was not the case, a vastly different set of social dynamics became apparent.

Taken together, these community decision organizations, and others like them but not in our sample, are thus able to define the social problems they are addressing, define the nature of what "must be done" in order to solve them, control the intervention strategies that are brought to bear on them, evaluate the results of their interventions, and exercise large measures of control over the way their respective fields and activities are conceived for purposes of public discussion.

These are rather formidable characteristics. Combined with the indefinite nature of the respective responsibilities and accountabilities of these CDOs, they make "success" or "failure" in any usual sense of effective task performance extremely difficult to identify. They also offer an even greater relief from the pressures of accountability by providing an excuse for apparent failure as well as a remedy that only adds to the organizations' aggrandizement—the expansion and more perfect coordination of services and service delivery patterns.

The Interorganizational Field
as an Ecological System

The interorganizational field thus presents a sort of ecological balance, much along the lines outlined in Norton E. Long's article on "The Local Community as an Ecology of Games."[6] It is an adjustment of relatively autonomous organizations, including community decision organizations, sharing a broad area of consensus based on their grounding in a common institutionalized thought structure, which both provides for them and gives them their legitimation. This balance is a constantly modified adjustment involving a division of labor based on common definitions of social reality, and on different competencies with only relatively minor differences of opinion as to what those competencies are or where they are appropriate. The specific division of labor is suited to the continued viability of the individual organizations, enabling them to have access to the resources necessary for their viability and to continue to exercise hegemony within their respective fields.

Since the relationships across service fields are not so clearly defined and delineated as the relationships within service fields, the multifield CDOs reflect a less determinate rationality and a less secure legitimation, and require more overt interaction in order to resolve the many unresolved problems of agency domain which occur as efforts are made to develop new linkages across service fields. As we shall see, this circumstance is reflected in their high rate of paired interaction and has a bearing on the nature of that interaction, as well.

But even across service fields, an ecological adjustment in the sense described above has been worked out and forms an implicit context for the interaction. This ecological adjustment in turn conforms to, and hence is supported by, the institutionalized thought structure described earlier in this chapter. There is, as a consequence, a large area of common agreement on what constitutes problems, how they shall be defined, what shall be done about them, and—roughly—who shall do it. This area of consensus is only to a small extent based on anything as explicit as specific interagency agreements or contracts. Nevertheless, it provides many of the common resolutions to problems which make specific ad hoc interaction unnecessary, especially at the level of the community decision organizations.

Hence, the interactional field of community decision organizations may be described as ecological in the sense that it is not deliberately administered but simply arises out of the interaction of individual actors; but this does not imply that it is not organized. It is highly organized, even though that organization is based on mutual tacit agreement rather than on specific organizational or interorganizational structures. In this sense, our findings support almost (but not quite) completely the lucid description of an ecological system contained in Robert R. Mayer's important theoretical article on "Social System Models for Planners."

"The characteristic structure of an ecological system," writes Mayer, "assumes equality among the individual elements; that is, no one element has prescribed power or authority over another. . . . However, the counterpart of a stratification of elements may emerge. Some may achieve dominance by virtue of their greater influence over the common resources which are the basis of the ecological system." He goes on, however, to differentiate collectivities from exchange and ecological systems, since

collectivities, unlike ecological or exchange systems, are bound together by common goals or values. This quality is expressed through boundary maintenance which determines who shall and shall not participate in the system, and through the power and authority granted the inclusive system to enforce collective interests. The exchange and ecological models take on all comers who wish to interact or who share some common resource. The system has no inherent power or authority which can hold it together. Reciprocity dictates the systems's persistence.[7]

The point where our conclusions diverge from this important statement lies in the alleged impotence of the ecological field described by Mayer to define boundaries, establish common goals, and exercise cohesive power. For it is precisely this process which takes place within the ecological field of CDOs. And the fact of its operation helps explain much of our data that would otherwise be much less explainable. Significantly, it is not through the deliberately established multifield CDOs that this takes place, but rather simply in the process of mutual adjustment among individual organizations.

We think we can pinpoint the difference with Mayer more precisely. Mayer points out that in the background of every such ecological system "there is always some latent, more inclusive system which can impose its goals and norms," and that "parties external to the partial conflict of an ecological system may experience disutilities which stimulate them to act as an inclusive system and to force some collective goals on that ecological system."[8]

What we have found in the case of the ecological system of CDOs is that for the most part, these "goals and norms" of the more inclusive system do not have to be imposed on the CDOs by third parties, since these CDOs have their very legitimation and their very domains firmly established within, and consonant with, these inclusive system norms and goals, which we have described as the "institutionalized thought structure." And it is the common adherence to these goals and norms of the inclusive system which makes interaction unnecessary in any but the most minimal sense. This minimal interaction consists of occasional contact at the margins of concern, which constitutes a scanning device through which each organization is constantly reassured that each other organization is acting within the goals and norms of the inclusive system and within the live-and-let-live norms of the interorganizational ecology.

The acceptance of common norms makes for placidity in the interorganizational field. In this respect, our findings are highly supportive of a speculative assertion by Emery and Trist. In their description of the characteristics of turbulent organizational environments, they speak of the difficulty faced by individual organizations in achieving stability. They speculate that a solution may arise in the form of emerging "values that have overriding significance for all members of the field." In their treatment, these values appear to be very much like the interorganizational consensus discussed above, including the norm of live-and-let-live through mutual adjustments at the margins of organizational domain which do not threaten any organization's core rationale. In their own terms, Emery and Trist point out that as such values emerge, they help to bring order and stability and predictability out of large classes of events.

By this transformation a field is created which is no longer richly joined and turbulent but simplified and relatively static. Such a transformation will be regressive, or constructively adaptative, according to how far the emergent values adequately represent the new environmental requirements.[9]

Parenthetically, in raising the question whether such field placidity based on common values is regressive or constructively adaptive, the authors do not indicate whether they mean to the individual organizations' viability, or to some more inclusive system, or whether they assume the two to be identical. In Chapters 5 and 6 we consider the placid field's impact on innovation and responsiveness, and will address this question there.

The "partial conflict" referred to by Mayer is the widely presumed situation of competition for scarce resources among organizations whose goals as such are not necessarily incompatible. But even on the level of individual organizational domain, including access to necessary input resources, the respective prerogatives of the individual organizations have been worked out with each other over time, in accordance with the institutionalized thought structure.

In fact, the competitive struggle for scarce resources was not found to be the principal occasion of domain contest among the community decision organizations of this study. In an analysis of the 141 action episodes on which intensive data were gathered, J. Wayne Newton, of the project staff, located 57 action episodes containing contest over domain. The largest group of these was not contests over input resources, which accounted for only 15 instances, but over autonomy in decision making, which accounted for 35 instances. In this light, the usual characterization of interorganizational contest as "competition for scarce resources" apparently needs considerable refinement.

We have already stressed the importance of the continuity of the individual CDO's domain with the local interorganizational field and the supporting institutionalized thought structure. Later, we shall give attention to three components of organizational rationale: technical rationale, administrative rationale, and institutional rationale. We allude to them now only to remind the reader that our concept of domain includes the organization's claim to operate with these rationale components—roughly, doing what it is especially equipped to do, in the way in which it is organized to do it, and in relation to the entire interorganizational field. This is a much broader concept than that of "service field," which is the usual conceptualization of domain. Since much of the interaction that does take place among the CDOs is related to domain, this relationship of organizational rationale to domain should be kept in mind.

Perhaps the most important global aspect of the interorganizational field is this basic agreement on definitions of social reality and social problems, respective agency domains, and ground rules for interaction, within which interaction is limited both in frequency and in the scope of the issues involved. In this framework, the basic problems of the city are seldom addressed.

It becomes extremely banal, a breach of good taste, to raise questions about whether agency programs have any direct, tangible impact on any large group of slum area residents. Indeed, the most noticeable impacts are the unfavorable ones, such as forced relocation, running of elevated highways through low-income areas, and preemption of low-income dwellings for public land use. Such actions become "problems" only at the point that a dissident group threatens to make trouble. Until that point, rather than being defined as problems, they are simply side effects of the "solutions" to other problems such as rapid vehicle transportation routes in and out of the central city, maximization of land usage, improvement of the city's tax base, etc. In Chapter 6, we shall deal with the structures and processes through which these community decision organizations are brought into a degree of responsiveness to the wishes and needs of poverty area residents. Meantime, in the absence of such input from poverty area residents (and even, as we shall indicate later, in its presence) the inter-CDO ecology presents a remarkably stable reality beneath the dramatic but superficial manifestations of great disorganization, high interaction, and individualistic competitiveness. It constitutes a situation much like that addressed by Theodore J. Lowi under the rubric of "political man."

Lowi points out that the aggregate impact of political man's negotiating and bargaining is inadvertently conservative. This is so not because of his ideological position, but presumably because of the reciprocal relationship between what Lowi calls quiescent periods, which call political man forth to positions of leadership, and political man's own interaction style.[10]

The above dynamics have a direct bearing on the characteristics of the interorganizational field, which shows much of Lowi's "quiescence." Since this field constitutes an ecological adjustment worked out over time and sustaining the same basic ground rules for interaction, even where different issue outcomes are desired, and since the basic ground rules of "live-and-let-live" and the basic definitions of the issues on which the organizations may differ are nevertheless similar because of their unanimous acceptance of the institutionalized thought structure, individual organizations can afford not to interact on many issues that affect their interests. They have constant assurance that most issues in which they have interest will be resolved in a way that is satisfactory to them, even if they do not intervene, and that whether or not any given issue is resolved in exactly the way they would prefer it, the resolution will be one that will not hurt them lethally. The system of relationships virtually guarantees this.

Manifest and Latent Functions
of the Interorganizational Field

From the above, it can be concluded that the structuring of the interorganizational field operates to "protect" these community decision organizations from the possible adverse effects of change. It is not suggested that the interorganizational field was deliberately structured with such considerations in mind. Indeed, one thing that makes this interorganizational field of CDOs both interesting and important is precisely that it is not deliberately structured, either by the CDOs themselves or by anyone else. Such lack of deliberate structure has been widely accepted as a partial reason for the need for coordination and has constituted part of the rationale behind such programs as Community Action and Model Cities. Even though the interorganizational field was not deliberately structured in a certain way, its consequences are much the same as though it had been so structured. The point is important and merits further attention.

In examining it, Merton's concepts of manifest and latent functions are of great usefulness. Merton defined manifest functions as the objective consequences of a social practice or belief which contribute to the adjustment or adaptation of a social system and which are both intended and recognized. Latent functions, on the other hand, are objective consequences contributing to the adjustment or adaptation of a social system which are neither intended nor recognized.[11]

The manifest functions of the individual community decision organizations are those of facilitating coordinated planning in their respective functional areas so that services, broadly considered, will be delivered in appropriate fashion to those who need them. Innovation is widely accepted as desirable. It is necessary to improve the quality and nature of the direct services offered, so they will be more effective, and it is considered necessary to achieve the benefits of coordination, so that innovational modes of coordination are likewise widely heralded as desirable. Responsiveness, another of this study's principal variables, is considered important for various widely held reasons enumerated in Chapter 6. The practical problem, on this basis, becomes "How do you get the organizations to set aside outmoded and ineffective methods of operation, and to adopt newer, more potentially effective ones? And how do you bring about coordination so as to exploit new opportunities for joint endeavor and prevent needless confusion, contention, and wasteful duplication?"

What is usually overlooked in pursuing this and related questions on the level of the individual interacting organizations is the latent functions performed by the patterned interaction of these organizations within the institutionalized thought structure described above. Some of these functions will be enumerated here, as a necessary context for interpreting the specific findings regarding key propositions tested in this research.

First, coordinative efforts, including the allotting of special funds for coordinated programs such as the Community Action and Model Cities programs, have the effect of confining activity in the pertinent functional fields to the operating agencies already on the scene, and of protecting them from possible competition from new agencies. Such new agencies as are created customarily come under the influence, if not the control, of these existing agencies. Coordinative efforts provide a mechanism that assures the taking up of new programs and the confronting of new possibilities and problems in a way that is compatible with the existing social and thought structure. Rose's study of community action agencies in twenty cities gives an extensive account of the operation of this process in CDOs of that type.[12]

Second, the common institutionalized thought structure provides substantial assurance that challenges to existing agencies will be prevented, discouraged, interpreted, dealt with, or resolved in ways that, though they may indicate minor gains or losses for one or another of the CDOs, will not threaten their organizational viability.

Third, in defining how problems will be conceived and how they will be dealt with, the local interorganizational ecology exercises important social control functions, most importantly through the process of problem definition, but secondarily through the ability to control the methods used to deal with problems, and to ward off possible alternative approaches that would jeopardize part or all of the institutionalized thought structure.

In affirming innovation and responsiveness, the aura of positive sanction for these goals is sustained, and it is possible to give massive evidence of progress in these areas while at the same time assuring that the innovation and responsiveness are kept within comfortable limits. The "heat is taken off," both through explaining the upsetting anomaly of widespread, systematic poverty amidst affluence and declarations of war against it—explaining the anomaly essentially in terms of the marginality of the problems and their locus in the deficiencies of marginal individuals unable to "make it" in the otherwise healthy mainstream— and through giving the aura of massive concern and effort to remedy untenable social conditions. The price paid for these considerable advantages to the CDOs is the virtual assurance that the new programs will be ineffective in addressing core problems of structured inequality.

Against this institutional backdrop of latent functions, the position, constraints, and *Spielraum* of individual organizations can be more adequately understood, and their behavior better assessed. It is customary in some quarters to deride these organizations for seeking their own best interests and deliberately choosing to promote their own maintenance needs rather than choosing activities and programs that would more effectively accomplish their manifest tasks, especially as regards the condition of the poor. Yet what is overlooked in this allegation is not only that the CDOs' technical rationale is adapted to certain modes of operation and not others, but that their room for maneuver is strongly confined, conceptually within the existing institutionalized thought structure and programmatically by their location in the interorganizational field. In the rare circumstances when a CDO moves beyond these constraints on innovation or responsiveness or both, strong sanctions are brought to bear against it. Hence, for the individual community decision organization, the interorganizational field operates not only as a buffer and support, but also as a definite constraint.

Organizational Rationale

Organizational rationale constitutes the how and why of an organization's operation within its environment. For analytical purposes, we divide it into three components.

Technical rationale involves the specific competencies that the organization's functions require, the methods, presumably based on empirical experience and/or scientific knowledge, which are applied by appropriate members of the organization in order to perform the operations that are considered its principal function.

Administrative rationale is the series of principles and procedures through which the coordination of different parts of the organization is brought about and sustained in order that it may perform its manifest functions. It includes organizational structure, authority-flow, and all deliberately maintained ways of doing things other than the purely technical aspects of the organization's operation. This is meant to include processes that mediate between the organization and the environment as well as maintenance activities within the organization itself.

Institutional rationale deals with the enduring aspects of the organization's position in its environment. This includes its manifest purpose and the legitimation of its right to its claimed domain within the interorganizational field, which in turn includes its manifest goals, channels of access to resources, service field, type of activity, service population, and geographic area. Together, these three components comprise an organization's rationale—the manifest how and why of its existence and activities.[13]

A community decision organization's rationale also performs latent functions. For example, it provides a means through which initiatives brought by citizens groups can be defined, channeled, and if necessary transformed—transformed from possible threats to the individual organization and to the interorganizational field into problems which, even though they may afford some discomfort, can be dealt with on the organization's terms and without jeopardizing its position within the interorganizational field.

This latent function is particularly apparent in connection with technical rationale, which is determined largely by the dominant professional orientations to which the community decision organizations are committed. In each case, there have grown up professional, expert "ways of doing things" which are acknowledged and certified and supported not only within the specific community decision organization but, by tacit agreement, among the various community decision organizations. The technical rationale performs both a manifest and a latent function. Manifestly, the technical rationale provides an expert, sophisticated, and presumably effective manner of rationally confronting the problems an organization's manifest goals address. Its justification appears virtually self-evident. But the latent function of the technical rationale is also to provide a mechanism by which the organization molds the conception of its problems in a way in which it can deal with them without threatening its own viability. Hence, technical rationale operates in a manner that has definite and important impact on both the process of citizen participation, which this study considers from the standpoint of organizational responsiveness, and the process of innovation.

Not only do organizational innovation and responsiveness take on a rather different significance when they are considered from the standpoint of the interorganizational field and its supporting institutionalized thought structure, but so do such processes as interorganizational contest, cooperation, and coordination. For depending on whether one views the interaction from the standpoint of the individual CDOs or from the standpoint of the entire configuration of their combined interaction, quite different meanings and implications are involved in the conceptualization of contest and cooperation, and quite different assessments are made as to what shall constitute the term *coordination* and as to just how much coordination is found to be occurring, and with what results.

What may look like major contests at the level of the individual organizations may look like minor episodes in a continuous process of domain readjustments at the margins among CDOs whose individual viability is sustained by the basic consensual configuration of which these minor adjustments are an important sustaining part. Their contest is analogous to a game of chess on a rainy afternoon. In any particular game, each side wants to win, but the contest over who shall win the individual games is minor compared with the cooperative activity of playing the game, with benefits usually exceeding costs for both sides, regardless of who wins or loses.

Further, as we shall indicate, the view of coordination likewise takes different dimensions. What looks like a situation of virtual anarchy and disorder, as largely autonomous organizations carry out their individualized activities in overlapping fields, turns out to be remarkably stable, patterned, and systematized as one looks at the same data from the standpoint of the aggregate level, the interorganizational field. And as we shall see, much of the coordination that takes place does so not within the rubric of formal coordinative mechanisms, but through this very process of mutual adaptation at the margins, in processes involving not only cooperation but also contest, when viewed from the standpoint of the individual organizations. Such activity is recognizable as coordination only from the level of the interorganizational field.

The consideration of specific findings from the standpoint of alternative paradigms is possible in this study only because of the fortunate circumstance that the methodology of the study provided for the systematic gathering of both specific quantifiable data, on the one hand, and of more qualitative narrative data relating to structure and processes on the other hand. The methodology of the study is described in the Appendix. Some of the implications of the study's findings and interpretations for methodology, particularly as regards the selection of major analytic paradigms, will be considered in Chapter 8.

**Interaction Among Community
Decision Organizations**

A popular conception of the crowded interorganizational field on the metropolitan scene is one of great disorganization and highly competitive struggle among organizations for the scarce resources needed to perform their respective tasks. The presumed anarchic condition is widely bemoaned in the professional literature, as new ways are sought to attack the problem of bringing order out of the existing chaos produced by literally hundreds of agencies going their own way. In such a crowded field of overlapping organizational domains, competing claims, and convergent and divergent goals, interaction is presumably very high, and agency officials speak of the huge drains on their time taken in interacting with other agencies. Further, since resources are limited, and since goals often diverge, there is supposed to be a constant struggle among organizations to gain and maintain access to scarce resources and to enhance their respective domains.

We begin this chapter by asserting that the data from our intensive study indicate that the usual picture, depicted grossly above, is highly distorted. In the nine cities of the present study, and among the six organizations studied, the picture that comes through is not one of chaos, but of a high degree of organization; interaction between these organizations is surprisingly moderate in frequency; and the interaction is characterized much more by cooperation than by contest.

The period of intensive field work from July 1968 through August 1970 was characterized by two relevant circumstances. First, it was a period of great turmoil in the cities, with an increasingly heightened awareness of the "crisis of the cities." The riots of 1967 had not initiated this awareness, but they certainly made the social problems of the inner cities a salient public issue and created a new sense of urgency. Second, this was the very period when seventy-five American cities (followed by an additional seventy-five a year later) were tooling up for and carrying out their Model Cities programs, programs that placed a high priority on comprehensiveness, concentration, coordination, and citizen participation. Coming as it did on the heels of the Economic Opportunity program, Model Cities posed a stimulus to coordination, an opportunity to enlarge budgets and expand domains, and a presumed threat to already existing organizational domains.

The paucity of interaction among the community decision organizations of this study is illustrated by the experience of the nine field research associates in gathering data for the action episodes. Data on organizational interaction came from three sources: the schedules, the action episodes, and narrative data other than the action episodes. The action episodes are best described by a brief excerpt from the instructions to the field research associates:

For the purpose of this study, an Action Episode is a relatively short-range interaction between two or more CDOs . . . An Action Episode is initiated by a CDO when an issue or situation arises calling for interaction with another CDO to achieve a desired outcome. . . . The type of interaction may range from cooperation at one end of the continuum to conflict at the other. The effort around the issue or situation achieves a resolution in some manner; the interaction around the issue or situation subsides as the Action Episode is finished.

Field research associates were asked to report, following a detailed outline, on three such episodes for each CDO. Episodes of interaction with another of the sample CDOs were preferred, but not required. At the time, the FRAs had been working intensively with these organizations for nearly a year. Nevertheless, they reported great difficulty uncovering three such episodes for each organization. Further, they reported great difficulty generally in finding instances of inter-action in connection with the organizational schedules and the narrative reports. They did report a large amount of informal interaction of the nature of an occasional telephone call or a chance conversation at a luncheon.

The generally low indication of CDO interaction, even under intensive field-work scrutiny, will be further documented presently in this chapter, especially in terms of the paired interaction analysis. The action episode experience is given here simply to illustrate what is meant by a low level of interaction. For here were organizations for each of whom Model Cities was a relevant development, organizations with overlapping domains, organizations presumably competing for scarce resources, organizations charged with achieving coordination and with bringing about desirable change in areas that overlapped to a great extent, organizations stimulated especially by the Model Cities program to participate in joint planning for change.

The surprisingly small amount of interaction becomes more readily under-standable in terms of the ecological system characteristics of the interorgani-zational field as outlined in the preceding chapter and extended in the final sections of the present chapter.

The Extent of CDO Interaction

Let us turn now to the limited interaction that did take place within the protective interorganizational ecology. The number of interactions in which each CDO type was involved is presented in Table 3-1.

These figures are based on the "paired interaction" analysis about which a word of introduction is in order. For the paired interaction analysis, instances of

Table 3-1
Number of Interactions by CDO Type[a]

Model cities agency (MC)	207
Community action agency (CAA)	187
Public school system administration (ED)	167
Health and welfare planning council (HW)	119
Urban renewal agency (UR)	100
Mental health planning agency (MH)	84
	864

[a]These figures are based on 53 rather than 54 CDOs (no Model Cities Schedule from Oakland MC) and hence on 130 rather than 135 possible pairs of CDOs. They include data on 97 of these possible pairs (MC-CAA, MC-ED, etc.), the remaining 33 pairs involving either no data or insufficient data. A careful check indicated that "no data" and "insufficient data" actually reflect a condition of virtually no interaction.

interaction were taken both from the narrative data and from the formal CDO schedules. The narrative data were combed for twenty-three different subvariables of interaction. The narrative data included the 141 action episodes that by definition involved one of the study's CDOs, and field research associates were instructed to select action episodes which in addition involved other sample CDOs if possible. Ninety-five of them did. These are all included in the count. Also, twenty-four items on the CDO schedules were likewise systematically recorded. The field period covered twenty-six months in which field research associates in each city were in constant contact with the CDOs. A time-consuming process of data aggregation and judgment produced the findings both on paired interaction "frequency" and on the "type of interaction" (cooperation/contest). The procedures are described in the Appendix. The paired interaction thus involves not only episodal interaction (including the 141 action episodes) but instances of such structured interaction as overlapping board membership, lending of staff, etc.

The comparatively high interaction count for the Model Cities agency is even more marked when one considers that only eight of the nine Model Cities agencies are included in the count, and that these agencies were only beginning to develop their full potential during the period of the study.

Table 3-2 gives the number of interactions for each possible pair of CDOs, summed up from the nine-city data. Figure 3-1 portrays the same data in graphic form.

From Table 3-2 it can be seen that the pair of CDOs that interacted most often was the Model Cities agencies and the school system administrations. Although the community action agencies interacted most frequently with the Model Cities agencies, their next most frequent interaction partners were again the school system administrations.

Table 3-2
Number of Interactions by CDO Pair Type

MC-ED	58
MC-CAA	52
CAA-ED	49
CAA-HW	44
MC-UR	39
MC-HW	29
MC-MH	29
CAA-UR	23
ED-MH	22
ED-UR	20
CAA-MH	19
ED-HW	18
HW-UR	16
HW-MH	12
MH-UR	2
	432

Several aspects of these findings are consonant with the theoretical formulation developed in Chapter 2 and which we continue to develop in this and subsequent chapters, in relation to the specific findings of the study.

The first aspect was mentioned at the beginning of this chapter. The amount of interaction among these community decision organizations was surprisingly small. The study yielded a total of 432 interactions between all pairs of organizations. This total is based on fifty-three rather than fifty-four CDOs. Because two organizations are involved in each pair, the total interaction count registered by the fifty-three CDOs was just double this amount, 864. This makes a total of just over sixteen interactions for each organization, on the average, and between six and seven for each of the organizations with each other. This was over a period of twenty-six months. To be sure, there were great differences in interaction counts for different pairs of CDOs, as indicated in Table 3-2, but the total and averages were as indicated. We are confident that we missed few if any interactions that developed into sizable issues, involved joint planning in any systematic way, committed a major share of the organizations' attention or resources, involved collaborative activities, or developed into serious disputes. It was such interaction that the study pursued, since interaction that does not meet one or more of these characteristics must be considered essentially inconsequential or marginal. No attempt was made to gather systematic data on the number of chance meetings between people from two CDOs, or the occasional telephone calls, conversations on the golf links, or whatever. We are aware that such informal encounters were frequent, and that they play an important function in

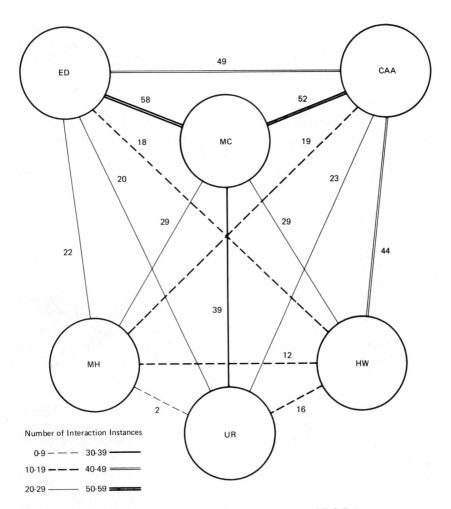

Figure 3-1. Number of Interactions Between CDO Pairs

reinforcing the existing consensus between organizations as to where their respective domains extend. Such encounters are akin to the "sounding out" process as described by Thompson and McEwen, a process that occurs quite deftly, informally, and often so subtly that a third party, even if he observed the process, might not realize what was going on.[1]

What makes this finding of little interaction important is the fact mentioned earlier that the period of the field study was one in which the emerging Model Cities program was presumably stirring up a ferment in these cities, as a new CDO sprang up with comparatively large resources and with a domain area that overlapped those of all the other CDOs. The entire Model Cities program was predicated on the desirability of coordinated efforts across a broad scope of service fields. The program required "the most effective and economic concentration and coordination of Federal, State, and local public and private efforts to improve the quality of urban life."[2]

We return now to analysis of the interaction that did take place. First, we note that the two organizations with the highest interaction counts were the two multifield organizations—the Model Cities agencies and the community action agencies. This finding is quite consonant with our theoretical statement that relationships between organizations are most highly regularized and routinized within specific interest fields, largely through the respective CDOs that head them up. A CDO charged with a specific interest field has less reason for interaction with other CDOs than a CDO charged with making a coordinated effort across a number of interest fields. Both the MC and the CAA fall into this latter category. According to this explanation, other CDOs interact less because their primary concern with their own service field presents less occasion for them to interact with other CDOs.

The high interaction count of the school system administrations merits special examination. These organizations are the largest of all the CDOs, both from the standpoint of annual budgets and from the standpoint of number of personnel. Although they are specifically charged with a single service field— public education—their domain involves some degree of overlap with all the other CDOs. After the Model Cities agencies and the community action agencies, they constitute the next most frequent interaction partner of the urban renewal and mental health planning agencies as well. Their particularly high interaction with the Model Cities and community action agencies reflects their extensive domain overlap with them; also, both organizations have been important sources of possible new funds for the school as well as sources of possible threats to their service domain.

In almost every city, ED loaned staff and space to MC. ED was a major contributer to the development of the education component of the Model Cities program in several cities. Interaction took place on such programs as Career Opportunities, vocational rehabilitation, and hot lunches. At the same time, ED was able to ward off or blunt attempts by the Model Cities citizens groups or by the Model Cities agencies themselves to stimulate parent involvement and citizen participation in the operation of the school system.

Likewise, the interaction of the school system administrations with the CAAs was characterized by programs that constituted sources of funding for the school system as well as possible challenges to its domain. The ED-CAA interaction was not only relatively frequent, but it involved the largest component of contest of all the CDO pairs (see Table 3-7). Interaction took place around such issues as Title I programs, Head Start, summer programs, New Careers programs, and Job Corps.

As an example of these often testy relationships, in one city some school pupils held a meeting in a community action agency facility to discuss a school guidance counselor's use of physical force. The school system pressured the poverty agency to stay out of the case and called upon the local congressman to support its position. Meanwhile, a parent committee made formal complaints about the counselor. These complaints led to a transfer of discipline functions from the guidance counselor to the vice-principal and the organization by the school administration of a largely ineffectual assessment committee. The school system administration served notice that in the future it would not accept such infringements on its domain, and the parents and students were left frustrated and apathetic.

Hence, the picture that emerges is one of a relatively stable field characterized by a modest degree of interaction which is stimulated by opportunities or threats that appear sufficiently important for the organization to take action. The high interaction count of both the MCs and the CAAs is explainable not only in terms of their multifield nature, but also because, partly for reasons of their multifield nature, partly for other reasons, they presented both opportunities and threats to the other CDOs. At the same time, they were seeking, themselves, to establish their niche in the local interorganizational ecology, and in doing so rubbing up against the other, more well-established CDOs and undergoing with them a process of mutual adjustment that gradually determined the borders of their legitimated domains.

Conventional organizational theory suggests that organizations interact with each other in relation to their need for scarce resources. If organizations could acquire the necessary resources independently of each other, there would be no occasion for interaction. Presumably, then, organizations with needs for related types of resources could be expected to interact more with each other than organizations whose needs were quite unrelated. Such related needs are implicit in the concept of domain overlap. In an attempt to penetrate systematically the relationship between frequency of interaction and domain overlap, an analytical proposition was formulated: *The greater the domain overlap between organizations, the more frequent is their interaction.* The proposition was found to be strongly supported by the interaction data.

To test this proposition, the fifteen possible interaction pairs were sorted into three groups according to their degree of presumed domain overlap. Then, the average frequency of interaction between pairs in each of the three groups was computed. The highest domain overlap group included only one pair, the CAA-MC, whose average interaction frequency was 6.44. The seven pairs in the group with medium domain overlap had an average frequency of 4.46. The seven pairs in the groups with low domain overlap had an average frequency of 3.06. The differences were in the conforming direction and were significant at the .001 level.

Hence, domain overlap is strongly associated with interaction among these CDO pairs and helps account for the differences in amount of interaction between specific CDO pairs across the nine cities. That the aggregate of all such interactions is nevertheless relatively low is attributable, we believe, to the tacit understandings that have been worked out over time—even among organizations with overlapping domains—as to access to resources within these overlapping areas. The interactions involve marginal adjustments to the existing and gradually self-modifying domain consensus within the interorganizational field.

From the outset, it had been assumed that the Model Cities program would constitute both a threat and an opportunity for these CDOs. But quite aside from the Model Cities program, it was assumed that much organizational interaction would be attributable to responses to opportunities or threats. Hence, a second analytic proposition was formulated: *Strong interaction is stimulated by threats to organizational domain, but not by opportunities for domain enhancement unaccompanied by domain threats.* This proposition is a crucial one, because it begins to describe what the interaction that does take place is all about, and to assess the relative importance of threats and opportunities in generating interaction.

It will be recalled that we define domain as the organization's locus in the interorganizational field, including its manifest goals and its channels of access to task and maintenance resources. For our CDOs, this includes the service field, the population or actors to be served, the geographic area of operations, and the degree of autonomy they exercise in performing their functions in accordance with their organizational rationale. A threat to any of these is a threat to the organization's domain, and an opportunity to enhance any of these is an opportunity to enhance the organization's domain. For purposes of assessment, strong interaction means interaction involving many and/or intensive interorganizational events related to an issue. A heavy investment of staff resources in such interaction is considered an indicator of the "strength" of the rating. In assessing this investment, the resource potential of the organization is taken into account; what is considered a heavy investment of resources for a small organization might represent a light investment of resources for a large organization.

Since the proposition relates to specific instances of interaction, the action episodes were taken as the data base for its testing. Action episode issues were classified according to whether they presented opportunities or threats, or did not; and whether the accompanying interaction was weak or strong. The results are shown in Table 3-3. This table also makes a distinction between threats to the CDO involved and threats to its interaction partner.

Table 3-3 indicates that opportunities alone seldom engender strong interaction. In thirty-one out of forty-nine cases where opportunities were not accompanied by threats, weak interaction ensued. But where opportunities were combined with threats to another organization, they engendered strong interaction in twenty-two cases out of twenty-eight. Hence, it is threats which are most strongly associated with strong CDO interaction—threats either to a second organization engendered by a CDO's pursuing some opportunity to enhance its

Table 3-3
Opportunities, Threats, and Strength of Interaction

		Strong Interaction	Weak Interaction	Totals
Opportunities for CDO	Not constituting threat to interaction partner	18	31	49
	Constituting threat to interaction partner	22	6	28
Threats to CDO		26	8	34
Neither opportunity nor threat for CDO		4	14	18
Totals		70	59	129

$$X^2 = 27.0 \quad \text{d.f.} = 3 \quad p = <.001$$

domain, or threats to the domain of the CDO itself. Here again, systematic quantitative analysis lends additional support for an assertion whose primary support lies in a more qualitative examination of the interaction dynamics based on the narrative data.

The Nature of CDO Interaction

So far we have reported findings on the amount and strength of interaction among these CDOs but have not yet addressed the type of interaction. By type of interaction is meant interaction as characterized by cooperation at one extreme and contest at the other.

Episodes of interaction between community decision organizations take place in regard to certain issues. By issues are simply meant the subject matter, problem, or enterprise that occasions the interaction. In each case it is some combination of circumstances which each organization is seeking to bring about or to prevent. And in each case, it is possible to ascertain the respective position of the participating organizations with regard to the outcome they desire from the issue—"what they are trying to do." Two or more organizations may desire the same outcome, or different outcomes, on any particular issue. This constitutes the basis for the definition of interorganizational cooperation and contest. *Cooperation is interaction between organizations directed at achieving the same issue outcome. Contest is interaction between organizations directed at achieving contrary issue outcomes.* It will be recalled that the action episode study specifically involves instances of the movement of two or more organizations into interaction with each other around a particular issue, terminating with the resolving of the issue and/or the ceasing of the organizational interaction around it. But the 141 action episodes of the study are simply a select group of such instances of interaction, chosen especially according to a systematic procedure for special study following a prescribed outline of variables. The definitions of cooperation and contest above have also been employed with other instances of interaction and structured relationships, both in the narrative data and in the formal data schedules.

Although the procedure involved in applying this conceptual scheme to the interaction between pairs of CDOs in the study was not easy, it was possible to attain a high degree of similarity of judgments among the three judges who engaged in making independent assessments. It was recognized that even on the same issue, organizations might interact in different modes—agreeing, for instance, that the "pie" is wanted but each desiring a larger "cut" than the other is willing to concede. Such mixtures of process at different levels of issue-oriented interaction are taken into account in the paired interaction methodology, which provides for assessing different admixtures of cooperation-contest. Data from the CDO Schedules and from the narrative reports (including the action episodes) were employed in the assessment of paired interaction. (See the Appendix.)

As can be seen from the above definition of *contest*, the term includes interaction that is often described as competition, as in the frequent global referral in the literature to organizational interaction as "competition for scarce resources." The term *competition* is used in a number of different ways by sociologists and economists. The present study makes a distinction between secondary contest and primary contest (conflict), which will be described later in this chapter. Most instances of what might be called competition (even allowing for the various usages of that term) are classified in this study as secondary contest. The distinction between primary contest (conflict) and secondary contest is, we believe, more useful for purposes of the present study than a distinction between competition and other types of contest.

We noted above that both cooperation and contest depend on the issue outcome interests of the organizations involved. Of course, if an organization has no particular interest in a given issue, it is not likely to interact at all. But even if the issue is of some interest to the organization, that organization may still not interact on the issue. It may expect that the issue outcome it desires will result even if it does not invest its resources in the issue interaction. Or it may be convinced that the desired outcome cannot be brought about even with such an investment of its resources in interaction. Or it may conclude that while the desired outcome might be brought about through its own intervention, the required investment of organizational resources would exceed the benefits to be derived from the favorable issue outcome.[3]

As already indicated, the data for the paired interaction came both from the narrative reports, including the action episodes, and from the schedules. Interaction between pairs of CDOs was judged on a five-point scale extending from virtually pure cooperation to virtually pure contest. The points on the scale are:

1. cooperation
2. mostly cooperation, with some contest
3. approximately equal cooperation and contest
4. mostly contest, with some cooperation
5. contest.

In order to determine the point on the scale which characterized the overall interaction of any given pair of CDOs, the instances of interaction from the data were abstracted and judged independently by three different judges for each item of data and summarily for the pair. The few differences of judgment were resolved through negotiation among the judges. Table 3-4 shows the number of CDOs of each type whose predominant interaction style was classified under each of the five points on the scale. Thus, one can see how many of each type CDO interacted predominantly at a given level with respect to cooperation and contest.

Table 3-4 indicates that the community action agencies showed the greatest proportionate amount of contest. In predominant interaction style, no CAA showed cooperation with no contest. Four CAAs showed mostly cooperation with some contest, three showed equal components of cooperation and contest, and two showed mostly contest with some cooperation. They constitute the only CDO category that contains no instance of unmixed cooperation. And they are the only CDO category to contain as many as two organizations characterized by mostly contest with some cooperation. The data presented in

Table 3-4
Predominant Interaction Styles of CDOs

	CAA	ED	HW	MH	MC	UR	Totals
1. Cooperation with no contest	0	2	1	2	1	2	8
2. Mostly cooperation with some contest	4	2	4	1	2	4	17
3. Equal cooperation/contest	3	4	1	1	5	0	14
4. Mostly contest with some cooperation	2	1	1	0	0	0	4
5. Contest with no cooperation	0	0	0	0	0	0	0
Total CDOs classified	9	9	7	4	8	6	43
Not classified	0	0	2	5	1	3	11
Totals	9	9	9	9	9	9	54

Chapter 6 indicate that there is one predominant reason why the CAAs turn out to have the highest relative proportion of contest in their interaction with other CDOs: they have been more responsive than the other CDOs to the needs and wishes of poor people and more sensitive to the participation of the poor as part of their input constituencies. It may seem surprising that the Model Cities agencies, coming later and with an even more explicit provision for the participation of poverty area residents, would not show a greater tendency toward contest than the CAAs. In Chapter 6, we indicate the tremendous importance of qualitative differences in types of responsiveness. Some of the responsiveness is highly perfunctory, some is relatively forceful. But in all types, the CAAs as a group are highest.

We have seen that strong interaction is positively associated with domain threats. But that relationship says nothing of the nature of that strong interaction. From the narrative data it seemed quite apparent that the interaction associated with domain threats was generally contestful, rather than cooperative, in nature. The relationship of domain threats and the nature of the interaction they occasioned was systematically checked through the action episodes, and the conclusions from the qualitative analysis of the narratives were confirmed. Domain threats were overwhelmingly accompanied by contest, while the action episodes in which no domain threats were present were overwhelmingly accompanied by cooperation. Table 3-5 presents the figures.

The quantitative analysis bears out the relation between contest and domain threats. A related proposition was suggested by an assertion of Levine and White. In their study of exchange between organizations, they stressed the importance of domain consensus as a basis for organizational exchange.[4]

One might anticipate that much of the contest among these community decision organizations would relate to their contrary claims in areas of overlapping domain. This is suggested in our analysis of the relationship between opportunities, threats, and strong interaction a few pages back. By the same token, the implication from the Levine and White study is that domain consensus should promote cooperation, at least in that it constitutes a basic precondition of exchange.

With such considerations in mind, an analytic proposition was formulated for

Table 3-5
Domain Threats and Nature of Interaction

	Cooperation	Contest	Total
Domain threats	12	58	70
No domain threats	59	12	71
Totals	71	70	141

$$X^2 = 61.4 \quad \text{d.f.} = 1 \quad p = <.001$$

testing: *The higher the domain consensus between two community decision organizations, the more cooperative will be their interaction.* Action episode data were employed in testing this proposition. To avoid contamination, an extremely inclusive definition of domain consensus was employed, which tended if anything to operate against the hypothesis:

Domain consensus refers to agreement among actors as to the appropriateness of their role in the interaction. For example, if several organizations are competing for a subcontract, they each hope to get the contract but they may agree that the other bidders are acting appropriately. Instances of domain dissensus, on the contrary, must involve some challenge to the appropriateness of one actor's role.

Nevertheless, the proposition, as tested by X square, was found to hold with a significance at the .001 level. Here again, the results from the quantitative findings are in keeping with the overall theoretical position of a stable interorganizational ecology characterized by little interaction which is at the margins of threats to organizational domain. This particular proposition indicates the relationship between domain consensus and cooperation, domain dissensus and contest.

Table 3-6
Domain Situation and Nature of Interaction

	Cooperation	Contest	Total
Domain consensus	62	31	93
Domain dissensus	9	39	48
Total	71	70	141

$$X^2 = 29.1 \quad \text{d.f.} = 1 \quad p = < .001$$

Organizational Stake and Position

When one examines the specific action episodes characterized predominantly by contest, it becomes apparent that the publicly stated reason for contest on an issue may not account for the whole basis of the organization's interaction. The publicly stated issue outcome desired by the organization, along with its supporting arguments, constitutes the organization's *position* on the issue. The organization's position is usually stated in terms of the substance of the issue itself, rather than the organization's own needs as an organization. On the other hand, these issues may affect organizations advantageously or disadvantageously according to how they are resolved. They may affect an organization's viability—at least at the margins—by having a favorable or unfavorable impact on some part of the organization's domain. Such considerations constitute an organization's *stake* in an issue, as distinguished from its position on that issue. For example, the community action agency and the school system administration may contest over the content and procedures to be used in the Head Start program. This is the public issue; this is their difference in position on that issue. But their stake in the issue may be their respective desire to control the program and the funds connected with it, and to keep the other CDO in a position where it can exercise little control. Later in this chapter, we examine some of the dynamic processes operating in such contest situations between CDOs.

An analysis of the action episodes in the light of the above considerations indicated that forty-five were found to involve at least some degree of contest over issues of substance; in addition, many more were solely domain contests. But even among the action episodes involving contest over substantive issues, there were almost always issues of organizational stake. Organizations, in other words, were interacting, when they interacted, to protect their viability as well as to secure a substantive outcome which they could affirm.

In Chapter 2, a distinction was made between manifest and latent functions, and this distinction was applied to *the level of the interorganizational field* in which CDOs interact. One can summarize that treatment by saying that the interorganizational field functions manifestly to address the social problems of the city with increasing effectiveness as a goal to be pursued through a more perfect coordination of services. It functions latently to protect the community decision organizations in their respective domains and to help them channel possible threats to their viability into definitions, prescriptions, and actions that are in accord with their continued viability, to minimize dissension among them, and to control civil unrest.

We can tie in the present analysis with that earlier analysis by saying that in CDO interaction, the manifest function at *the organizational level* has to do with addressing issues in terms of the performance of the tasks for which the organization is legitimated, in accordance with its technical, administrative, and institutional rationale. The latent function has to do with the organization's stake in the issue, as distinguished from its position on the issue. The relationship holds not only for contest episodes, but also for cooperative episodes, since in the latter the organization's stake is furthered through cooperation. Such episodes involve issues where the respective stakes of the interacting CDOs are furthered by the similar issue outcome, rather than contrary issue outcomes.

Secondary Contest and Primary Contest (Conflict)

The definitions of contest and cooperation have proved serviceable both from the standpoint of theoretical conceptualization and methodological operationalization. As indicated by the findings presented so far, it is possible to employ the definitions for purposes of quantitative treatment. Yet this gross, global analysis of cooperation and contest processes may lead to undue emphasis on unimportant distinctions and failure to recognize the important distinctions that should be made.

In Chapter 2 we pointed out that the same processes take on quite different significance when viewed from the organizational level or when viewed from the level of the interorganizational field. So far in this chapter, we have been considering interaction primarily from the organizational level, and we have defined contest as interaction for contrary issue outcomes. But we have repeatedly pointed out that most organizational interaction takes place within a basic interorganizational consensus that derives from and continuously reaffirms the institutionalized thought structure, affirms a set of norms governing contest situations, and affirms the legitimacy of the contesting organizations. It thus assures their viability no matter what the issue outcome, since the issues of interaction are kept to those that affect CDOs only at the margins of their viability, not at the core. In this respect, it is easy to place undue emphasis on the distinction between cooperation and contest. (And it is easy to overlook the fact that much contest performs an important allocational function for the interorganizational field. (See Chapter 4.) Both cooperation and contest, in these circumstances, have the latent function of supporting the interorganizational field, which in turn assures the continued viability of the individual CDOs.

In this context the question arises as to whether there are not circumstances or issues in which this essentially protective and basically cooperative interaction (even in contest) is shattered, cases where the stakes are higher, both for the individual CDOs and for the protective interorganizational field in which they operate. Let us be explicit about the kinds of circumstance or behavior which would depart from this set of usual interactional processes. Consider some of the possibilities of departure from the procedures described so far in this chapter.

1. An organization might challenge another organization not only over a specific issue but over its very legitimation, making a lethal threat to its continued viability.

2. An organization in a contest situation might violate the accepted norms for interorganizational contest, employing methods that constitute a threat to the usual system of minimizing conflict and confining it to marginal matters.

3. An organization might challenge and attack the interorganizational field structure and the institutionalized thought structure that sustains it.

Our theory, as it has developed, asserts that any of these possibilities would bring a drastically different set of interaction processes into play. For this, to use an earlier analogy, would constitute not merely a hard-fought contest to see who wins a particular chess game; it would constitute a threat to the game itself. It is one thing to fight hard to win a game; it is another thing to overturn the chess table. The issue then becomes: Do you support the chess game itself, or do you threaten it? Dropping the analogy, the issue becomes: Do you affirm the interorganizational field structure with its supporting institutionalized thought structure, or do you combat it?

Such instances are not only theoretically possible and important; they have occurred in the present study. And they involve such a different set of interorganizational dynamics that, to repeat, the important distinction is not between cooperation and contest, but between types of contest that support the existing interorganizational field structure and those that attack it. For the former, types of contest that support the existing interorganizational field structure, we employ the term *secondary contest*. *Primary contest*, on the other hand, comprises those interaction processes in which a CDO engages in one or more of the three contest behaviors just enumerated: challenging another organization's legitimacy at the core, violating the accepted norms for interorganizational contest actions, or attacking the interorganizational field structure itself. Such contest is so radically different from the great bulk of the contest that takes place that it perhaps would be preferable to use a separate term for it. We shall therefore use the term *conflict* in most instances, in place of the term *primary contest*. This usage of the term *conflict*, though specific to CDO interaction in relation to the institutionalized thought structure, is consonant with usual sociological formulations emphasizing a breaking of usual norms governing opposition processes, an attempt to destroy—rather than merely to compete with—the opponent, or simply "intense" opposition.

The category of conflict is not important numerically, for nearly all the inter-CDO contest we encountered in these nine cities was of a secondary nature. The instances of primary contest are very few, being confined almost exclusively to a single organization, the Oakland Economic Development Council, Incorporated (OEDCI), the Oakland community action agency. Other instances of interaction briefly manifested one or another of the three characteristics of conflict, but they were more sporadic.

A many-sided example of such incipient threat of primary contest was contained in several provisions of the original Model Cities plan in one city as drawn up by the neighborhood board and submitted to the city council. It provided for an experimental guaranteed income program, for turning over large measures of control of schools to model neighborhood residents, for participation in police-community programs, and for financing the training of 2000 construction workers from the model neighborhood. Various pressure groups, including the unions representing the teachers, police, and construction workers, along with various organizations including the school system administration and the police department, were able to redefine the issues in more conventional terms, resulting in a modification of all these programs so that their threat to existing groups was minimized. The reason this and other sporadic primary threats did not develop further was that in other cases as well, such threats were blunted and finally terminated within the existing organizational field structure, according to a set of simultaneous or successive dynamic processes that we shall turn to later. Only in the case of the OEDCI did a CDO persist over a sustained period of time in following a set of interaction procedures that involved all three of the characteristics of conflict.

Yet, even on the level of secondary contest, the issues, though marginal, still exist, and they engender occasional vigorous contest. Approximately half of the action episodes involved the reporting CDO in contest, and these were nearly all instances of secondary contest. Here are a few examples of such secondary contest involving CDOs:

The community action agency in one city developed an employment program with federal funds, and with the school system administration as one of the contracting agencies. The community action agency's personnel committee insisted on a greater role in the board of education's hiring policies and personnel practices. The board of education, though, was willing to give the community action agency only an advisory role. This latter agency held up the funding, pending a settlement, and the board of education eventually agreed to a joint committee.

In one city, a health and welfare council demanded review rights on the community action agency's proposal for federal funding of a health program in a particular area. The council planned a comprehensive five-county study, but the community action agency did not want to wait so long. The council promised to complete its study and institute a program in that area within a year, and on that basis, the community action agency withdrew its proposal.

In another city, a health council which had been left out of the Model Cities mental health planning sought to perform a role in such planning, but the Model Cities agency stalled and eventually declined this offer of help and participation. The council then called upon the regional office of the federal Department of Health, Education, and Welfare, which affirmed its legitimation in the health planning field and forced the Model Cities agency to grant the health council a larger role in planning and review.

One sees in such examples the development of contest at the margins of service domain and the attempt to maintain organizational autonomy. In each case, these are contests that each organization hopes to win, but can afford to lose.

For purposes of the paired interaction analysis, not only the formal action episode materials but also other narrative materials and materials from the CDO Schedules were used as the data base. Table 3-7 presents the extent of cooperation/contest characterizing each pair of CDOs summated for the nine cities, using the five-point cooperation/contest scale described earlier. It also repeats from an earlier table the interaction count for each pair.

The pairs are listed in descending order from most to least contest. The column on interaction counts helps point up a relationship that exists between frequency of interaction and type of interaction. There is a marked tendency for

Table 3-7
Nature and Amount of CDO Paired Interaction

CDO Pair	Nature of Interaction	Scale Point No.	Interaction Count
ED-CAA	Mostly contest with some cooperation	4	49
MC-ED	Equal cooperation/contest	3	58
MC-CAA	Equal cooperation/contest	3	52
CAA-HW	Equal cooperation/contest	3	44
MC-UR	Equal cooperation/contest	3	39
HW-MH	Equal cooperation/contest	3	12
MC-HW	Mostly cooperation with some contest	2	29
MC-MH	Mostly cooperation with some contest	2	29
ED-MH	Mostly cooperation with some contest	2	22
ED-UR	Mostly cooperation with some contest	2	20
CAA-MH	Mostly cooperation with some contest	2	19
CAA-UR	Cooperation	1	23
ED-HW	Cooperation	1	18
UR-HW	Cooperation	1	16
MH-UR	Not classified	–	2
	Total		432

(Correlation between degree of contest and frequency of interaction: Spearman's rho equals .64)

high frequency of interaction to be associated with greater proportions of contest in the interaction. One can observe this by noting the drop in interaction count as one goes down the cooperation/contest scale from point 4 to point 1. The correlation of .64 is reasonably high. This particular finding was not anticipated in the form of an analytic proposition. To place it in the context of the present analysis, one might say that while there is little overall interaction, and while that interaction is predominantly cooperative, those CDOs that do interact more frequently with each other are more likely to be interacting over domain issues constituting minor threats to their respective viability.

Here are a few examples of such contest on issues constituting minor threats to a CDO's viability:

The community action agency in one city had selected the health and welfare council as subcontractor for a homemaker services employment program. A community action agency subcommittee was upset about the low wages the council was paying on the project and tried to have the contract canceled. The council raised the wages, but the community action agency decided to take over the program anyway, and to work out other program difficulties itself, involving such things as seniority and tenure.

In another city, the health and welfare council offered the local share of money for a federal grant for social planning submitted by the regional council of governments. The regional council then took over control of the project, contrary to the original agreement as the health and welfare council had understood it. The aggrieved council protested, eventually to Washington, but did not receive the needed support to wrest a measure of control over the planning project from the regional council of governments.

The three examples of secondary contest given a few paragraphs back also constitute illustrations of minor threats to CDO viability, since that is what such contests are usually about.

Organizational Response to Threats

Since the issue of domain threats as the occasion of interaction looms large in the analysis of interaction among the CDOs, the question of *how* CDOs behave in these contests over domain threats merits further exploration. In this exploration, the dynamic aspects of interaction processes as recorded in the narrative data have proved an indispensable resource.

Thompson characterizes complex organizations "as open systems, hence indeterminate and faced with uncertainty, but at the same time as subject to criteria of rationality and hence needing determinateness and certainty."[5]

Their behavior when faced with uncertainty indicates a strong tendency to strive to make the unstable situation a stabilized one, to try to convert the nonroutine situation into routine components, and in the process to avoid any undesirable change in their domain situation. We now come to the relationship that this somewhat abstract introduction has been leading toward: *In seeking to attain its desired issue outcome in contest episodes, the organization's principal strategy is to seek to impose its own organizational rationale as the only appropriate basis for the issue's definition and for its resolution.* The organization thus gains a double measure of protection against the issue outcome affecting it adversely. First, the issue is defined within the institutionalized thought structure and therefore its resolution will not hurt the organization badly, no matter how poorly the contest goes. Second, the issue is defined in terms of its own organizational rationale, including its own areas of competence and noncompetence, of constraints and possibilities. Therefore, although one resolution might be more desirable than another from the organization's standpoint, any resolution will acknowledge the organization's areas of operation and ways of doing things. The threat that may have loomed comparatively large from the standpoint of the individual CDO, thus turns out to have been exaggerated, for the outcome is brought very close to what the organization originally desired, or if not, it is at least sufficiently compatible with its viability that the organization can "live with" it fairly comfortably.

In his study of the Tennessee Valley Authority, Philip Selznick was concerned with threats to organizational viability as he formulated his conception of *cooptation*. He defined cooptation as "the process of absorbing new elements into the leadership or policy-determining structure of an organization as a means of averting threats to its stability or existence."[6] In the light of the preceding analysis it can be seen that Selznick's concept of cooptation, which has been widely adopted even in the popular language surrounding citizen participation, is a means toward assuring that the problem will be defined and resolved in a way satisfactory to the organization. Through absorbing possible opponents of the organization or its position, the organization strives to assure that these opponents are brought to see the problem from the organization's point of view. This process is not always without cost, as Thompson and McEwen have pointed out, for it may limit the organization's autonomy in its decision-making process.[7]

Our analysis of the data from nine cities indicates that a broader definition of cooptation is more useful than that given by Selznick. The definition includes Selznick's concept of cooptation, but includes other types of cooptive action as well: *Cooptation is the process through which an organization succeeds in defining problems which appear to threaten its stability or existence in such a way that the actual resolution of the problems will be amenable to its continued stability or existence.* The way it does this is by imposing a definition of the problem which is consonant with its organizational rationale. One means through which this process may occur is through the preemption of leadership elements that might otherwise constitute a threat. Such preemption strengthens the organization's definition of the problem and makes it more likely that the organization's definition will prevail, since it is now supported by leadership from the potential opposition, whose position is therefore correspondingly weaker. This type of cooptation, corresponding to Selznick's conception, we call "personnel cooptation," since the organization seeks to impose its definition through absorbing personnel from the possible opposition. This type of cooptation was especially noticeable in the relation of the CDOs with citizens groups, and we shall discuss it further in Chapter 6. But we point to three other types of cooptation as defined above. These three types are directly related to the three analytical components of organizational rationale introduced in the preceding chapter: technical, administrative, and institutional.[8]

An organization's *technical rationale* is a frequent source of interorganizational contest because the technical rationale concerns itself with how activities should be carried on and who within the organization should perform them, usually a matter of professional expertise, and always a matter of jobs and of budgets. An organization's technical rationale enables it to insist that it has the knowledge, the skill, and, even, the ethical base from which programs should be operated. Some organizations, such as the public school system and the urban renewal agency, possess highly determinate technical rationales compared to the indeterminateness of the technical rationales of the poverty agency and of the

Model Cities agency. As a result, *technical cooptation* may occur, for example, when a CDO of indeterminate technical rationale accepts the definition of the appropriate technology to be used in dealing with a problem espoused by a CDO with a determinate technical rationale, and, by so doing, removes itself from contention for operation of a program. Or it may be overwhelmed by the technical expertise mustered up by the more determinate organization.

As an example, in one city the Model Cities organization developed a set of plans for urban renewal in the model neighborhood. The housing authority, which included the urban renewal agency, had not participated. But when it inspected the plans, it claimed they not only contained inaccuracies but were technically inadequate. It insisted that such technical competence was available through its own staff and its own planning operations and prevailed on the Model Cities agency in effect to give up its own plans in a negotiated relationship that clearly put the planning operation in the control of the housing authority.

An organization's *administrative rationale* is concerned on the one hand with those activities that mediate between the environment and the technological tasks and on the other with essential maintenance activities. The administrative rationale deals not only with support, internal and external, for task and maintenance activities, but also with acceptance of those routines and procedures deemed necessary to sustain them. *Administrative cooptation* takes place when a focal organization succeeds in getting another organization to define a contested issue in terms of the focal organization's administrative rationale.

A deputy superintendent of schools, on an apparently routine meeting at the regional office of the Economic Opportunity program, found the local community action agency officials there for the purpose of demanding parent control and paraprofessional roles in the Head Start program the school system had been running. The education man convinced the community action agency people to participate in joint staff meetings to review the situation. During these meetings, the school system administration emphasized the constraints under which it operated vis-à-vis the teachers union, the state education law, and the upholding of professional standards. Once these constraints were accepted as a basic and unchangeable part of the total situation, the school administration was assured that the agreement that emerged from the meetings would be one with which it could live with only minor inconvenience, if any.

The institutional component of organizational rationality, or the *institutional rationale*, relates, first of all, to its legitimacy, its right to exist, based upon greater or lesser support in the community for the functions it performs. Another aspect of an organization's institutional rationale is its domain, its locus in the interorganizational network. Domain includes an organization's manifest goals, its channels of access to resources, its service field and type of program, its service population, and its geographic area. *Institutional cooptation* occurs when a focal organization succeeds in getting another organization to define a contested issue in terms of the focal organization's own institutional rationale, and thus to acknowledge the focal organization's primary rights to the domain.

In one city, the Model Cities agency developed a manpower program to be funded by the Department of Labor. It abruptly encountered the fact that the community action agency, which had been particularly active in manpower programs, was seen by the Department of Labor as the agency legitimated to make decisions in the manpower field. It would not fund the program without the community action agency's sign-off. The community action agency insisted upon protracted negotiations and a reaffirmation of its own hegemony in the local manpower field, to which the Model Cities agency acceded. The interaction led, incidentally, to a much more explicit allocation of roles between the two organizations, an example of coordination through contest.

Note that there is a difference between defining an issue in terms of the organization's legitimated domain, and then letting the resolution of the issue develop whichever way it does, and engaging in a dispute over whose definition of the domain question will prevail. Cooptation relates to the definition of the issue, not to its resolution.

It appears that organizations with more determinate rationales are at an advantage in contest situations, since they can muster claims to expertness and to "generally accepted" principles in support of their positions. For example, the school superintendent in a dispute over curriculum can point to a whole shelf of technical books on curriculum construction. If the dispute regards administration, he can likewise point to a whole shelf of books describing his administrative rationale. The community action agency has no such shelf of books to point to, nor does the Model Cities agency. The situation regarding institutional rationale is analogous.

The result seems to be that organizations with determinate rationales are able to employ these types of organizational cooptation more readily than organization with less determinate rationales.

In such analyses, quantitative tables are somewhat premature. Yet it is interesting, and probably no coincidence, that in the 141 action episodes, the most frequent cases were instances of cooptation of an indeterminate rationale organization by an organization of determinate rationale. By contrast, the case of an organization with determinate rationale coopting another organization with determinate rationale was much less frequent, as was the case where an organization of indeterminate rationale was able to coopt another organization of indeterminate rationale. The fourth possibility, that of an organization of indeterminate rationale coopting an organization of determinate rationale, did not occur at all.

In the present study, the community action agencies and the Model Cities agencies were the ones with less determinate rationales. Even with this handicap in their interactional position, they were nevertheless able to contest successfully on a number of issues. This was so because they had special access to two other types of leverage from outside the local interorganizational system. On the one hand, being federally supported agencies and controlling the funds thus made possible, they could and frequently did call upon federal officials of their respective agencies at the regional or national level to support them in their side of a contest and to help them impose their definitions, or at least see that their definitions were given substantial consideration in the resolution of the issues.

As an example, in one city the school administration had offered two citizen planning committees an opportunity to join in planning a dropout prevention program. The plan was to include parents and dropouts on the project board. But when the school administrator who had helped develop the plans left his position, the school system administration backed down on the provisions for such participation on the project board. One of the citizen planning committees then succeeded in having the proposal rejected by the U.S. Office of Education because of its failure to comply with requirements for citizen involvement.

The other source of leverage for these two CDOs coming from outside the CDO interorganizational structure was the leverage of organized groups of poverty area residents. Both the community action agencies and the Model Cities agencies had special relationships to organized groups of poverty area residents. Such groups were a much more acknowledged part of their input constituencies than they were of other agencies. Thus, they could bring to bear in various contests whatever authoritativeness came from their claim to represent "the people" as over against "the bureaucracies." And in specific instances this claim could be backed up with demonstrations of citizen support that carried with them a background hint of coercion in the aftermath of the 1967 riots. This leverage was far from absolute, and as we shall see in Chapter 6, this citizen participation was not an unmixed blessing to the CAAs and MCs, because it was frequently directed at these organizations themselves. Nevertheless, the backing of organizations representing poor people was on occasion an effective resource.

As an example, in one city the community action agency's subcommittee on education sought with relatively little success to bring about certain changes in the administration of the school system. It held a citizens' meeting out of which arose six specific proposals which it subsequently presented formally to the school system administration at a meeting of the board of education. The board did not officially respond to these six proposals, but soon afterward the school system administration put three of them into operation.

In pointing out the importance of the organizational contest strategy of seeking to impose the organization's own definition on the issue or of calling in outside resources such as federal agency officials and local organizations of the poor when the CDO is at a disadvantage in pursuing this strategy, we do not mean to minimize the other important factors in these contest situations, such as the relative power of the organizations involved, and the resources they can bring to bear on any interaction issue. Rather, it is to point out the importance of determinateness of rationale and the manner in which such determinateness aids the organization in getting its way without having to apply the more overt types of contest strategy, including calling in federal officials or local citizens organizations.

System-Maintaining Processes of the Interorganizational Field: Preventing, Blunting, and Repelling

One of the anomalies of the urban turmoil of recent years, including the events that took place in the nine cities of this study during the study period, is that with so much apparent toil and trouble—as reported for example in the daily news—so little change has actually been brought about in the local interorganizational structure of CDOs. What of all the changes that were presumably taking place? And what of the impact of the struggles surrounding citizen participation? Were they largely without substance? We shall examine these questions in Chapters 5 and 6 respectively, along with other findings regarding innovation and participation. Suffice it to say here that the impact has been slight and that the individual community decision organizations both as individual organizations and aggregately as an interorganizational field structure have shown a remarkable degree of persistence and stability. We have already presented in Chapter 2 some of the dynamics that assure this stability of the interorganizational field. In the present chapter we have addressed the manner in which the individual organizations encounter threats to their viability, and have remarked on the circumstance that most such threats are of a distinctly minor nature and do not constitute a lethal danger to the organizations' viability.

The interaction between the two levels is of course reciprocal. The interorganizational field structure protects the organizations in their individual interaction and in their need for continued viability. At the same time, the behavior of individual organizations has the aggregate effect of preserving the major configurations of the interorganizational field and the institutionalized thought structure that supports it.

There has been very little conflict, which by definition constitutes a threat to the interorganizational field either through attacking the core legitimation of the CDOs or by violating the norms for conducting interorganizational contest or by attacking directly the interorganizational field configuration and the institutionalized thought structure on which it is based. Hence, the interaction has been confined to processes that are well within the requirements for the stable operation of the interorganizational field. Threats to the "system" are extremely rare. How can this be accounted for?

We can analyze system stability in terms of three "lines of defense" which protect the interorganizational structure as such from attacks that might threaten it in a major way. The three lines of defense can be called *preventing,* *blunting*, and *repelling.*

Preventing

The system is protected from major threats because the socialization of individuals makes it unlikely that such threats will arise. We follow the usual definition of socialization as the process through which individuals learn to internalize the norms of a social group or system. One does not have to go all the way with Parsons in order to recognize and acknowledge that the acceptance of common norms is an important element conducing to system stability. The prevailing definitions of social reality, social problems, and social intervention strategies are learned in the process of socialization of both the rich and poor, by "volunteers" and professionals, at the same time that an attitude of abhorrence is learned in regard to activities or plans that constitute major violations of these social definitions. Hence, it is no coincidence that most policy suggestions or widely heralded "innovations" remain well within the bounds of the existing institutionalized thought structure and constitute not a threat to it but a support of it. They constitute "fine-tuning" of a system whose major dimensions (whether or not they are understood) are accepted and which presumably needs only minor adjustments here and there, adjustments that, as we have seen, are largely in the nature of some type of services or therapy for the poor and some type of "increased coordination" for greater effectiveness on the part of the agencies.

We shall examine the substance of the innovations that took place in the CDOs during the study period in Chapter 5. For the present, we summarize by saying that most proposed changes were changes of minor points within the interorganizational field structure and did not constitute a serious threat to the major configurations of that structure, and that the most important social dynamic assuring this was the process of socialization into acceptance of the major outlines of the existing thought structure as part of the process of "growing up" to become a "normal" adult. In this process, the norms of the system had become internalized, even by those who were displeased with the system's operation, such that it did not seriously occur to them to question the major outlines of the system.

Blunting

The blunting of threats to the interorganizational structure was performed by individual organizations that constituted the immediate target of these threats. Primary threats—that is, threats to the organizational field structure itself— seldom arose because of the socialization process, the structure's first line of defense. Where they did arise, having permeated, as it were, that first line of defense, they were usually blunted by the target organization.

Thus, in the development of the multifield Model Cities programs during the planning process, plans were pushed in a number of cities, usually at the behest of organizations of the poor, for types of program that began to constitute major threats to the existing interorganizational structure. Such plans involved popular local neighborhood control of the police, or of the schools, or the establishment of substantially funded agencies that threatened major competition with one or more of the existing social agencies, or massive replacement of "qualified," "certified" personnel by paraprofessional personnel from among poverty area residents, or large proportions of control over the resources and activities of existing agencies. Any of these, if pushed beyond a certain point, might have constituted major threats to the existing interorganizational structure. What these efforts had in common was that they began to approach actions that redefined the nature of social reality and social problems, seeing the latter not as mere aberrations consisting of inadequate people on the margins of an otherwise healthy and essentially wholesome social structure, but rather as major defects in a system that generated social problems and required major changes.

Despite the extensive "rhetoric" in which such conviction was often voiced, comparatively few such instances arose. Most of those that did were blunted or simply defeated, with all parties accepting the defeat as a normal and legitimate part of the community decision-making process. Often, however, these proposals did not develop so far as to have to be contested by means of a vote of the city council or by a veto, say, from the appropriate regional or federal office, or through a major test of strength between one of the CDOs and the group or organization making the proposal.

Rather, the target CDO was usually able to apply its organizational rationale to the issue and impose its definition of the issue upon the interaction, thus effectively blunting the threat. For example, a given program had to be under the technically competent supervision of a professional physician, social worker, or educator. Or a given proposal offered as an alternative to an urban renewal or highway plan was not technically competent. In this way, the technical rationales of the organizations could be brought into play in the interaction, often with persuasive effect, so that what might have otherwise developed to the stage of a vigorous contest was "nipped in the bud."

Likewise, an effort to demand more hiring of poverty area residents in a given program came up against the agency constraints of civil service, or of agreements with a union, or it constituted a violation of the state education law, or it was not feasible in terms of prevalent goals and priorities and resources as these were embodied in the existing structure. Or it simply was not the way things were done by those who were in the positions legitimated by the community for doing them. Thus, the administrative rationales of the organizations were likewise brought into play in the blunting process.

Of great importance in the blunting process was the legitimation afforded these CDOs as the arbiters of what might and might not be permitted or encouraged or prevented from happening in their respective service fields. In this, they were supported by the wide acceptance of their manifest function of bringing about coordination within their respective fields, of avoiding wasteful duplication of services. Such legitimation had the side effect of permitting these organizations a virtual veto over what programs would be developed in their service fields, under whose auspices, with what technologies, administrative procedures, etc. The wide acceptance of their right to order their service fields and to prevent useless duplication and waste had the latent function of preventing competition, thus protecting and reinforcing their domains. The Model Cities Administration, even under the Johnson administration, was committed to working through and with existing agencies. This policy was justified as the only effective way of bringing about social change. Although the reasoning may seem somewhat paradoxical—that one works for change by supporting the existing agencies—the logic was that special ad hoc agencies would be able to accomplish little outside their own programs. If the efforts were to make a lasting impact, they must make it on the established interorganizational structure, through inducing change in its components. The usual method of inducing such change was to offer them federal funds provided that they did thus and so.

The Nixon administration placed even greater stress on working with the existing agencies and avoiding the setting up of new agencies wherever possible. What this all amounted to was a strong dynamic supporting the institutional rationale of the CDOs, their right to be doing what they were doing in their respective fields. This underlying institutional legitimation of the existing interorganizational structure was an important component in the blunting process; its effect was to filter new proposals through the existing organizational rationales of the community decision organizations, thus enabling them to define the problems, define the issues, and with overwhelming success impose their desired resolution on those issues.

One other aspect of the process by which potential threats to the interorganizational structure were blunted was the underlying leitmotif of the services strategy, the rationale of *therapy*. The social definition of problems of poverty, poor housing, and the rest as inhering largely in the defects of those who suffered from them suggested therapy, in one guise or another, as the appropriate strategy for approaching their problems. Indeed, even the struggle of neighborhood residents to gain a measure of influence over neighborhood institutions, including service programs, was considered by many to have a positive value not because it would produce desired change in those institutions, but because it would have a therapeutic effect on "alienated, powerless" neighborhood residents. Once they had overcome this feeling of alienation and powerlessness, they would be better able to cope with the situation that this very alienation and feeling of powerlessness had helped to bring about. By this means, citizen participation came to be seen as an experience that would do poor people good, and should therefore be suffered patiently by the agencies, rather than as the gradually strengthening expression of the interests of an increasingly organized citizen constituency.

From this institution-maintaining perspective, the person who attacks the institutionalized thought structure becomes by definition a problem. He must be dealt with. He must be helped to see where he is wrong, whether for ideological reasons or reasons of feasibility. The problem lies with him. This was nowhere more apparent than in the rash of research that broke out in the aftermath of the 1967 ghetto riots. Numerous well-funded research projects were developed to study the characteristics of the ghetto rioters, on the implicit assumption that these people were "different" from those who did not riot, and in this difference lay the roots of the problem. Special "youth service" programs were sponsored during subsequent summers, an understandable part of the services approach to dealing with the problems of the inner cities.

Writing in the year after the ghetto riots, S.M. Miller and Martin Rein warned that "if a socio-therapeutic orientation is not guarded against, it insidiously gains ascendancy. The black struggle of today may change this picture and reduce the likelihood of socio-therapy suppressing the drive for social change. But there is no assurance that protean socio-therapy will not dominate."[9] The data from the present study, which covered the experience of the subsequent two years, indicate that "protean socio-therapy" prevailed, as will be shown in Chapter 5.

Repelling

Our data indicate that the vast bulk of organizational interaction took place around issues that involved no threat to the interorganizational structure. Most contest occurred well within the definitions of social reality supplied in the institutionalized thought structure, and according to the norms of live-and-let-live which protect both the interorganizational structure and the individual CDOs. Only relatively rarely did issues develop which began to constitute a potential lethal threat to an individual CDO and/or to the interorganizational structure. These threats were usually blunted through personnel or organizational cooptation, or through prevalence of the CDO's position in the community decision-making process. Seldom did they permeate this second line of defense.

But the question arises as to what the response would be in those cases where a threat to the system is made and persists and does not yield to prevention or blunting. Though such cases are infrequent, the question is important, for its answer helps us to gain a more complete understanding of the operation of the interorganizational field. Let us be clear about the seriousness of the issues under consideration. We are talking about attacks on the interorganizational structure, attacks that threaten the very persistence and legitimation of the interorganizational structure, attacks that it has not been found possible to prevent or to blunt. Sterner measures must be taken if the interorganizational structure is to persist. The iron fist must now make itself felt through the velvet glove. The threat must be destroyed.

From a quite abstract standpoint, Berger and Luckmann have conceptualized the dynamic situation. They point out the importance of therapy as a method for dealing with challenges to any given social construction of reality. But when therapy fails, then the challenge must be destroyed through annihilation. The ideas expressed in the threat are assigned "an inferior ontological status, and thereby a not-to-be-taken seriously cognitive status." They continue: "Whether one then proceeds from annihilation to therapy, or rather goes on to liquidate physically what one has liquidated conceptually, is a practical question of policy."[10]

If the threat arises from an organization, there are several paths this "physical" annihilation may take. But basically, they reduce to two; the organization can be either transformed or destroyed. It can be transformed, for instance, by changing its internal power structure, replacing its leadership, etc. It can be destroyed by outlawing it—though subsequent enforcement measures must be adequate to make the ban effective—or by cutting off its resources at one or more vital points.

Among the fifty-four community decision organizations of the present study, only a single instance arose of a persistent and direct attack involving the three components of primary contest, or conflict. The development of this conflict, occasioned by the Oakland Economic Development Council, Incorporated, the Oakland CAA, is recounted at length in Chapter 7. In that instance, the attempt was made to transform the organization, and when this attempt failed, the organization was destroyed through cutting off its vital resources. More specifically, the OEDCI was finally disqualified by the Office of Economic Opportunity from being the recipient of OEO funds. This action did not immediately destroy the organization, but it removed its legitimation within the local interorganizational structure to occupy its domain—in our terms, a lethal blow to its institutional rationale—and cut off the major part of its financial resources, at the same time setting up a new community action agency, quite independent of the old one, to take its place—a new CDO which was more firmly under the control of the city council. The reliance on reinforcement from a more inclusive system here—the federal OEO office—illustrates the linkage in thought and social structures between different system levels.

Such clear-cut examples of primary contest do not arise frequently, but they indicate the hard core of determination and potential destructive response to system threats that it has not been found possible to prevent or blunt. It should be noted, however, that like other possible applications of force, the very existence of the possibility has the impact of helping prevent the necessity for its use. It acts as a deterrent, a deterrent which, along with the milder and less noticeable processes of preventing and blunting, had the effect in nearly all cases of keeping the interorganizational interaction well within the accepted definitions of social reality and social problems and the accepted, protective "live-and-let- live" norms for organizational interaction among CDOs.

Summary

There is relatively little important interaction among these CDOs.

The interaction that does take place occurs in relation to both opportunities and threats, with the threats usually accompanied by strong interaction.

In specific interactions, a CDO's stake is governed by the anticipated effect of alternative issue outcomes on its viability. Its position on an issue is dependent on its stake in the issue, but is formulated in terms of the performance of its manifest tasks.

In addition to the employment of cooptation in Selznick's sense (*personnel* cooptation), these organizations employ technical, administrative, and institutional cooptation (*organizational* cooptation) as means of warding off domain threats.

Secondary contest occurs on matters of issue outcome difference between CDOs. It takes place according to well-defined norms of live-and-let-live and within the confines of the prevalent institutionalized thought structure, which emphasizes social problems as inhering essentially in the victims, at the margins of an otherwise healthy social order, for whom improved social services and greater coordination among organizations constitute the remedy.

Secondary contest occurs principally around domain threats.

While at the organizational level secondary contest is at times serious and vigorous, at the level of the interorganizational field it operates as an adjustive mechanism defining and redefining the ongoing domain consensus rooted in the institutionalized thought structure and worked out in such interaction between organizations with overlapping domains.

The stability of the interorganizational field is maintained by the three processes of preventing, blunting, and repelling actual or potential threats to the structure of the interorganizational field.

In the course of this long chapter on interaction among CDOs, relatively little has been said about coordination. Yet, much of what has been reported has a bearing on the question of coordination among CDOs, to which we now turn.

Interorganizational Coordination[1]

Concerted attention in this study to coordinative activities among CDOs over an extended period of time has produced a series of findings which in some respects reinforce what is already known, and in other respects come as a challenge to widely held points of view.

The major findings and conclusions on coordination can be summarized:

A substantial amount of coordinative activity takes place unevenly among these CDOs. A large proportion of this activity takes the form of structured arrangements for coordination without reference to any specific objective other than coordination. A still larger amount takes the form of ad hoc, goal-oriented coordinative activities, both short term and long term. These somewhat different kinds of activities, which we shall call *structured* or *ad hoc* as the case may be, are characterized predominantly by cooperation.

Although we have made no quantitative breakdown, we have been impressed by the importance of *short-term* ad hoc coordinative efforts within the total coordination picture. These efforts take two forms. One is the widely recognized *coalition*, where organizations pool a share of their resources (usually an extremely small share) to bring about some mutually desired outcome, such as the development of a new program. The other is less widely recognized, but nevertheless of great importance—the activities set in motion primarily by a single organization which has a particular objective for which it must gain the assent or cooperation or resource sharing of a number of other organizations. This process we call *mobilization.*[2] The process fits loosely into Etzioni's conception of mobilization as "the process by which a unit gains significantly in the control of assets it previously did not control." Such ad hoc mobilization is an important source of coordination, although it is frequently overlooked because of an implicit equating of coordination with "structured" coordination alone.

A more focused analysis of structured coordination indicates that most of the structured coordination among these community decision organizations is without tangible outcome of any kind and presumably very largely a waste of time and community resources.

A significant proportion of coordinative instances takes place not only outside of formal coordinating structures, but in a process of contest rather than cooperation. Failure to recognize them as instances of coordination results from a faulty or inconsistent identification of the term with cooperative activities. The equating of coordination with cooperation is an important source of confusion.

67

We have been unable to find in our data any substantiation of the claim that the Model Cities program increased either the frequency or effectiveness of coordinative activities among CDOs during the study period.

The above findings on structured coordination and its results are more readily understood, we believe, from a paradigm that views the interaction from the standpoint of the interorganizational field rather than from a paradigm that views the interaction solely from the standpoint of individual organizations pursuing their own autonomous courses. From the organizational level paradigm, much interaction that performs a coordinative function is overlooked, not being recognized as coordination. Further, the findings are quite consonant with a theoretical conceptualization of the interorganizational field of CDOs as an ecology organized through mutual adjustment at the margins of the domains of the respective CDOs, within norms that protect their individual viability even in cases where coordination through contest results in a decision that has an adverse effect on a given CDO's domain.

More importantly, our conclusion is that even if such efforts to improve the possibilities of coordination within the existing interorganizational field were much more frequent than they were found to be, and even if they reported tangible positive outcome in a much higher proportion of instances than they now do, the effects would be only minimal. From the interorganizational field perspective developed in Chapter 2, the achievement of, say, 10 percent or even 50 percent greater efficiency in the disposition of resources by these organizations would have a minimal effect on the problems of the inner cities, and hence the concentration of attention on ways of enhancing such efficiency has the latent effect of distracting attention from the fact that the structural aspects of the problems of the inner cities are not being addressed by these organizations. This point is further elaborated in Chapter 5 and reviewed in Chapter 9.

Coordination through Cooperation

Lack of conceptual clarity may vitiate systematic efforts to study coordination. Many studies do not give a formal definition, but simply enumerate types of specific activities (for instance, joint committees) which are presumably coordinative. In some cases, definitions are given that are virtually indistinguishable from definitions of cooperation, such as "working together for common goals."

The concept used in the present study is based on the process of concerted decisions and actions. We define *interorganizational coordination* as a structure or process of concerted decision making or action wherein the decisions or actions of two or more organizations are made simultaneously in part or in whole in some deliberate degree of adjustment to each other.[3]

As will presently be seen, coordination as so defined is distinguished from cooperation; for although much coordination takes place within a context of cooperative interaction, some coordination takes place within a context of contest rather than cooperation. We will first present the findings on coordination through cooperation. Parenthetically, most treatments of coordination in the literature are confined to this type of coordination.

It is well to remind the reader that we are here concerned with coordination between and among CDOs, and not with coordination within the service field of any specific CDO. CDOs are, themselves, coordinating mechanisms for their respective fields and presumably bring about various amounts of coordination within those fields; but that is not the subject of the present study. Rather, this study is concerned with coordination among the coordinators, among the CDOs. This being the case, coordination by superordinate authority is not relevant to our data, in that there is no superordinate authority authorized to make coordinating decisions among the study's CDOs. If the study's focus were on coordination within service fields, superordinate authority would be relevant, as exemplified by the school system administration's authority to make coordinative decisions among the various schools in the public school system. Not all CDOs exercise superordinate authority as their principal means of effecting coordination, as illustrated in the federative collaborative methods of the health and welfare councils and in the negotiating-contracting methods of the urban renewal agencies.

The very absence of an authority structure to coordinate the efforts of the various CDOs makes coordination among them problematic and raises the question of how it occurs. The data of this study show that coordination takes place among CDOs primarily by structured and ad hoc cooperative procedures, but occasionally by contest procedures. We consider first the cooperative procedures, both structured and ad hoc.

Structured.—Formal, enduring structures for concerted decision making not directed at a specific goal or program includes such coordinative mechanisms as interlocking board membership, liaison staff, and the sharing of facilities for purposes of facilitating coordination generally. Such coordination is of a deliberate, self-conscious nature in that its purpose is purely to establish a structured relationship between the CDOs of the pair.

Ad hoc.—Structures for interaction around specific goals. Examples would be the development of a jointly sponsored program, such as a transportation program set up by the Model Cities agency and the community action agency, or the activity through which an urban renewal agency helps a school administration locate a new school site. It also includes more enduring structured relationships which are goal-specific, rather than general, such as the lending of personnel between CDOs for purposes of a specific project.

Roughly, what these two types of coordination represent is the difference between general, all-purpose coordinative structures and special arrangements that develop around an individual program or activity. A special classification and count of such instances was made, as they applied between pairs of CDOs. The number of ad hoc instances recorded in the data totalled 238, somewhat more numerous than the instances of structured coordination, which totalled 203 between CDO pairs. In addition, there were 189 instances of coordination which included other organizations in addition to the interacting pair of CDOs. These 189 instances were not included in the structured versus ad hoc breakdown, which is restricted to pairs of CDOs without third parties. They are included, however, in the total count of CDO pairs involved in instances of cooperative coordination, bringing the total to 630. Using this total count, Table 4-1 gives the number of instances of cooperative coordination between pairs of CDOs for all nine cities.

Table 4-1

Instances of Cooperative Coordination, by CDO Pair Type

MC-CAA	72
MC-ED	69
ED-CAA	67
MC-UR	62
CAA-HW	57
MC-HW	42
ED-MH	36
ED-UR	36
CAA-UR	33
UR-HW	33
MC-MH	31
CAA-MH	28
ED-HW	28
HW-MH	24
MH-UR	12
	630

In coordination, just as in the case of number of interactions (Table 3-2), the pairs made up of the Model Cities agencies (MC), the community action agencies (CAA), and the school system administrations (ED) show the highest counts, although their order is slightly different. Generally speaking, the order of frequency between pairs on structured and ad hoc coordination follows the general trend of the order of frequency of interaction. This is hardly surprising, since these two variables overlap considerably, much of the interaction falling within the definition of coordination, and much of the coordination (though not all of it) falling within the definition of interaction.

Even though the Model Cities organizations were only in their early stages of development during the study period, they totaled the largest count of cooperative coordination of all the CDOs. The others follow in a not unexpected order, indicated in Table 4-2.

The cities of Detroit and Manchester were included in the nine-city purposive

Table 4-2
Instances of Cooperative Coordination by CDO Type

Model cities agency	276
Community action agency	257
Public school system administration	236
Health and welfare planning council	184
Urban renewal agency	176
Mental health planning agency	131
	1260[a]

[a]This total is double that of Table 4-1, since two organizations are involved in each instance of paired interaction.

sample of this study so as to yield some exploratory indication of the effect of scale on these inter-CDO relationships. We have not reported the findings on these two cities in the presentations on cooperation/contest, since generally they did not seem to have any special significance. But in connection with coordinative activity, both structured and ad hoc, the cities show an unexpected relationship. Detroit is highest in frequency of coordination between pairs of CDOs, as might well be expected, accounting for 119 of the 630 instances reported in Tables 4-1 and 4-2. Manchester, instead of being lowest, as might have been expected if city size and frequency of paired coordination are positively correlated, was actually higher than any other city except Detroit. As best we can determine, this represents a substantive difference, not attributable to possible overreporting in the case of Manchester, a possibility that was looked into. We believe our findings actually represent what was going on in these cities regarding coordinative activity. It is of course impossible to generalize from this exploratory aspect of the study to the situation in other cities not included in the sample. The high coordination in Manchester may be purely adventitious and not representative of smaller cities generally. On the other hand, it is also possible that there is a curvilinear relationship between city size and coordinative activity between pairs of CDOs, a relationship that is U-shaped. It may be that smallness of size is conducive to high coordinative activity for a somewhat different set of reasons than largeness of size is conducive to high coordinative activity. On frequency of overall *interaction*, as defined in Chapter 3, Detroit was the highest by far, while Manchester was fourth out of the nine cities.

Returning to the findings on structured versus ad hoc coordination, we made note that the ad hoc coordination instances are more numerous than the structured instances, although the difference is not great. This throws some light on the question of the extent to which coordination among organizations (in this case CDOs) takes place through structured arrangements which are presumably conducive to coordination (but which may or may not actually lead to concerted decision making and to tangible outcomes from such decision making), or through the interaction generated around specific, ad hoc issues. The answer, in the case of these CDOs, is: Both, in approximately equal proportions.

In connection with the ad hoc type of coordination, which brings organizations together for concerted decision making around a specific issue, we have noticed two major ways in which this occurs. At the one extreme, the issue is a joint endeavor virtually from the start. Two or more organizations are mutually interested in some particular issue and begin to interact and concert their decisions around it. The issue may be a contract between them, which is mutually beneficial. Or they may set up an interaction process in order to pool their efforts toward accomplishing some mutually desired objective, such as the development of a new agency, or a new set of services, or a joint program. This can be called a *coalitional* approach to ad hoc coordination. It is, we believe, what most people have in mind when they refer to what we call ad hoc coordination.

But there is another type of ad hoc coordination that we believe is equally important. This is what, for lack of a better term, we call *mobilizational* coordination. In these instances, a single organization sets out to pursue some objective. It may be the addition of a new service, or the award of a new contract, or the expansion of its own program. But it recognizes that it needs the support of other organizations in order to accomplish its objective. It may need financing, access to a building, some borrowed staff, or assurance that clients will be referred to it. Likewise, it may need to overcome potential or actual resistance to its objective on the part of one or more organizations. As a result, it sets about systematically interacting with other organizations in a decision-making process which, if successful, adds up to the securing of the help it needs from other organizations, often with some quid pro quo. In effect, it is coordinating the various pertinent organizations—or parts of the various pertinent organizations—around its own objective. It performs, in other words, an entrepreneurial function in the sense that it gathers together the resources and forges the ad hoc relationships that enable it to pursue its objective.

This type of activity is often simply overlooked or disregarded, because conventional concepts of coordination do not include it. The result is the impression of the interorganizational ecology as largely uncoordinated, when actually, coordination of this type is going on much of the time. And in such cases, since an organization is aggressively interested in a particular issue, the likelihood that some tangible result will follow from the coordinative effort is greater than if the coordination were simply "to establish better relations," to "keep in touch," etc. This circumstance is especially important in the light of the analysis of the results of structured coordination, which were largely negative.

The Results of Structured Coordination

Consonant with the initial interest of the project in structured coordination, a special analysis was made of the results of such structures. We are here referring to instances of overlapping board and committee membership between CDOs, the lending of staff, and the sharing of facilities for the purpose of facilitating coordination rather than a specified goal. As reported earlier, there were 203 instances of such structured, enduring, non-goal-oriented relationships. The study included data not only on the presence of such mechanisms, but also on what happened, if anything, in and through them. Since these 203 instances involved CDO pairs, and the same questions were addressed to each CDO of a pair, there were 406 possible affirmative answers regarding definite *results* from such coordinative structures. The affirmative answers were classified into a number of categories, which we now consider briefly in sequence:

Program (35 instances). This category was the highest, with 35 instances of the structured coordination actually leading to the realization of a program by the two CDOs.

Resource exchange (32 instances). This included exchanges involving such items as facilities, consultation, labor, funds for new programs and for hiring or training personnel.

Communication (29 instances). In the broad interpretation of the term *results*, this category of improved communication was included as a positive result when it was claimed as such by the respondent. This included such relative intangibles as "keeping in contact better," "kept us more aware of the role of the other CDO," etc.

Influence on other CDO (29 instances). This category includes cases where the coordination was stated to have influenced the activity or the operating rationale of another CDO. For example, an urban renewal agency asserted that the loan of a planner to the Model Cities agency helped get that agency to "do things our way." Interestingly, *all 29 reported instances of influence through structured coordination were one-way; the respondent CDO influenced some other CDO, never the reverse.*

Negative results (21 instances). This included cases where no positive response was reported and where negative responses were given, chiefly characterized by termination of the relationship because of dissatisfaction of one or both of the parties.

Hence, from a total of 406 possible reports of structured coordination, only 125 instances of positive, tangible results were elicited, and 29 of these were simply references to improved communications and hence largely insignificant. In addition, there were 21 reports of negative results.

These findings raise further questions. Perhaps the most important question has to do with the tremendous apparent attrition involved in structured coordination, the predominant number of instances where "we coordinated," but "nothing happened."

Coordination through Contest

The importance of the distinction made in Chapter 2 between an interorganizational paradigm that focuses on the individual organizations and a paradigm that focuses on the interorganizational field becomes apparent in a systematic conceptual analysis of coordination. At the level of interaction between individual organizations, the concering of decisions usually takes place through cooperation that is voluntary because it is seen as compatible with the viability of each individual organization and furthers the interests of one or more of them as well; or is imposed through power exerted by one over the other; or is imposed through external authority. CDOs work toward common ends as a result of a concerted decision that is either voluntary or imposed. By such a means, for example, decisions are made as to the allocation of scarce resources among them as well as the division of labor in performing their operational activities. In our conception, these are simply marginal adjustments in domain. They conform to the conventional conception of coordination.

But if coordination—the concerting of decisions regarding allocation of resources and functions—is viewed from the level not of the individual organizations but of the interorganizational field that includes them (or some other inclusive system, such as the community), then it becomes apparent that this process may take place, and indeed does often take place, in contest as well.

A concerted decision is made, for example, in the contest of a school system administration and a community action agency for control of an educational program. From the standpoint of the contesting agencies, this of course is not recognizeable as coordination. But from the standpoint of the community, it is a concerted decision as to who shall do what, a very important aspect of what is usually meant by coordination. In most cases, though, it is not thought of as coordination because of the failure to define coordination carefully, the failure to be clear about the system level that is the point of reference, and the consequent equating of coordination with cooperation. The opposite of coordination is neither contest nor cooperation, but separate or fragmented decision making, the result not of interaction, but of noninteraction—at least on the issue involved.

Let us consider this distinction between coordination and its opposite, noninteraction. The activities of actors in contest are brought much more closely into relation with each other than the activities of actors who are acting without regard for each other. The actions of two tennis players require large degrees of coordination in order to keep the ball whizzing rapidly and skillfully back and forth across the net. The fact that they are doing so with somewhat different desired outcomes in mind is of great importance; but it does not detract in the least from the extremely interrelated nature of the overt behavior. Theirs is a type of "coordination in contest," a type Sumner called "antagonistic cooperation" and which he applied even to situations of international warfare, where closely interrelated efforts of antagonists are likewise present.[4] But the point at issue is perhaps best captured by Simmel: "Both forms of relation—the antithetical and the convergent—are fundamentally distinguished from the mere indifference of two or more individuals or groups. Whether it implies the rejection or the termination of sociation, indifference is purely negative."[5]

Such a process of conceptual analysis indicates that coordination, or the concerting of decisions, takes place in either cooperative or contestful interaction. Lack of coordination arises from lack of interaction concerning the substantively related decisions made, decisions made in what Simmel calls "indifference," as opposed to "sociation."

This "antagonistic cooperation," which Sumner describes, seems paradoxical only when one ignores the two possible levels of analysis: that of the individual organization and that of the more inclusive system. What appears as—and is—contest at the organizational level may perform a coordinative function at the interorganizational field level. Some examples:

A school system administration had run the local Head Start program with some assistance from the community action agency. Later, when the community action agency changed its policies, it tried to take over the Head Start program, giving various reasons for the change, including the alleged excessive overhead charged by the school system administration. The latter organization reluctantly acceded, relinquishing the program.

In a different city, the Model Cities agency, the community action agency, and a city official discussed the citizen participation component of the Model Cities program. The community action agency did the planning for this component, but the Model Cities agency was critical because an agency with which it had friendly relations had been excluded from the planning process. The Model Cities agency then created a citizen participation component similar in many respects to the one planned by the community action agency, but without giving that agency credit for the planning or a role in the new mechanism.

In a third city, the health and welfare council tried to convince the city govenment that it was the appropriate agency to oversee the development of the Model Cities citizen participation component. Just as it appeared to have succeeded, the community action agency called a community meeting out of which there developed an independent organization claiming to represent the citizens of the Model Cities area. This body gained approval as the Model Cities citizen component, thus defeating the health and welfare council's efforts.

These examples clearly demonstrate the manner in which interorganizational contest frequently operates to perform allocative coordinational functions through concerted decision making. The allocative decision is concerted in that the decisions and/or activities of the organizations are carried out in relation to each other. The difference from cooperative coordination lies in the fact that the concerted decision arises out of contest, where different and incompatible outcomes were desired by the participating organizations.

A further analysis of such instances[6] indicates that four types of situation regarding coordination through contest are revealed in the 141 action episodes. Although they are not mutually exclusive, they warrant separate listing:

1. The organizations establish mechanisms to achieve coordination of activities despite continuing contest.

2. The contest is resolved through a division of labor and/or resources which is less than satisfactory for at least one of the organizations.

3. In the contest, one organization gains control over the pertinent part of another organization's activities, thus being able to adjust the other organization's decision making and activities to its own.

4. In the contest, one organization induces another to accept its organizational rationale—or some aspect of it—in such manner that it becomes the principal benefactor of the coordinative decision that is made.

Thus, a type of coordination often overlooked occurs in many of the contests over domain that take place. But whether structured or ad hoc, whether cooperative or contestful, such episodes of concerted decision making have the effect of constant modification of the structure of the local interorganizational field in terms of minor domain shifts at the margins of the viability of the individual CDOs. The issue regarding coordination, then, is not so much one of structural mechanisms versus chaos, but of coordination taking place in both structured and ad hoc modes, with ad hoc modes including not only cooperation but also contest. The common plaint for "more coordination" is thus misconceived. The real issue would seem to be: Which type of coordinative activity yields optimal outcomes in which kinds of situation; and—optimal for whom?

The Coordinative Impact of Model Cities

Most of the Model Cities agencies got underway at about the beginning of the twenty-six-month field period. Since one of the purposes of the Model Cities program was coordination, the question arises as to how much coordination it engendered, and with what effect. The present study was not directed specifically at that question, but it did produce some sets of data that give an indication of how effective the coordinative efforts of these agencies were in the first two years of their existence.

As already indicated (in Table 4-2), the Model Cities agencies were the highest of all CDOs on cooperative coordination, both structured and ad hoc. So there is little question that they were engaging in coordinative activities, in accordance with their manifest purpose. The data indicate that their relationships to the community action agencies, the school system administrations, and the Urban Renewal authorities were particularly active. Hence, a new agency had arisen which engaged in a high degree of coordinative activity with the other CDOs of this study. One may ask whether this coordinative activity had the effect of stimulating further coordination among pairs of CDOs in the study. That is, were the other CDOs more likely to coordinate activities with each other as a result of the Model Cities agencies' presence and activities?

Two sets of data cast doubt on the effectiveness of the Model Cities agencies in stimulating coordination between other CDOs. First, the CDO schedules from which most of the data on coordination were provided were administered both in 1968 and in 1970. (The 1970 figures are given in Table 4-1, since the 1968 figures did not include the nascent Model Cities agencies.) One would expect the 1970 coordination to be the larger in numbers, if the Model Cities agency was making a major impact on inter-CDO coordination during the two years of the study period. Yet the total inter-CDO coordination was less, rather than greater, in 1970 than it had been in 1968.

A second set of data is more directly relevant to the nature of the inter-CDO coordination in which the Model Cities agencies engaged. These data indicate that the Model Cities agencies' relations to the various CDOs were directed at furthering the Model Cities agencies' own programs, and not at stimulating interaction between CDOs in matters other than Model Cities programs. In the Model Cities agency schedules (CDA schedules) the Model Cities agencies were asked if they had attempted to set up linkages between community agencies outside of the formal Model Cities coordinative arrangements. No schedule was available from Oakland. Of the other eight Model Cities agencies, six indicated no such attempts. (Interestingly, Manchester was one of the two that did indicate such attempts. It indicated three attempts to bring organizations together across service fields. This suggests a possible accounting for the inordinately high rate of coordinative activity in this small city. There are fewer organizations, to be sure. The interorganizational field is not so crowded. But perhaps for that very reason, CDOs are more likely to come in contact with each other than in larger cities where, by comparison, they represent more or less independent "empires.")

Hence, it appears that most of the Model Cities agencies were engaging in high rates of interaction with other CDOs, but around their own programs, in more or less direct reciprocal relationships, which did not have the effect of stimulating greater interaction and coordination among the CDOs with each other on matters other than Model Cities programs.

Some Observations on Coordination

In the light of these findings on coordination, a larger question is suggested: Why is coordination taken unquéstioningly as a desideratum by both administrators and social scientists working in this field? Is all coordination *ipso facto* desirable? Apparently, there exists a widely held implicit assumption that the answer is "Yes." Yet, as previously indicated, it is an open question whether organizations that desire the same issue outcome will invariably further their own interests (disregarding for the moment the interests of an inclusive system) by concering their decisions, whether on a structured or an ad hoc basis. Even Mayer Zald, who is most explicit on pointing out the importance of the "costs" of coordination, in some cases high, in some cases low, does not go so far as to question its overall desirability. "No argument is made *for* fragmentation and low coordination," he writes; "instead, there are costs and benefits to *both* integration of services and autonomy of services. Only if these costs and benefits are seriously weighed can anyone estimate the value of different *degrees* of coordination and integration under varying *structural* arrangements."[7] The assumption seems to be that the benefits will exceed the costs in all coordination, so long as it is the appropriate *degree* of coordination for the situation.

In pointing out the costs of coordination, Zald is not alone. Sjoberg argues not only for the existence of contradictory functional requirements within social systems, but that these contradictory requirements (which "coordination" would presumably even out or eliminate) may be essential to system maintenance.[8] In a similar but more explicit vein, Landau asserts the importance of duplicative functions which appear redundant but which constitute second-line safeguards to the adaptability of the system, and which are eliminated (through effective coordination) at the system's peril.[9] Terreberry maintains that "it may well be that coordination *per se*, in the static sense usually implied by that term is dysfunctional for adaptation to turbulent fields." She points out that this very criticism has been leveled at local councils of social agencies (the health and welfare planning councils of the present study).[10]

Elling indicates the need for research as to whether specific sets of organizational arrangements to promote coordination may have the effect of restricting or fostering innovation.[11] Mott indicates the ineffectiveness of efforts at coordination by peer group, but asserts that the alternative, coordination by hierarchy, tends to reduce the areas of discretion necessary to professional personnel, decreasing their creativity and requiring increasing reliance on rules and regulations, thus increasing rigidities and hampering the free flow of communication. It also provides greater likelihood of "inappropriate" actions by central decision-makers relatively remote from specific problems being resolved.[12]

Yet the quest for coordination goes on with the implicit assumption that it is always desirable. Part of the paradoxical commitment to unexamined coordination is attributable to the lack of specificity as to what the term shall mean, as well as to confusion as to whether the alleged benefits are to the individual organizations or to some more inclusive system, or both. Quite obviously, the wide recognition of the fact that interorganizational coordination of some types at least may operate to the detriment of a more inclusive system is amply illustrated in the presence of antitrust legislation, and in the doctrine of conspiracy in restraint of trade, just as it is implied in Shaw's dictum that all professions are a conspiracy against the public.

In treating the subject of coordination, most investigators confine themselves exclusively to the manifest functions of coordinative efforts and not to their latent functions or side effects. (In Chapter 2, we indicated some of the ways in which the overall cooperative nature of the interorganizational field performs protective functions for the individual CDOs.) One such side effect of coordination among nonprofit organizations is to reduce competition. The attempt to eliminate the "chaos" of presumably "uncoordinated" interorganizational relationships often takes the form of eliminating "unnecessary" duplications in functions, thus presumably effecting "economies." The reduction of competition among nonprofit organizations may have diverse effects on different parties, which effects would seem to be essential components in any careful assessment of the costs and benefits of a particular coordinative arrangement. A realistic and inclusive consideration of these side effects might indicate that the advantages to the coordinating organizations which accrue through the side effect of effectively disbarring new, competing, alternative organizations with different strategies for combatting the city's social problems may far outweigh the purported advantage of effecting economies or improving service delivery. Who benefits? and at what level? Who pays? and at what level? The question certainly needs to be addressed rather than ignored.

As mentioned in Chapter 2, there is a tendency for "coordination" to displace other possible strategies for a more effective engagement with the city's social problems. In the juvenile delinquency field, in the manpower field, in the alcoholism and drug addiction field, in the mental illness field, it is easy to make the illogical jump from noting that ameliorative efforts are ineffective and that they are uncoordinated to the assumption that existing services would constitute an adequate approach to such problems if they were only sufficiently coordinated.

Again, for better or worse, the quest for coordination often results in a tendency toward creating authority structures for concerted decision making. Two sets of circumstances contribute to this. One is the experience in numerous instances that individual adjustment and voluntary collaboration "don't work." The other is inherent in the developing technology for decision making. As observers like Robert Boguslaw[13] and Aaron Wildavsky[14] have pointed out, such technologies as systems analysis and program budgeting are virtually predicated on the assumptions of central decision making through authority structures. The attempt to consider all factors at once, to weigh them rationally, assumes a consistent basis for weighting necessary for the centrally made decision. Otherwise, as soon as different preference scales enter the situation, the process becomes one of negotiation, rather than the central decision of an individual decision-maker. Hence, systems analysis and program budgeting as an aid to central decision making require corresponding authority structures. The issue is reflected in the strong current drive by the federal government to strengthen the authority of the municipal executive over such relatively autonomous agencies as housing authorities, urban renewal authorities, and boards of education.

Failure to recognize that coordination, in the sense of allocational decisions at the level of the local interorganizational field, may take place through contest as well as through cooperation helps contribute to an exaggerated misconception of the "chaos" that presumably exists in the absence of formal coordinative mechanisms. Our data indicate that the effectiveness of these formal mechanisms may be largely overrated; that the importance of ad hoc coordinative efforts and of coordination through contest may be underrated; and that there is much more orderliness, regularity, conscious division of labor, and general domain consensus among these organizations than is usually recognized. It is a domain consensus that is constantly sustained and renewed by adjustments at the margins of organizational domain, adjustments brought about to a large extent through the moderate secondary contest described in the preceding chapter.

5　Innovation

Three overriding circumstances form the background for understanding the behavior of the community decision organizations under study in this book in connection with the objective of innovation.

The first is the ambiguity that prevails regarding the meaning of the term, and hence the nature of the presumed objective.

The second is the pervading assumption that innovation is good and is to be desired, even though a reduction of the term's ambiguity often brings high disagreement about the desirability of any specific innovation.

The third is the characteristics of the interorganizational field which help define what is meant by innovation in the actual operating situation and in doing so tend to channel the thrust toward innovation into routinized channels.

These three circumstances help make understandable the findings from the study of innovation in community decision organizations reported here.

Community decision organizations are the principal administrators for the guidance and development of change at the community level in their respective interest fields. The rationale behind the expectation that community decision organizations will initiate change is quite simple. Circumstances and conditions are in a constant process of change, and some organizational adaptation to these changes is necessary in the normal course of events. But more than that, new approaches are believed necessary because customary programs are widely considered inadequate to cope with mounting urban problems, let alone to prevent them.

The Model Cities program was specifically developed to help localities bring about changes in their manner of addressing a broad spectrum of problem areas, areas that involved all of the CDOs of this study. The legislation called for "programs containing new and imaginative proposals," and every city that applied for admission to the program was instructed explicitly to summarize the "innovative characteristics of the proposal."

An early objective developed by the Model Cities Administration was that of "institutional change" that would involve new types of programs and new types of administrative arrangements. Hence, a deliberate stimulus to innovation was provided by the Model Cities program with its objectives and administrative requirements and with its inducements in the form of additional funds for the cities whose applications and subsequent plans passed muster. Great ambiguity surrounded the meaning and implications of the term *institutional change* and led to the most contradictory assumptions as to what was to be brought about, and how.

81

The importance of including the extent and type of innovative behavior in an interorganizational study such as this derives in part from the immediate relevance of innovation to the struggle of the cities with their social problems and with the degree of effectiveness or ineffectiveness of various federal and local efforts to stimulate innovative ways of dealing with these problems. But the process of innovation is pertinent, as well, to an adequate theoretical understanding of interorganizational behavior. For innovative behavior by any of these community decision organizations does not take place in a vacuum. Conditions and developments in the interorganizational field can be expected to exercise some influence on the innovative process of any particular organization, as well as being affected by it. One organization's innovation may have the side effect of enhancing another organization's viability, or may be detrimental to it. More pointedly, in the case of community decision organizations, at least, the attempt to understand the dynamics of the innovation process without reference to the nature of the interorganizational field, and each organization's position in it, can lead only to trivial results, which may be misleading as well.

Ambiguity in the Concept of Innovation

The ambiguity prevailing in the use of the notion of innovation as an objective to be achieved is of immediate importance in that according to how the term is defined, the same set of findings may be interpreted to indicate a large amount or a little amount of innovation in a specific time period, or innovations that are important or innovations that are trivial, or innovations that directly address the problems of the central city or innovations that have only a remote relation to those problems. More important, as innovation becomes more specifically defined, the general, tacit assumption of the desirability of innovation often rapidly dissolves.

Most prevalent definitions of innovation are so formulated as to obscure such major issues as these. A brief review of some current definitions illustrates this point. Perhaps the most widely quoted definition of innovation is that given by Barnett: "An innovation is here defined as any thought, behavior, or thing that is new because it is qualitatively different from existing forms."[1]

Innovation in organizations is treated under various concepts. Simon approaches it in connection with innovative program building, and treats it from the standpoint of decision making.

We can call program-building innovative when two conditions are met: (1) finding the answer to the new problem involves difficult search, problem-solving, and learning activities; (2) the initiation of the new program—the recognition of opportunity or need—comes largely from within the organization as a result of systematic scanning of its environment and sensitivity to problems and challenges.

Simon goes on to discuss the differences between such "creative problem-solving" and other types of more routine decision-making.[2]

Gore pursues a similar path in differentiating routine, adaptive, and innovative decisions, the last being "a major change in activity and operation which leads to a change in goals, purposes or policies."[3] Whisler likewise uses an organizational definition: "An organization is innovative if it is the first to do something that no other organization has done before."[4] Wilson uses "tasks," in the sense of the full-time activities of one member, as the basis for his definition of innovation: "An innovation (or, more precisely, a major innovation, since we are not concerned with trivial changes) is a 'fundamental' change in a 'significant' number of tasks."[5] Victor A. Thompson, on the other hand, gives a much broader definition: "By innovation is meant the generation, acceptance, and implementation of new ideas, processes, products or services. Innovation therefore implies the capacity to change or adapt."[6]

None of these definitions takes into account the direction of the development that is to be considered an innovation. Yet implicit in the way they are used is the assumption that innovation is desirable. They seem to say, implicitly: "Well, perhaps not all the changes that would meet my definition are desirable, but we needn't be explicit about this, for we all acknowledge that this is what is meant, and we all know what is desirable." And on this basis they go right on to examine the preconditions of innovation, as though all innovation that meets their definition were desirable.

Much the same blurring of the issue occurred in the developments concerning Model Cities with which the community decision organizations were involved. At the level of the basic legislation, at the level of the administrative promulgations, at the level of the local Model Cities agencies, at the level of the CDOs, and at the level of the citizens groups, innovation was taken as something to be striven for. Yet there was little clarity as to the qualitative nature of the changes desired. It was simply assumed to be a matter of removing the constraints on innovation and providing inducements. Developments would then take place which might be expected to have major impact on "improving the conditions of living" in poverty areas.

Yet, the qualitative nature of the changes to be induced remains of crucial importance, and it requires further consideration here. Once it is examined, the simple assumption that innovation is desirable proves untenable. The innovation that is talked about as desirable is innovation that meets certain criteria. Since these criteria are nowhere made explicit, the assumption is usually allowed to continue until such time as a specific innovation is considered by someone to be unsatisfactory. In the absence of such explicit instances, the question of the need for criteria is ignored; and where the question of desirability arises, it may be answered by indicating that of course the change must make the organization more viable or help it to accomplish more effectively or efficiently its manifest goals.

It is difficult to conceive any organizational situation so bad that any conceivable change would be desirable. This being the case, it seems impossible to ignore the directionality of change in any adequate consideration of innovation. Qualitative differences must inevitably be addressed.

In his article on innovative and allocative planning, Friedmann writes: "Innovation appears as a leap into a new state of affairs, an event that leads to the structural transformation of an existing situation . . . it appears *as a form of action intended to change the nature of reality*, rather than as a thought process preliminary to action—the master plan, the capital budget."[7]

Hence, in conceptualizing innovation it is important to acknowledge the difference between those changes that provide a qualitative difference, such as in a major reorganization of thinking or a structural transformation of the existing situation, and those that do not. Friedmann is emphatic on this point. Yet he says little about the substantive direction of the qualitative change.

In considering the qualitative nature of innovation, another important aspect involving these community decision organizations has to do with participation in decision making, especially on the part of citizens who are the "targets" of much of the action that stems from these organizations and the related organizations within their respective interest fields. Particularly pertinent is participation by low-income residents who have been largely shut out of the decision-making process in the past. Part of what is usually meant by "the need for innovation" in the urban field is the need for new ways of providing for such participation. And, of course, the Model Cities program made such participation mandatory as a precondition for the funding of local programs. Here the qualitative dimension is particularly important. For there are vast differences in the forms of participation as well as in the impact, potential or actual, which these formal provisions for participation make in actual practice. Hence, any considered treatment of innovation in these organizations must be concerned not only with the citizen participation aspect, but with the nature of that participation as well. To omit the qualitative dimension here is to confuse the important with the trivial and to treat them as equivalent.

A third qualitative dimension of innovation in the case of these CDOs relates to the basic manner in which they define social reality, social problems, and the means of changing them. Barnett contends that to be an innovation, a thought, behavior, or thing must be "qualitatively different from existing forms." What would seem basic to the innovative process would be not only the adoption of some new practice (whether invented or borrowed is a still different issue), but the extent to which the new practice represents an important reorganization of thinking—a new way of visualizing the area in which the innovation occurs. In Chapter 2, we have described the basic orientation toward social reality of these CDOs pointing to the existence of an institutionalized thought structure that defines social reality and social problems and prescribes the manner in which such problems are to be attacked. It also legitimates an organizational structure and a set of technologies to be used for addressing these problems. In the case of inner city poverty and related problems, the diagnostic paradigm employed is that of individual deficiency, and the intervention strategy is that of "providing social services." Failures of the intervention strategy are interpreted as attributable to inadequate services—inadequate either in amount or because they are not sufficiently finely tuned to the mentality and needs of the service recipients, or because they are not sufficiently coordinated and are poorly packaged. The implied remedies are obvious.

A major reorientation of the diagnosis of urban poverty and related problems would call for a different set of intervention strategies as well. Such a major reorientation would constitute innovation in a much more meaningful sense than simply making incremental changes in service delivery systems based on the same definitions of social reality held in the past. Hence, it is important to consider alternatives to the prevailing paradigm. An alternative paradigm was available for development during the time of this study. Its major outlines had been fairly definitely formulated, and indeed it was even utilized in the problem diagnosis included in some of the original planning grant applications submitted by individual cities for admission to the Model Cities program. The alternative paradigm (which for convenience can be called Paradigm II, to distinguish it from the prevalent paradigm described in Chapter 2 (Paradigm I)) sees the poverty problem not as one of an aggregate of deficient individuals in need of services but rather as a characteristic of the American institutional structure, which is so organized as to "produce" inequity in distribution of power and wealth and opportunities, and through these inequities to "produce" poverty.

These differences in problem diagnosis and implementation have been treated elsewhere by two of the authors.[8] A shift from one of these paradigms to the other, insofar as this is implemented in program or organizational structure or relations with other organizations, must therefore receive appropriate attention in any system for judging organizations on the variable of innovation. Just as a new scientific theory is more innovative than the day-in-day-out research expanding the implications of an existing theory, so a major new explanatory paradigm is innovative in a quite different way from simply a new device for expanding or perfecting existing approaches in the social problems field.[9]

But in addition to its newness, one might expect that innovation that includes a switch to an alternative explanatory paradigm would involve a set of interaction dynamics somewhat different from innovation that Kuhn describes as the "mopping up operations" of normal science, the incremental expansion of knowledge within the same scientific paradigm.

One may of course ask how an idea (in this case an alternative explanatory paradigm) can be relatively widespread despite—or perhaps because of—its highly ambiguous qualities. It could be accepted verbally not only by some of the more militant and change-oriented among poverty area residents, but also among agency leaders. They, too, could talk of "the need for structural change" or "the need for institutional change" or "a broader distribution of power" or of "income redistribution" precisely because the terms were highly ambiguous. It was only as these changes came to be defined in program development and operation that the qualitative difference in orientation was recognized. Far from being commonplace, the alternative paradigm has truly revolutionary implications. But in most instances, an initial orientation toward Paradigm II encountered the blunting process described in Chapter 3 and was gradually transformed into a services orientation compatible with the already existing institutionalized thought structure.

Three Types of Innovation

Preliminary analysis of the narrative data and of the Major Change Schedules used for recording data on innovation suggested the importance of incorporating the issues raised above into the treatment of innovation. Fortunately, the Major Change Schedule made this more refined analysis possible. The schedule had been designed to elicit "major changes" in four separate areas: policies and programs, organizational structure and administration, relations with other organizations, and a residual area. In each case, the informant was the organization's executive director or his designate. Changes in any of these areas, as recorded in the Major Change Schedules, were considered innovations. The analytic proposition that incorporated innovation as one key variable were tested using alternative definitions that separated out the important qualitative distinctions discussed above. The general concept of innovation was differentiated into three types: primary innovation, secondary innovation, and gross innovation. The analysis based on these distinctions brought out important relationships which would have been obscured in a more general treatment.

Primary Innovation

Primary innovation involves a change in organizational behavior which reflects a redefinition of urban problems from an emphasis on individual deviance or deficiency (Paradigm I) to an emphasis on the dysfunctions of the institutional structure (Paradigm II). This definition incorporates Friedmann's concept of a change in the perception of reality with the specific addition of the direction in which consequent actions should be taken. Like primary contest, it involves a qualitative break with the prevailing analytical paradigm. It thus comprises activities constituting a direct challenge to an established organization not only over a specific issue but over its very legitimation, thus constituting a lethal threat to its continued viability; or it departs from the accepted norms for interorganizational contest, employing methods that constitute a threat to the usual system of minimizing conflict and confining it to marginal matters; or it attacks the interorganizational field structure and the institutionalized thought structure that sustains it.

In the empirical situation, behavior described as primary innovation took the form of explicit basing of strategies on a rejection of Paradigm I; withdrawing of financial support (through contracts) of various social service organizations, on the basis that their programs were irrelevant to the problems of the poor; organizing poor people to confront various established agencies in the governmental, educational, and social service fields around issues of power and resource distribution; and organizing new and competing organizations under the control of poor people in order to contest with the established agencies in their legitimated domains.

The instances of primary innovation were rare, being confined principally to a single community decision organization which is treated in detail in Chapter 7.

Two additional types of innovation were examined. They both included only changes that remained within the prevalent analytic paradigm. They thus differed qualitatively from primary innovation. They also differed from each other on the intensity of the change within the prevailing paradigm. Secondary innovation included only the relatively more substantial changes, while gross innovation consisted of only minor changes.

Secondary Innovation

This includes changes in definition of the nature of the social problems being addressed, (but changes that remained within the framework of Paradigm I), or definite movement in the direction of substantive participation of slum area residents in decision-making processes.

This category of innovations included many different kinds of development. Specific illustrations will help give a more definite notion of the kinds of changes which were going on.

A health and welfare council moved from its customary social service planning activities into the field of comprehensive health planning. A mental health agency switched its emphasis from hospitalization of psychotic patients to intensive, family-oriented intervention in the community setting. An urban renewal agency changed its conception of housing needs for black and Puerto Rican families, and modified its building plans accordingly. Such changes are classified as changes in problem definition within Paradigm I.

A mental health agency began to employ nonprofessional poverty area residents for various positions, including counseling. A school system began to engage students and parents as research aides. A community action agency built in career ladders and training programs for nonprofessional personnel. These changes exemplify innovations in hiring practices and staffing patterns to accommodate more low-income people.

A mental health agency set up a layman's screening committee of poverty area residents as part of its hiring procedures. A school system established citizen groups in the Model Neighborhood area to have a role in the hiring of new teaching staff. A community action agency formed a neighborhood corporation to help administer its services, with neighborhood residents having a key role in decision making. These instances exemplify changes that afford poverty area residents a substantive voice in the organization's decision making.

A Model Cities agency stimulated the city government to reorganize in order to avoid bureaucratic delays in providing services. An urban renewal agency forced construction companies that worked on urban renewal projects to employ a larger number of blacks. A community action agency pressured the regular service agencies to provide services for the poor. These instances exemplify formal efforts by a community decision organization to direct another organization's activities toward problem redefinition or toward greater employment of low-income people or a greater substantive voice by them in decision making.

These examples indicate that changes classified as secondary innovation were changes which were more than merely ritualistic or purely administrative, in that they constituted problem redefinition within Paradigm I or a relative degree of substantive participation as distinct from mere administrative involvement.[10]

Gross Innovation

This is the most inclusive category of innovation. It includes the vast bulk of changes listed on the Major Change Schedules, after duplicate reports (under different categories) had been weeded out, including only the relatively infrequent primary and secondary innovation. Examples will indicate the comparatively superficial nature of such changes, as contrasted with primary and secondary innovations:

A community action agency instituted a summer youth program which included work-training components. A Model Cities agency established a weekend and evening college whose time schedule was adapted to the time limitations of many prospective students. A health and welfare council set up task forces on public welfare and citizen participation. These exemplify changes in agency programs.

A health and welfare council added youth and consumer representatives to its board of directors. A school system added a Title I advisory group with representation both from agencies and from parents. A community action agency reorganized itself on a divisional basis in order to achieve a more logical flow of decision making. These are changes in organizational structure and administration.

A school system entered into a cooperative relationship with a business firm for experimenting with the development of electronic teaching methods. A mental health agency developed collaborative relationships with a Model Cities agency for the use of Model Cities supplemental funds to help finance a mental health center. A Model Cities agency took over a major role in mental health planning from a mental health agency. These represent changes in relationships to other organizations.

A Mental Health agency changed its problem definition from prevention to the provision of services. A community action agency made a deliberate attempt to reduce its dependency on federal funding. A health and welfare council changed its emphasis from a process orientation to one of substantive problem solving. These exemplify changes of various types, including relatively modest redefinition of problems.

Findings on Three Types of Innovation

As can be seen from the above examples, gross innovations are changes involving purely administrative matters, or a modest addition of neighborhood resident input with no assurance of a change in power relationships, or modest changes in program, well within Paradigm I. Secondary innovations, on the other hand, represent changes of a more substantive nature. Primary innovation represents an abrupt departure from usual definitions and intervention strategies.

When the total number of innovations is broken down in terms of these more refined definitions of innovation, the numbers of instances under each type present a striking contrast:

Table 5-1
Instances of Three Types of Innovation[a]

Primary Innovation	3
Secondary Innovation	44
Gross Innovation	559
Total Innovation	606

[a]These figures include fifty-two organizations. No Major Change Schedule was available from the Oakland Model Cities Agency and the Denver Community Action Agency.

The implications of this breakdown are far-reaching. They take on meaning as one considers them against the three basic circumstances stated at the outset of this chapter: the ambiguity of the term *innovation*; the assumption that "innovation" is desirable but the disagreement over the desirability of innovations when made more specific; and the interorganizational field process of channeling proposed innovations into routinized patterns.

The examples given above of different instances of gross innovation indicate their essentially minor nature. It should be recalled that they were given in the responses of agency executives or their designates to an extensive questionnaire on "major changes" which gave them opportunities both broad and detailed to enumerate the important changes in the preceding two-year period. The changes they reported make extremely dull reading, and in most cases it is difficult to imagine any significant impact of these innovations on the problems of the inner cities.

Our own findings regarding these community decision organizations are substantiated by other, analogous findings, made quite independently of the present study. Stephen A. Waldhorn, who directed the Model Cities Service Center that was established by the National League of Cities and the United States Conference of Mayors, published an article with Judith Lynch Waldhorn which assessed the Model Cities program. They reported in highly negative fashion on the innovation achieved in connection with the Model Cities programs across the country. Even with an inclusive and undifferentiated conception of innovation, they reported that innovation in programming "was achieved only in a few Model Cities." The Department of Health and Welfare had solicited from its Washington desk officers examples of new uses of health, education, and social services funds by Model Cities agencies (which would also include programs by other agencies funded by Model Cities money) in 1970, nearly three years into the Model Cities program. Almost no examples were produced.[11]

An extensive report was issued by the Model Cities Service Center in June 1971. It was designed as a report on progress to date in the Model Cities programs across the country. It is replete with instances of presumably significant aspects of administration and programming in the many different problem areas included in the Model Cities purview. The items give the impression of much change and numerous specific innovations; but when examined carefully, the newness in most cases involves superficial changes, and few of the developments reported would be classifiable as anything but "gross innovation" as described above.[12]

"Generally," conclude the Waldhorns, "local government staffs and citizens seemed unable to escape conventional or fashionable solutions to problems. Thus most Model Cities programs were mixtures of conventional services and current fads, such as housing development corporations and multi-service centers."[13]

The use of three differentiated subcategories of innovation in the analysis of our quantitative data throws light on a number of important questions regarding the innovative process among community decision organizations. One such question is the importance of intraorganizational variables as presumably "causing" innovation, in contrast to variables that concern the organization's relation to other organizations within the interorganizational field. Another question relates to the extent to which innovation is associated with cooperation, or contest or conflict with other organizations.

Generally, our findings indicate the dubious value of making generalized statements about "innovation" among these CDOs. It is only as one goes beyond a simple conception of innovation and examines the relationship between various subcategories of innovation and other significant variables that a coherent theoretical framework for understanding the concomitants of innovation emerges. The relationship to other variables which are shown by gross and secondary innovation suggest that the difference between these two types of innovation is largely quantitative; they represent a dichotomy produced by breaking a quantitative continuum at an essentially arbitrary point. But the contrast between these two types and primary innovation is both striking and important. Yet, without the use of refined subcategories of innovation, and using only a quantitative analysis, the small number of instances of primary innovation would have been lost in the analysis.

From the analysis of the narrative data, a description of the overall dynamics in the interorganizational field regarding innovative behavior begins to emerge. For the most part, this analytic description is substantiated by quantitative findings regarding certain of the key relationships involved. In presenting our analysis, we shall focus on the three overriding circumstances enumerated at the outset: ambiguity as to the meaning of innovation; assumption that innovation is desirable; and the relation of the interorganizational field to the definition and implementation of innovation.

Let us begin with an assessment of innovation as a product. In two years of pursuing their activities under the stimulus of the Model Cities program, these six types of organizations produced numerous instances of what they categorized as "major change." The total of such changes reported, by types of community decision organizations for the nine cities, is given in Table 5-2.

It should be kept in mind that these total innovation scores include primarily types of changes which are either purely administrative or involve only extremely modest steps to provide for citizen participation or to redirect the

Table 5-2
Total Innovation Scores by CDO Type[a]

Community action agency	136
Public school system administration	132
Model cities agency	106
Mental health planning agency	101
Urban renewal agency	72
Health and welfare planning council	59
Total Innovations	606

[a]These figures include fifty-two organizations. No Major Change Schedule was available from the Oakland Model Cities Agency and the Denver Community Action Agency.

nature of their program. The total of 606 innovations includes only 44 sufficiently significant to be classified as secondary innovation, according to the criteria listed earlier. Generally, secondary innovations represent changes that represent a more substantive participation by poverty area residents or a redefinition of the problems being addressed, though still within the major outlines of the institutional thought structure.

Table 5-3
Secondary Innovation Scores by CDO Type[a]

Community action agency	12
Public school system administration	9
Urban renewal agency	9
Mental health planning agency	7
Model cities agency	6
Health and welfare planning council	1
Total secondary innovations	44

[a]These figures include fifty-two organizations. No Major Change Schedule was available from the Oakland Model Cities Agency and the Denver Community Action Agency.

The CDO types range themselves in similar order on both gross and secondary innovation, with the urban renewal agency constituting a modest exception. (In both this and the preceding table, the Model Cities agencies' scores should be interpreted in the light of the fact that these organizations were only in their early stages of development during the period covered. Hence, their *rate* of innovation may well have been higher than indicated.) There was a tendency for the number of gross innovations to vary differently with the frequency of interaction with other CDOs, but this tendency was hardly discernible in the case of secondary innovation.[a]

Primary innovations were so infrequent as to be unsuitable for statistical treatment. The three primary innovations all occurred within the same organization. Their number would hardly merit explicit treatment, from the standpoint of a quantitative approach. Yet, their qualitative difference from other instances of innovation is great. Much can be learned from a sustained analysis of these qualitative differences, the dynamic interactional situation within which they arose, and the dynamic interactional situation they precipitated. They are treated extensively in Chapter 7.

From the remarkably skewed distribution of these three types of innovations, one begins to get a grasp of what is taking place. The innovations have virtually all been of the nature of incremental refinements of existing technologies and organizational structures. The widely held notion that "innovative programs"

[a]The corresponding Pearsonian correlation coefficients were .37, significant at .01 level for gross innovation and .16, not statistically significant, for secondary innovation.

would make a marked impact on our urban problems assumed more than this. It assumed that changes would be brought about which would constitute new, more effective substitutes for existing organizational structures and procedures.

The ambiguity regarding innovation is well illustrated in the widely proclaimed objective of "institutional change," mentioned earlier in this chapter. "Institutional change" appeared to many impatient and disaffected poverty area leaders to constitute much more of an open door to basic structural changes in their environment than was indicated by a strict interpretation of the context in which the term was used in official policy documents.

As the institutional change objective became implemented, however, it encountered the blunting process described in Chapter 3. Proposed changes that dealt with the distribution of power and resources in the cities' poverty areas suffered an attrition by which they were confined to changes in service delivery patterns and to largely advisory but essentially powerless modes and structures of participation. In this manner, a proposal for a measure of control over police actions by poverty area residents was transformed into a police auxiliary program under police control. A proposal for a guaranteed income program was transformed into a study of public welfare programs. A health council which was to afford poverty area residents a large measure of control over health services both in the model neighborhood and throughout the city was transformed into an auxiliary and subordinate appendage of the local comprehensive health planning unit. A Model Cities program including new neighborhood corporations as components under the control of the organization that represented citizens in the model neighborhood area became transformed into program components primarily under the control of the existing social agencies.

The local interorganizational field operated, in each case, in such a way that the new developments that occurred were new only in the most superficial aspects of agency programs—such as storefront mental health units, multiservice centers, and citizen advisory councils. Much of the dynamics of this slippage has been described in Chapters 2 and 3. More specifically, in connection with innovation, the study's narrative reports abound with examples of specific mechanisms of the blunting process. It was comprised, in different instances, of various combinations of the following components:

1. modification by local superior authority, as when a city council approved a proposal only after it had been modified into substantial conformity with the interests and programs and technologies of the legitimated agencies;
2. modification by extracommunity authority, through the regional or national officials of the Model Cities Administration, Office of Economic Opportunity, or the various federal departments whose programs were involved, principally Health, Education and Welfare; Housing and Urban Development; and Labor;
3. technical cooptation, as when the proposal was modified in accordance with

the professional standards or technical requirements asserted by one of the legitimated agencies;

4. administrative cooptation, as where the proposed organizational structure of a new program was modified to meet the administrative constraints and interests and procedures of existing agencies;

5. institutional cooptation, as where the legitimated agency in whose generally accepted domain a specific proposal fell asserted its ultimate right to determine the major outlines of programs that would be mounted in its domain, and thus succeeded in modifying the proposal; and

6. the advice of advocacy planners, who quite regardless of where their loyalties or their ideologies might lie, often found themselves advising their clients to give in on some innovative aspect, for reasons either of substance or strategy.

In the majority of instances, however,—we allude specifically to the 243 separate projects approved for the first year Model Cities action programs in the nine cities of this study—the proposals did not precipitate these types of blunting, since they were not sufficiently threatening to any established agency or any established practice or interest group to require modification.

While the one-to-one correspondence is not perfect, there is considerable substantiation for a statement that brings together much of the substance of the present chapter on innovation as well as the chapter on organizational inter-action.

1. Cooperation tends to be associated with gross innovation and with the preventing process.

2. Secondary contest tends to be associated with secondary innovation and with the blunting process.

3. Primary contest (conflict) tends to be associated with primary innovation and with the repelling process.

The relationship of innovation to any set of other variables is obscured by any conceptualization that neglects to differentiate between types of innovation. This is exemplified by testing the simple analytic proposition: *The greater the innovation in an organization's program, the greater the amount of contest in its interorganizational relationships.*

We had expected this proposition to be supported, being inclined, with Thompson, to suppose that "conflict generates problems and uncertainties and diffuses ideas. . . . Conflict, therefore encourages innovations."[14] In this statement, Thompson was alluding to intraorganizational conflict; but there is little reason to suppose that the same relationship might not apply to an organization's external relations. Further, quite deductively, it seemed reasonable to expect that innovations in turn might disturb the ecological balance among organizations and might involve side effects that would impose a threat on the viability of other organizations, thus generating contest. This proposition was tested quantitatively, using as indicators the total program innovation score of each of the fifty-four organizations, omitting nonprogram innovations such as those in organizational structure. The other variable was the score of each organization on the cooperation/contest scale (see Chapter 3). These indicators are, then, the amount of an organization's program innovations and its degree of contest with other organizations.

On this undifferentiated measure of innovation, the proposition was not supported by the data. Actually, the small correlation coefficient of $-.14$ was in the opposite, or nonsupporting, direction, but not statistically significant. From this undifferentiated treatment there appears to be no significant relationship between the amount of innovation and the amount of contest between these organizations.

More refined analysis of the data on innovation, however, revealed quite a different set of findings. When secondary and primary innovation are separated out from gross innovation and related to the cooperation/contest variable, the relationships are both strong and revealing. These relationships were tested using the action episodes as a data basis. These are episodes of relatively intense interaction (see page 38). All but seventeen of the 141 action episodes involved innovation of some sort. These 124 action episodes were classified as to whether they involved gross or secondary innovation, or primary innovation, and they were cross-classified as to whether the interaction was primarily of a cooperative or contest type. Table 5-4 presents the results with respect to the 121 instances of gross and secondary innovation involved in these action episodes, and Table 5-5 presents the remaining three instances of primary innovation. Earlier, (Table 3-5), a strong relationship was indicated between domain threats and the nature of CDO interaction. Thus, in Table 5-4 here, the gross and secondary innovations are likewise classified as to whether they involve domain threats to either of the interacting community decision organizations.

The table indicates that gross and secondary innovations may or may not be associated with contest, largely depending on whether these innovations constitute threats to an organization's domain. Where they involve threats, these action episodes indicate that they engender contest. Where these innovations do not involve domain threats, however, they are usually accompanied by cooperation as the dominant mode of interaction.

A substantive examination of the nature and flow of events in these action

Table 5-4
Gross and Secondary Innovations, Domain Threats, and Nature of Interaction

	Cooperation	Contest	Total
Domain threats	12	45	57
No domain threats	57	7	64
Total	69	52	121
$X^2 = 56.9$ d.f. $= 1$ $p = < .001$			

episodes throws light on these relationships. Many instances occurred in which the development of a new program or the establishment of a new relationship involved two of these organizations in a cooperative venture. The instances that involved contest, however, were usually cases where one organization developed an innovation that posed a threat to the other organization, either through invading its program domain or threatening its resource base. The threats were seldom major, but nevertheless sufficiently strong to engender the mild form of contest described in Chapter 3.

The innovations that involved cooperation virtually all constituted expansions or refinements of generally approved practices or arrangements, constituting purely incremental, rather than qualitative changes. They represented the kinds of "new" developments that arise out of a basic acceptance of existing definitions and activities. They are thus innovative in only a superficial sense. Even the small number of secondary innovations do not represent basic departures from accepted definitions and practices. Thus, in reference to the preventing, blunting, and repelling processes described in Chapter 3, they are largely of the preventing type; no threat arises, because they are well within accepted procedures and within the accepted organizational domains. Rather than threatening the domain consensus, they contribute to it.

Some of these innovations, however, do generate at least a mild form of contest—what we have called secondary contest. Such contest, though it may be quite serious, affirms the institutionalized thought structure, affirms a set of norms governing contest situations and their resolution, and affirms the legitimacy of the contesting organizations. It is contest, nevertheless, in that it consists of interaction in order to bring about different and mutually incompatible issue outcomes.

In the case of secondary innovations, a somewhat larger proportion generate issues around which such secondary contest takes place. These are innovations that, though still remaining within the accepted norms of the institutionalized thought structure, may challenge the domain of another organization at the margins (without threatening its very existence). Through such secondary contest, as well as through cooperation (which is more prevalent with these innovations), the continuous process of successive adjustments to new situations is carried out in a manner that minimizes friction among the partly competing organizations and that assures the essential stability of their respective domains in their mutual interrelationships. It is in these secondary innovations that the blunting process is most apparent—the process of modifying potential threats either through organizational cooptation or through overt forms of secondary contest.

The situation is drastically different in the case of primary innovation. It may appear ludicrous to construct a table that includes only three instances, all by the same organization. But precisely this is done in Table 5-5, because of the revealing nature of the empty cells in the table.

Table 5-5
Primary Innovations, Domain Threats, and Nature of Interaction

	Cooperation	Contest	Total
Domain threats	0	3	3
No domain threats	0	0	0
Total	0	3	3

All of these instances involved primary contest engendered by the Oakland Economic Development Council, Incorporated (OEDCI), the community action agency in that city during the period of the field study. This agency was explicitly committed to a Paradigm II approach, thus challenging directly the institutionalized thought structure described in Chapter 2. It developed action strategies consistent with this approach, and hence not in accord with the accepted norms governing contest. The contest was primary both from the standpoint of the qualitatively different strategies employed by this organization and of the qualitatively different response these strategies engendered in the interorganizational field. The sequence of events is described in greater detail in Chapter 7.

Table 5-5 dramatizes the point that of fifty-four organizations studied over a period of more than two years, only one organization produced substantial indication of primary innovation. The hundreds of other innovations reported in response to the Major Change Schedule were all of the gross or secondary type, all based on the prevailing definitions of social problems and of the services strategy, all consisting of minor modifications of existing methods and procedures.

Table 5-5 also dramatizes the point that these three instances of primary innovation all involved threats to the domains of other established organizations, and all engendered conflict. What it does not show is the qualitatively different nature of the conflict—contest that, unlike the other instances in this study, was not confined within the "live-and-let-live" norms prescribed by Paradigm I for organizational interaction, but rather constituted a direct challenge to the very legitimation of other organizations and a threat to their continued viability. It employed methods of confrontation different from and opposed to the Paradigm I norms governing organizational interaction, maximizing rather than minimizing conflict, and directing it at core matters rather than marginal matters. It involved an explicit rejection of the interorganizational field structure and the institutionalized thought structure that sustains it.

In turn, this primary innovation was met with increasingly hard and increasingly lethal pressures, terminating in the destruction of the organization's status and support as the official community action agency. It both employed,

98

and became the target of, strategies that went beyond the usual norms of contest interaction. In the estimation of the other organizations, apparently, it had broken the social contract and opened up a Hobbesian war of all against all. In this war, it was destroyed.

Intraorganizational Variables and Innovation

We were interested in the relation of a number of intraorganizational variables to innovation. These included organizational decision-making context (whether unitary or federative); leadership style of the chief organizational executive (whether charismatic, bureaucratic, or collegial); the organization's program/ planning ratio, and its degree of professionalization. The first two variables did not show any statistically significant relationship to the three types of innovation. It was found that the higher the organization's ratio of program to planning, the greater the extent of gross innovation, although the relationship was modest. The correlation coefficient of .33 was significant at the .05 level. It held to an even lesser extent, for secondary innovation, where the correlation coefficient was .17, not statistically significant. The single organization that showed primary innovation was fourteenth among the forty-five organizations included in this particular test, thus being high in program/planning ratio and tending to lend suggestive support to the proposition.

It has frequently been suggested that an organization's innovativeness may be affected by its degree of professionalization.[15] With this consideration in mind, it was decided to explore the relationship between professional diversity and the three innovation definitions. As an indicator, the number of different types of professional occupation contained in the organization, rather than the number of individual professional personnel, was utilized. The distribution by CDO types is given in Table 5-6.

Table 5-6
Number of Professional Occupations, by CDO Type[a]

Community action agency	8.4
Model cities agency	6.7
Public school system administration	6.3
Mental health planning agency	5.4
Urban renewal agency	5.0
Health and welfare planning council	3.9

[a]The scores are arithmetic means for each type. Two CAAs and one ED were missing from this computation, and means were calculated accordingly.

The table carries few surprises, since one would expect the multifield CDOs to have broader representation of professional categories than the single-field CDOs.

An analytic proposition was developed and tested, using the individual CDO scores on number of professional occupations and the three definitions of innovation: *Innovation in community decision organizations varies directly with professional diversity*. The proposition was strongly supported for gross and secondary innovation, and even the one organization with primary innovation was somewhat higher than the average of all CDOs in professional diversity, thus supporting the proposition. The correlation coefficients for gross and secondary innovation were each .42, significant at the .01 level.

The two multifield CDO types (CAA and MC) are high on both professional diversity and innovation. With the quantitative methodology employed, it was not possible to separate out the effects of the multifield nature of these two CDOs from their degree of professional diversity. Hence, there is no assurance that the strong relationship found between professional diversity and innovation is not a product of the multifield nature of the organizations highest in innovation.

Except for professional diversity, the relationships found between these intraorganizational variables and innovation are highly modest and inconclusive. Before commenting on the significance of these findings, let us consider the question of the relation between the various types of innovation and interorganizational variables.

Innovation and the Interorganizational Field

There is considerable basis for supposing that the *dependence of community decision organizations on other organizations in the local interorganizational field for financial resources* might constitute a constraint on their innovation. In a study of the national Planned Parenthood Organization some years ago, Martin Rein found that the ties of these organizations to other organizations in the locality, particularly their dependence on local organizations such as the United Fund for financial resources, constituted a constraint on their program activities. Local branches that released themselves from such ties were able to perform more effectively.[16] Similarly, Levine and White found that health agencies not dependent on local resources for financial support did not engage in so much interaction with other local agencies as those that were so dependent.[17] In his study of the programs of twenty community action agencies, Rose found that broad local agency participation in the development and implementation of the antipoverty programs appeared to have a stultifying effect on the development of new social action programs.[18] Hence, the following analytic proposition was formulated: *Innovativeness in community decision organizations varies inversely with dependence on local community organizations for financial resources.* In order to test this proposition, a percentage of total operating budget from local organizations was calculated for each CDO, and these percentages were correlated with the amount of various types of innovation.

The findings for both gross and secondary innovation were in a supporting direction, but not statistically significant, with the correlation coefficients for gross and secondary innovation $-.28$ and $-.26$ respectively. The single organization showing primary innovation was not dependent on local organizations as sources of funding, thus tending to support the proposition. Here, again, the posited relationship does not make much difference except in the case of primary innovation.

The relationship between crisis and innovation should at least be addressed in its relation to these community decision organizations, although no analytic proposition was developed to test it. The notion that "necessity is the mother of invention" has been around a long time. Such necessity, when examined in terms of organizations, can be conceived as a condition that arises to threaten the continued viability of the organization. Such threats are usually referred to as *crises*. Friedmann writes of "the catalytic role of crises" in connection with innovative planning,[19] and March and Simon state, "The rate of innovation is likely to increase when changes in the environment make the existing organizational procedures unsatisfactory."[20] Wilson points to some contrary evidence: "The necessity theory was not supported by the facts. Being on the ragged edge of adversity did not appear to make firms more inventive or more adaptive; on the contrary, the prosperous firms seemed more willing to try new ideas."[21] He suggests that perhaps extremes of both adversity and prosperity may be associated with organizational innovativeness.[22]

The crisis theory has direct relevance to the present study, for it was assumed that innovation by these organizations would be stimulated by crisis in two senses. First, the broader context, indicated by the widely used expression "the urban crisis," comprised a troubled environment in the respective interest fields of these CDOs. The sense of growing urban problems and "the need for change" was so widespread as to make the very terms almost banal.

The second sense in which crisis applies to these organizations arises from the nature of the Model Cities program. It constituted, in itself, a crisis in that it set up a new community decision organization, the Model Cities agency, with fairly large amounts of financial resources at its disposal and with various types of power to influence the viability of these other CDOs either favorably or unfavorably. The necessity for adjustment to this new circumstance might well be expected to generate adaptive responses on the part of these CDOs which would be innovative in varying degrees.

Another related characteristic of the interorganizational field was the generation of pressure for change which operated on these organizations from outside sources. Community decision organizations such as those under study have been the subject of continual criticism for presumably being unwilling or unable to make the changes necessary to address the urban problems with which they are charged. The antipoverty program was initially set up, at least in part, to bypass such agencies as those of this study, on the basis of their lack of adequate potential for change. But the antipoverty program, as represented by the community action agencies, subjected itself to administrative cooptation by these agencies through its own subsequent adoption of the strategy of trying to change them through internal pressure to reform, rather than by-pass or replace them. The Model Cities program was likewise committed to bringing about "institutional change," but especially after the advent of the Nixon administration it committed itself to working with existing agencies and trying to change them, rather than setting up competing organizations of a supposedly more effective nature. Other federal programs have also sought to exert leverage for change in local organizations, as have the activities of social action groups of the poor and of various ethnic groups in the cities.

The question arises as to how much of the innovation this study uncovered was attributable to such external pressure from federal or state agencies or from social action groups. This is difficult to ascertain. Terreberry claims, "There is *no* systematic empirical evidence on the relative influence of internal versus environmental antecedents to organizational change. The empirical task here is to identify organizational changes, and the internal or external origins of each change."[23] This is, of course, easier said than done.

The Major Change Schedule employed in gathering data on innovation contained as its final question: "To what extent are any of these changes (in all sections of this document) the result of requirements imposed by organizations having authority or control over your organization?" The informants for this schedule were the agency executives or their designates. Of twenty-nine community decision organizations that registered one or more changes at the secondary innovation level, fourteen, or just under half, indicated that these changes occurred as a direct result of pressure from federal intervention or citizen pressure, or both. Our assessment is that this figure is highly conservative. But taken at its face value, it indicates that outside pressure was involved in about half the cases of secondary innovation.

Summary Analysis

In concluding this chapter, we return to the three overriding considerations enumerated at the outset: ambiguity regarding the meaning of innovation, naive assumption of desirability of innovation, and the operation of the interorganizational field structure in regard to different kinds of innovations.

In connection with urban reform, the ambiguity performs the function of giving the appearance of agreement where there is no agreement and thus making more credible the assumption that basic political issues are not involved, but instead merely technical considerations regarding how best to achieve mutually desired objectives.

In addition, of course, the ambiguity provides a source of confusion in assessing what is to be done and what will constitute actual progress toward stated objectives such as improving living conditions in slum areas. The importance of this confusion is apparent to anyone who examines the specific innovations these organizations made during the period covered. They were primarily technical and administrative refinements of existing intervention strategies, (largely social services), addressed essentially to improving the effectiveness of existing approaches rather than making any qualitative changes of approaches.

Granted the ambiguity, it was easy to become convinced that innovation was taking place at a rather impressive rate, without examining the largely unfounded assumption that the nature of the innovations was such as to make a tangible impact on the lives of any substantial number of poverty area residents.

Hence, the ambiguity contributed to the process by which changes that were presumably to be made in the institutionalized thought structure were modified in the actual situation through the system-maintaining operations of this same institutionalized thought structure. Innovation seldom posed even a potential threat to any of these CDOs whose legitimation was solidly rooted in that structure. Potential threats tended to be blunted into accustomed channels that enabled these CDOs to continue their control over their respective interest fields. The few innovations that could not be so blunted were vigorously combatted. As a result, the context and dynamics that were expected to produce meaningful innovation stultified the process and produced results that, however disappointing they might be in their prospects of improving living conditions for poor people, were quite acceptable in that the CDOs and their related agencies could live with them without great discomfort.

We have argued for the appropriateness of considering paradigm change as a meaningful accommodation of the qualitative dimension in innovation. The shift in focus from an analytic approach to the social problems of the inner city based on individual deficiency to an approach based on these problems as system outputs represents an appropriate qualitative change and one that is highly relevant to the condition of the nine cities of this study. Such an approach points not so much toward extension and refinement of services as toward institutional change. By institutional change we do not mean simply the incremental modification of structure and administrative procedures and operating technology of the present community decision organizations and their related organizations, but rather change on the level of reallocation of income and power. It also implies changes at the national level which are not within the scope of community-based strategies.

Changes that are not system-bound and system-constrained but that seek to escape routine procedures and refinements must of necessity pose a domain threat to existing organizations. They cannot be settled or reconciled on the basis of generally accepted administrative and technological realities, for they challenge these generally accepted realities. They are few because of the preventing-blunting-repelling sequence, of which by far the most important is the prevention that occurs as socialization. On the other hand, most of the changes initiated provide no special problems for agency domains, even marginally, and are characteristically the result of cooperative efforts. Even those that necessitate moderate adjustments at the margins can be handled in ways that, though contestful, are within the general cooperative system norm of live and let live.

In this context, the essentially inconclusive nature of this study's findings regarding the relation of intraorganizational variables to innovation is readily understandable. For the dependent variables of gross and secondary innovation are hardly distinguishable from the ongoing, routinized operations of the organizations involved. They tell us something of the nature of those operations, including something essentially superficial about the ways in which they may show differences from year to year in moderate adjustment to changing situations. In retrospect, it seems unreasonable to assume that they would vary systematically with organizational decision-making contest, or type of leadership, or program-planning ratio. On the other hand, the relatively high correlation with professional diversity may simply be an artifact of the circumstance that organizations that seek to establish programs across several interest fields have more adjustments to make in order to remain viable than do single-interest-field organizations. It may be unwarranted to assume that their greater professional diversity—reflecting their multi-interest-field status—bears a causal relation to their relatively high rates of minor change.

Conceivably, an infinite number of different paradigms would likewise represent a qualitative departure and hence constitute primary innovation. During the period of this study, the dysfunctional social structure (system output) paradigm was the only one in evidence—and that in only one organization, even though verbalization about the system output paradigm (without accompanying action) was more widespread. Its association with the repelling process and with conflict, as opposed to live-and-let-live contest, has already been treated.

Given these findings, it is difficult to see how serious innovation can arise from strategies that accept the existing institutionalized thought structure. Whence would they arise? And how would they escape the preventing-blunting-repelling sequence? It is equally apparent that the quest for innovation as it is pursued with and by these community decision organizations can be expected to confine itself to minor modifications in program, structure, and relationships which permit and support a continuation of essentially the same strategies based on the same analytical paradigm for understanding and responding to the social problems associated with poverty in the inner cities.

6 Responsiveness

Anyone at all familiar with developments in American cities over the past decade is aware of a tremendous ferment for urban reform in regard to the sensitivity of various local agencies to the needs and wishes of low-income people. Such sensitivity is here denoted by the term *responsiveness*, one of the principal variables of this study of community decision organizations.

In recent years there has been growing acknowledgment on the part of CDOs of the desirability of greater responsiveness on their part. Some of this recognition has appeared to be only minimal, and somewhat grudging at that. In other instances it appears to represent a more affirmative commitment. Not surprisingly, this growing acknowledgment on the part of organizations has occurred during a time when increasing demands were made upon them by organized groups of the poor. Such demands have in some cases themselves been part of a deliberate effort by the federal government to work toward greater responsiveness through the pressure of groups especially organized for that purpose. The Economic Opportunity program and the Model Cities program are notable for furthering the establishment of such groups to act as a stimulus to local agencies, as well as for other purposes.

Each of the CDO types of this study has found itself caught up in one way or another with these developments. Four of the six CDOs, each in its own way, have been objects of criticism because of lack of such responsiveness. Urban renewal agencies have been the focus of bitter attack because of their alleged disregard of the interests of poverty area people, either razing low-income areas and making low-income families homeless or more generally taking measures that "upgrade" residential properties to the point where the rents they command can no longer be met by their former tenants. City school systems have come under steady attack on the basis that they do not meet the needs of poverty area children, and that they are staffed by teachers who in the main neither understand nor identify with the people of the neighborhoods in which they teach, and that, as distinguished from the smaller suburban school systems, they represent large, remote, and inflexible bureaucracies that are virtually inaccessible to the citizens of the poorer areas. Mental health agencies have been challenged for making little or no provision for any kind of impact on policy and program from poor people, for the class bias of the treatment that individuals receive from mental health agencies in both diagnosis and therapy, and for their general remoteness from the major social problem concerns of the cities. Health and welfare councils have been accused of representing the interests of the

105

agencies themselves as well as the interests and values of an elite group of board members. They have been attacked for allegedly avoiding the major problems of discrimination in housing, education, the labor market, and the delivery of social services, in favor of a paternalistic view toward the poor.

These are only some of the ways in which these four types of CDOs have been caught up in the problem of responsiveness. As for the remaining two CDOs, the community action agencies and the Model Cities agencies were specifically created to help confront such problems in the CDOs and in other established service agencies in their respective fields. It was an express purpose of both the poverty program and the Model Cities program to bring about change in the "institutional structure" generally and more specifically in the sensitivity of these organizations to the needs and wishes of low-income people. An underlying issue in each case was just who would define the needs and wishes of low-income people, and through what procedure, as well as the question of just how these needs and wishes would be implemented in relation to the rationale of the pertinent organizations—technical, administrative, and institutional.

Citizen participation was accepted—with various degrees of enthusiasm or reluctance—by both the agencies and citizens groups as constituting a practical answer to the question of defining and acting upon the needs and wishes of low-income people. Yet the concept and the process contained two opposed conceptions of its objectives and its dynamics. Our own study has brought to the foreground the confrontation of these two drastically different conceptions of responsiveness.

The Movement for Participation

The movement for "participation," or more specifically, "participation of the poor," was supported on widely diverse grounds. Participation would help make programs more effective in accomplishing their objectives; it would reduce the likelihood of ghetto riots; it was necessary in order to establish truly democratic relationships between agencies and those served; it would help the poor to become more self-sufficient and "responsible"; it would build groups for participation in the pluralistic system of American politics out of those formerly excluded from it; it would reduce alienation and through this have an impact on delinquency, crime, drug addiction, dependency on public welfare, etc.; it would assure consent to and cooperation with agency programs; it would redistribute "power" more equitably; it would provide ladders for upward mobility.

Quite obviously, different emphases placed upon these different objectives of participation might be a source of friction and turmoil. Such an outcome was noticeable particularly during the years of the field research, when the citizen participation issue loomed large and caused contoversies not only directly in relation to the local Model Cities agencies, but in relation to the programs of other CDOs as well, both in their own right and through their involvement in Model Cities activities and contracts. But underlying the different emphasis placed on one or another objective of citizen participation was a more fundamental issue, one that cast doubt upon the assumption regarding the convergence of sensitive professional and agency opinion and responsible citizen opinion. This was the contradictory nature of citizen involvement and citizen action, which was overlooked because the same term—citizen participation—was used for both of them.

Our present task is not to assess the validity of these diverse alleged advantages of participation or of their aggregate merit. We simply note them as part of the social context in which responsiveness has attracted increased attention in recent years among CDOs.

The list of various objectives that citizen participation was to accomplish should be considered in relation to the background of social unrest among low-income people, blacks, and slum neighborhood residents which characterized the sixties. Not the least important aspect of that unrest was the great overlapping among the three categories just mentioned. The civil rights movement of the early sixties merged into the subsequent movement for "black power" and the related movement for "neighborhood control." The ghetto riots of 1967 were a signal that what had been accomplished through the community action programs was insufficient to cope with the unrest. There was a ferment for change. CDOs were not alone in experiencing this upsurge in the issue of responsiveness. In one way or another, direct service agencies, churches, universities, professional associations, even the military establishment were under similar pressures and took adaptive actions, large or small. These adaptations in the direction of increased responsiveness were quite obviously a response to the "pressure from the streets."[1]

A number of issues pertained more directly to CDOs. One of these issues centered around their essentially monopolistic nature and its implications for their accountability. While there is some limited competition at the margins between certain pairs of community decision organizations such as the six in our sample, they are for the most part characterized by fairly well-established domains in which their decision-making prerogatives are broadly accepted, in some cases being established by statute. This is particularly true of the singlefield CDOs. There is only one public school system administration, one health and welfare council, and so on. The two multifield CDOs have broader and less clearly defined domains and are more likely to find themselves in marginal competition with any of the other CDOs, and especially with each other. Generally, though, the extent of competition that CDOs afford each other is perhaps comparable to the competition between natural gas and electricity for heating purposes. But unlike so-called "natural monopolies" in the industrial sector, these organizations have neither the constraint of "running at a profit" nor of accountability to a regulatory commission.

So long as they could be accepted as operating "objectively" in the public interest, the issue of the accountability of these "monopoly enterprises" did not arise, but was left to the dynamics of the fiscal support process—through legislative budget committees, through federal funding agencies, through the donor's dollar, through taxes in the case of most boards of education, etc. But in the course of the past decade, there has been increasing questioning of the assumption that such CDOs operate impartially in the public interest. As this issue became joined, and as increasing attention was given to the growing problems of the cities, punctuated by ghetto riots, the pressure grew for these organizations to become more responsive to poverty area residents, or, in the more popular manner of expression, to "provide for citizen participation."

A characteristic closely related to the monopolistic nature of CDOs is that by definition they are legitimated for decision making on behalf of the community. In the past few years, this very legitimation has been challenged by citizen groups who in effect said that this legitimation was invalid because the CDOs did not represent their interests but instead furthered the interests of more well-to-do people, the industrial interests, the realty interests, and the interests of established bureaucracies. Only if they could gain some power over the decisions of these organizations that affected their lives could the poor continue to accept such organizations as justified in representing the broad community interest—including the interests of the poor.

A third factor had to do with effectiveness. In brief, city efforts in public education, in conquering poverty, crime, delinquency, drug addiction, and ill health were far from successful. Part of the reason, it was averred, was that the agencies engaged in such efforts did not really understand the nature of the problems they were addressing, and hence needed considerable input—accompanied by power—from poverty area residents. This input would not only make for improved programs, but pave the way for greater cooperation with these programs by poverty area residents.

Types of Responsiveness

What all of these issues surrounding the CDOs have in common can best be analyzed from the standpoint of organizational input and output constituencies. By *input constituency* is meant those people or organizations to whom an organization acknowledges a legitimate role in determining its policies and programs. By *output constituency* is meant those people or organizations whom an organization acknowledges a responsibility to serve. The two constituencies within the community decision organizations were largely insulated from each other, and the issue of responsiveness had to do with bringing them into closer relationship. These organizations were, in effect, responsible for serving one group of people, but were accountable to a quite different group of people for how they served the first group. While in many types of organizations this is not seen as a problem (e.g., the separate relationships to stockholders and to customers of a manufacturing company), it came to be considered increasingly inappropriate for CDOs, largely because of the reasons given above.

Participation, then, provided a structured mechanism through which the poor, as the recipients of agency services or the targets of their functions—and hence an important part of the output constituency of these organizations—could become a part of their input constituency as well. This was accomplished through various measures, and with varying degrees of intensity for different types of CDOs, as we shall presently indicate with data from the present study.

What the study sought to determine, then, was the extent to which, and the methods through which, the residents of slum areas became a part of the input constituencies of these community decision organizations. Hence, *responsiveness is defined as the acknowledgment by an organization of low-income people as a part of its input constituency.*

As one proceeds to operationalize this definition for purposes of research, certain aspects of responsiveness require elucidation. Perhaps most difficult is to distinguish the extent to which measures taken toward responsiveness are really meaningful, as opposed to being merely perfunctory. This question is understandably a current issue of considerable public attention and controversy. Reference was made in the preceding chapter to Selznick's useful distinction between substantive participation and administrative involvement. He pointed out that in the TVA experience, participation by local citizens was largely a matter of the latter.[2] The channels of participation are customarily set up by an organization in such a way as to help that organization further its goals, carry on its program, and maintain its viability. The officials of the organization are usually under definite constraints regarding the degree of flexibility they can employ. They must therefore be assured that such participation contributes to the organization's viability and to the security of their own position in it. They must keep the upper hand.

Depending in part on the degree of flexibility permitted the organizational leadership by regulations or by elements of its input constituency, organizational officials may or may not be willing or able to respond positively to needs and wishes expressed through participatory channels. Much of the urban drama of the past decade has been enacted in terms of the reciprocal testing of the meaningfulness of participation, on the one hand, and the need of organizational officials to maintain their own viability and that of their organizations on the other.

But just as organizational behavior takes place not in a vacuum, but in an environment with which it must come to terms, so likewise the participation of citizens in organizational participation channels takes place within an environment with which they must come to terms. The part of that environment most relevant to citizen participation is that of a social movement variously referred to as "neighborhood control," "black power," "decentralization," or "participatory democracy"—the "neighborhood movement." This social movement exists independently of the explicit participation channels provided by various organizations, although it is closely related to them. It is drastically different from the notion of the social development of neighborhoods as practiced in earlier decades by the settlement houses. It is a more ideologically conscious movement by poverty neighborhood residents to exert a larger degree of influence over the social institutions of the neighborhood, including public or voluntary social services, municipal services such as police or street cleaning, economic activity, housing conditions, renewal programs, and so on.

Hence, "citizen participation" in organizations such as the CDOs of this study comes to be the juncture of two diverse sets of goals and constraints, those of the organizational officials, and those of the neighborhood participants.[3] This represents a somewhat precarious balance between disparate sets of constraints, aspirations, and interaction styles.

So long as a disparity exists between the goals of the citizen participants and the officials, there remains the question of the "meaningfulness" of the participation, the extent to which it is substantive, rather than merely administrative, in Selznick's terms; or, in even simpler terms, the extent to which it "makes a difference" in the organization's policies and behavior. This being the case, any adequate investigation of the responsiveness variable must take systematically into consideration the impact of the participation on the organization.

The provision of formal, structural channels for participation, however, is not the only mode through which an organization responds, or fails to respond, to the needs and wishes of poverty area residents. In addition, there are often ad hoc occasions on which the wishes or demands of poverty area residents are presented to an organization—not from inside the organizational structure through formal participation, but from outside the organizational structure, through some form of confrontation with it. Such confrontation may vary all the way from a mild type of request by a few neighborhood individuals or a formally organized neighborhood association to a head-on test of strength with such dramatic tactics as sit-ins, boycotts, picketing, and so on.

An organization's responsiveness must therefore be assessed not only in terms of its structural provision for "participation," but also in terms of its manner of response to such ad hoc requests or demands from poverty neighborhood residents as they arise around specific aspects of the organization's behavior. Such interaction processes are generally thought of in terms of negotiations, although that term is usually employed for dealings between well-defined groups, while many of these ad hoc encounters involve much more diffuse and often highly transitory groups, without organized leadership structures, etc.

In such negotiations, as in any other type, the amount and forms of power that the negotiating parties respectively can bring to bear will influence the substantive outcome. Many types and channels of power are often operative, including the appeal to jointly held values, the threat of sanctions, the offering of inducements, the use of technical knowledge, the appeal to various governmental officials or to the media of public opinion, and so on. Since the power that neighborhood groups can otherwise bring to bear through conventional channels is often minimal in contrast with that of the CDOs, such groups often make use of tactics not deemed "acceptable" according to American middle-class norms for behavior in situations of controversy. They violate the norms of the institutionalized thought structure and, incidentally, may contribute to a backlash as the more established organizations respond with righteous indignation at the allegedly deplorable methods used by the neighborhood residents to put power behind their demands. This backlash may comprise both blunting and repelling elements. But whether these methods are norm-violating, in this sense, or norm-abiding, they involve requests and demands to which the organization responds in one way or another, manifesting greater or lesser sensitivity to the wishes and needs of the groups involved. Such behavior must also be taken into consideration in any adequate assessment of the responsiveness of these community decision organizations.

The effort made in this study to incorporate these nuances of responsiveness into the analysis has been rewarded; more refined analysis has uncovered vast differences in the dynamics and outcomes which would otherwise have been obscured. Responsiveness is defined as the acknowledgment by an organization of low-income people as a part of its input constituency. As with innovation, responsiveness is analyzed into three subcategories:

Gross responsiveness is simply a measure of structured participation—the formal provision the organization makes for participation of poverty area residents through advisory committees, board membership, and so on. It corresponds roughly to Selznick's "administrative involvement."

Secondary responsiveness involves substantive participation in the sense that neighborhood residents actually take part in bringing about changes in agency activities, either through formal participation structures or through ad hoc negotiations of various types.

Primary responsiveness involves changes in the organization's activity initiated by poverty area residents that are based on Paradigm II, that is, changes that convert program areas from those of giving services to people who need help to those of changing the pertinent aspects of the institutional structure so as to minimize or prevent the need for such services.

We shall state briefly the analytical framework that has emerged from our findings and then present a more detailed analysis.

The Counterposition of Citizen Action
and Citizen Involvement

The data can best be understood in terms of the interplay of the two sets of dynamics we have differentiated as citizen action and citizen involvement.

In this distinction, *citizen action* is the effort of low-income people to influence organizations to act in ways that give first priority to the needs and wishes of low-income people—as defined by low-income people—and to consider as secondary such constraints as organizational viability and rationale.

Citizen involvement is the orderly, channeled input into agency decision making by low-income people, through appropriate structures set up for this purpose. The decisions arrived at and actions taken as a result of such channeled input from low-income people are constrained by the viability needs of the organization and by the nature of its technical, administrative, and institutional rationale. Whether the organization provides such channels reluctantly or with enthusiasm, the assumption is that the organization will respond to such input within these constraints of viability and rationale. "Responsible" participation by low-income people implies an acceptance of these circumstances and a willingness to work within them.

The difference between citizen action and citizen involvement can best be described in terms of a number of characteristics: Objectives, direction of thrust, status of citizen participants, source of legitimation, resources available, tactics employed, and definition of "success."

Citizen action and citizen participation are differentiated from each other on each of these analytical aspects. Although these two sets of dynamics interact, we begin with citizen action, for that is where the impetus for the interaction lies.

The *objective* of citizen action is for target organizations to give first priority to the needs and wishes of low-income people—as defined by low-income people—with only secondary consideration to such constraints as organizational viability and rationale.

The *direction of thrust* is toward primary innovation, primary responsiveness, and conflict.

The *status of citizen participants* is that of adversaries, of citizens demanding their rights.

The *source of legitimation* of the participation is the claim to represent validly the needs and wishes of low-income people, as defined by low-income people. It is external to the target organization.

The *resources available* are potential external funds (usually federal) which can be blocked or delayed by citizen action, and the power, such as it is, which comes through organization.

The *tactics employed* are requests, demands, threats and acts of disruption, attacks on the target organization's legitimation, appeals to third parties (usually federal), and development of competing organizations.

The *orientation toward professionals and technology* is hostile. They are considered part of the problem.

"Successful" citizen participation consists in citizen control which "turns the agency around" by subordinating the constraints of organizational rationale and viability to the priorities of responding to the needs and wishes of low-income people.

Citizen involvement, on the other hand, has a quite different set of characteristics:

The *objective* of citizen involvement is for the organization to adapt to citizen action in ways that give first priority to the technical, administrative, and institutional rationale of the organization, and to its continued viability, constraining the organizational response to the expressed needs and wishes of low-income people to actions that are compatible with these first priorities.

The *direction of thrust* is toward gross innovation, gross responsiveness, and cooperation.

The *status of citizen participants* is that of clients, whose opinions are solicited as a means of considering changes to make the organization more effective.

The *source of legitimation* of the citizen participation is the formal provision for it within the structure of the organization and the continued recognition of it as "acceptable" and "responsible" by the organization.

The *resources available* are the organization's legitimated position within the interorganizational structure, its professional expertise, its command of a paid staff, (often rather large), and its accessibility to funds and support from local sources.

The *tactics employed* are prevention, blunting, and repelling.

The *orientation toward professionals and technology* is favorable. Technological solutions are the remedy for technological and other problems.

"Successful" citizen participation consists in "responsible" suggestions from low-income people that help make services more effective in meeting the needs and wishes of low-income people insofar as this can be accomplished without major inconvenience and without jeopardizing the technical, administrative, and institutional rationale of the organization or its continued viability.

Since issues arise in which these different approaches are in conflict with each other, there is a constant confrontation of the two sets of dynamics involved in citizen participation, in which the agencies attempt to control the participating citizens and to channel their inputs into acceptable form, and the citizens attempt to control the agencies so that their activities more adequately meet citizen needs and wishes. The tension caused by these two sets of dynamics is always present in citizen participation, but in some cases it is minimal, while at other times it breaks out as an overriding and dramatic confrontation.

The manner in which this dialectic of forces works itself out is quite different in circumstances of gross responsiveness, secondary responsiveness, and primary responsiveness. We shall analyze these differences by considering in each case the relationship between responsiveness and the nature of CDO interaction, the nature of innovation, and the preventing-blunting-repelling process. These are related to the two counterpoised dynamics of citizen involvement and citizen action in a definite and dramatic way. Citizen action, whose primary concern is the needs and wishes of low-income citizens, constitutes a force moving in the direction of an adversary role for the citizen participants, primary innovation, primary responsiveness, and, to the extent that it is not attenuated, conflict and eventual repelling. Citizen involvement, concerned primarily with preserving agency rationale and viability and the institutional thought structure that supports them, is a force opposing the dynamics of citizen action. It constitutes an attempt to contain citizen participation within the confines of the client role and of gross innovation, gross responsiveness, cooperation and preventing.

Thus, the thrust of citizen action is toward the right side of Figure 6-1; the thrust of citizen involvement is toward the left side of the chart.

Citizen Action →

← Citizen Involvement

CITIZEN ROLE	Clients	Constituency	Adversary
INNOVATION	Gross	Secondary	Primary
RESPONSIVENESS	Gross	Secondary	Primary
DOMINANT MODE OF INTERACTION	Cooperation	Contest	Conflict
MODE OF CDO DEFENSE AGAINST PARADIGM CHANGE	Preventing	Blunting	Repelling

Figure 6-1. The Thrusts of Citizen Participation

Gross Responsiveness

Gross responsiveness consists of the formal provision for participation by low-income people as part of the input constituency of a community decision organization. Operationally, it includes:

formal arrangements within the structure of the CDO which provide residents of poverty areas an avenue to influence CDO policies and programs (positions on board of directors, and other decision-making bodies);

informal processes *regularly* practiced by the CDO to give residents of poverty areas some form of policy and/or program review;

employment of poverty area residents by the CDO; and

formal relationships of the CDO with organized groups of poverty area residents.

In this study, the scores that individual CDOs received on gross responsiveness were derived by adding up the separate instances of each of the above for each CDO. In the scores on this variable, no consideration is given as to whether such provisions have any effect at all on organizational policy and programs.

As can be seen from Table 6-1 there was considerable variation by CDO types in gross responsiveness.

Table 6-1
Gross Responsiveness Scores, by CDO Type [a]

Community action agency	39
Model cities agency	29
Public school system administration	15
Urban renewal agency	14
Mental health planning agency	5
Health and welfare planning council	3
Total gross responsiveness	105

[a]The *n* for this table is 54.

For this and other responsiveness tables, it must be remembered that the model cities agencies were only beginning to develop as self-sufficient CDOs during the study period; consequently, their rate of responsiveness is not adequately reflected in these tables. A figure perhaps twice as large would no doubt be closer to what the scores would have been had they existed throughout the study period.

It is hardly surprising to see the community action agencies and the Model Cities agencies heading the list on gross responsiveness. Not only were they required by federal law to make provision for citizen participation, but federal administrative regulations spelled out in each case a definite set of requirements on which their continued funding hinged. Further, in each case their prescribed mission included the objective of promoting greater responsiveness among the agencies with which they made contracts and to which they allocated funds. They far surpassed the other CDOs in gross responsiveness. The strong federal prescription for citizen participation in the community action agencies and model cities agencies clearly had an impact on the rate of gross responsiveness.

A number of analytic variables were tested for their relationship to the gross responsiveness rate. One of these was the program/planning ratio. It might seem reasonable to suppose that organizations having a strong program component would be more task-oriented than the others, more concerned with "getting the job done." They might therefore be expected to be less responsive to the needs and wishes of low-income people, and less likely to make formal provision for some type of participation by them, than would organizations with a low ratio of program to planning and with perhaps more interest in the process of collaborative decision making. The findings, however, indicated exactly the opposite. *The higher the community decision organization's program/planning ratio, the higher tends to be its gross responsiveness.*[a] Hence, if there is any negative effect of a high program/planning ratio on the CDO's gross responsiveness, it is apparently more than compensated for by other considerations. As an example of such other factors, all nine community action agencies were in the upper half of the array on program/planning ratio, and they were required to make extensive formal provision for citizen participation.

Another significant positive relationship to gross responsiveness was indicated by professional diversity. The relationship may be stated as follows: *The greater the diversity of professional types in a community decision organization, the higher its gross responsiveness.*[b] This finding would seem quite understandable on the assumption that professional staff are more likely to take a "liberal" attitude about the desirability of citizen participation than are administrators and others who are not trained in a human services profession. We shall comment on this later, after we have presented our other findings. Meantime, the correlation should be interpreted in connection with the fact that it was the Model Cities agencies and community action agencies, the two multifield CDOs of the sample, which showed the highest professional diversity, but at the same time were under the most stringent requirements to provide for some form of citizen participation.

One of the analytic propositions most closely relevant to the evolving theoretical structure of the study concerned the relationship between responsiveness and the organization's situation in the interorganizational field. This proposition was developed in response to the narrative data and in connection with the continuing need for clarifying and refining concepts and operational measures. In these deliberations it was noted that on the one hand financial dependence on other organizations might form a constraint against providing any measure of substantive participation to low-income people, and on the other hand it was apparent that the chief impetus for increasing responsiveness came not from the CDOs themselves, especially not from the older, single-purpose CDOs, but rather from the poor and from the federal government. Hence, both independence from local organizations and funding from the federal government might operate to promote CDO responsiveness. The posited relationship was

[a]The Pearsonian correlation coefficient was .35, significant at the .05 level. Because the model cities agencies had not been in existence long enough to develop operational programs, they were not included in this computation.

[b]The Pearsonian correlation coefficient was .37, significant at the .01 level.

formulated for gross responsiveness as follows: *Gross responsiveness in community decision organizations varies inversely with dependence upon local organizations for financial resources.* The relationship was confirmed.[c] One might, of course, wonder whether this relationship again was accounted for by the community action agencies and Model Cities agencies which were largely independent of local financing and which had to provide for citizen participation in order to be financed federally. It was possible to check this statistically and to ascertain that the relationship holds, though somewhat weaker even though these organizations are omitted from the computation.

At the beginning of the study, a relationship was hypothesized between responsiveness and contest. It was assumed that actions taken to provide for citizen participation, and actions emanating from such participation, would be likely to be innovative and to disturb the domain consensus, posing possible threats to the viability of other organizations. But the analysis of the narrative reports that came in early in the study indicated that responsiveness, considered globally, did not appear to have such an effect. Nevertheless, a proposition was stated for systematic testing of the three different types of responsiveness. For gross responsiveness, the proposition states: *Contest interaction by a community decision organization varies directly with its extent of gross responsiveness.* This proposition was *not supported* by the analysis, which showed a quite random relationship between the two variables.[d]

The quantitative findings described above require interpretation and supplementation from the narrative materials. The narratives indicate that gross responsiveness was instituted in many cases with reluctance, and in other cases with an apparent positive willingness on the part of the CDOs to conform to the new trend and provide for "more citizen participation." In both types of circumstances, the presumption was that such participation could and should take place within a collaborative framework which would enable the organization to continue with its activities according to existing standards of administrative convenience and professional competence. Low-income people were thought of primarily as *clients* in the broad sense that they were people being served. Citizen participation's principal function was to help the organizations serve them better. This function involved not only the possible modification of agency programs the more effectively to serve the citizens (more sensitive procedures for relocation of families displaced by urban renewal projects, modification of the mental health clinic's visiting hours, or the establishment of storefront services in low-income neighborhoods), but also the enlisting of more understanding cooperation and utilization of services on the part of the citizens.

[c]The Pearsonian correlation coefficient was $-.49$, significant at the .01 level. The determinant variable was the percent of each CDO's total operating budget coming from other local organizations.

[d]The Pearsonian correlation coefficient was $-.03$, a weak *inverse* relationship, not statistically significant.

Excerpts from a document prepared by one of the health and welfare councils in its bid for a leading role in the citizen participation component of the Model Cities program give a somewhat extreme depiction of this approach:

The best way to define a "slum" is that it is a place where the people living there don't give a damn about the place. They are only aroused from their apathy when they are threatened with having to move without having a definite place to move to.

The acceptance of self-discipline by a neighborhood is slow to come by and only as the residents acquire knowledge of the benefits of self-imposed discipline. The road to achievement is a long one of education and encouragement from those outside the area.

What marks these neighborhoods apart is an inability of the individuals to utilize effectively the services available. Through ignorance, fear, and apathy they ignore existing services and will ignore or misuse new services unless they are patiently re-educated and motivated. It will not be enough to provide the service unless a direct effort is made to reach the people themselves.

Actually, little is known of the number of "problem families" within these neighborhoods or the number of relatively self-reliant families that can become the nuclei of re-established neighborhood self-sufficiency. This service will also provide the residents with the assurance that they will not be "rooted out" in a callous manner and that any displacement of them will be attended with provision for their future compatible with their needs.

If leadership in the community is to be recruited and encouraged, it is necessary to delegate power to local planning committees. In order that this power be identified with national mores and upwardly mobile aspiration, such committees must be provided with direction as well as support. Inter-agency committees made up of representatives of agencies serving the neighborhoods may well provide this guidance and support, provided they are staffed by competent personnel.

Because the success of the [model cities] program depends heavily upon local citizen's participation, there must be a planning for the education and organizing of the residents to make the most effective use of their new services, both physical and social.[4]

The document represents somewhat of an extreme in its conception of citizen participation as an essentially professional relationship to a pathological clientele and as a means of socializing or resocializing deviant citizens into accord with "national mores and upwardly mobile aspiration." Under the firm guiding and socializing hand of competent professional agency personnel, there is assurance that citizen participation will come up with the right answers, insofar as it gives consideration to anything at all but correcting the deficiencies of "problem individuals," "problem families," and "problem neighborhoods," to quote from their depiction in another section of the report.

Not all the CDOs of this study would subscribe to such a statement of the citizen participation objectives—particularly after the subsequent ghetto riots in the late sixties. Nor is it the language of the amended Economic Opportunity Act which encouraged community action agencies to make use of "neighborhood organizations" to assist "in the planning, conduct, and evaluation of components of a community action program."[5] The Model Cities Administration likewise was much more forceful in its requirement of citizen participation than the excerpts cited.

Nevertheless, citizen participation was acceded to by the vast majority of these community decision organizations on the assumption that it would not get out of hand, and that competent action by agency professionals and administrators would need to be complemented by *cooperation* on the part of "responsible" representatives of low-income groups. Hence, the formal structures established for such participation were for the most part purely advisory. The exceptions were the community action agencies and the Model Cities agencies, where such structures contained more or less clearly defined policy prerogatives as well. In some of the Model Cities agencies, the model neighborhood resident organization was set up with its own distinct identity, so that it could bargain with the Model Cities agency rather than constitute an integral part of it. Nevertheless, even here, the presumption was that the bargaining process would take place within the constraints of agency viability and rationale.

The notion that "responsible" citizen participation will produce cooperation and will produce "successful" results confined largely if not exclusively to gross innovation is illustrated in the following excerpt from the Citizen Participation Schedule filled out for a community action agency in a different city:

The target area residents at the beginning of the program and up to recently appeared to have developed a general frustration with the anti-poverty program. Anything they proposed seemed to be one that could not be funded by OEO. Their views were largely advisory and were usually ignored if they went contrary to priorities set by Washington and regional offices of OEO. The election in October, 1969, however, seemed to have turned out a group of action council members who through representation on the Board have become increasingly influential and understanding about the limitations in the program. Therefore, they are now moving responsibly toward the day when the Action Councils will become delegate agencies and operate the poverty programs.

There was a widely prevalent, largely unvoiced assumption that "responsible" citizen participation and competent professional conduct would produce agreements because there was no basic conflict of interests. And indeed, this assumption was widely supported by subseqeunt action, which indicated that even where there was considerable preliminary strife concerning the prerogatives of low-income groups in "citizen participation," the actual programs turned out to be basically conventional, emphasizing minor adaptations in the substance of services and their manner of delivery. As indicated in the preceding chapter, the "innovations" were for the most part not such as to disturb the interorganizational consensus. Where innovation did not pose domain threats, it was usually accompanied by cooperation, as already reported in Chapter 5. Indeed, in such cases it was usually the product of the cooperative interaction of two or more CDOs on programs that would enhance, rather than threaten, their viability.

From the standpoint of the citizen action movement, however, participation limited to gross responsiveness constituted cooptation.[e] For it was confined to giving legitimation to what the agencies would be doing anyway, or to providing merely advisory "input" that could be disregarded at the agency's own discretion. The greatest safeguard for agency viability, and by the same token the greatest assurance that little of substance would emerge from citizen participation, was the definition of the situation that reinforced the technical rationale of the agencies and that, through minor "innovative" adjustments in conventional agency procedures, gave the aura of great responsiveness to the needs and wishes of low-income people.

Where agency personnel did not recognize a conflict of interests, it was quite appropriate to use the cooperative process, to provide for participation on advisory committees, and to plan jointly for "improved services" under the guiding hand of agency professionals and administrators. In this context, the strong relationship between professional diversity and gross responsiveness is quite intelligible, for professional personnel with a "liberal" outlook could be expected to endorse the principle of citizen participation and to find, in actual practice, that responsible citizen participation posed no threat to them as professionals nor to the organizations that employed them. Likewise, they could be expected to be "innovative," provided the process through which innovations were considered and implemented was largely under agency control and provided the innovations were gross innovations, changes made in superficialities rather than at the core of organizational activities or viability.

Secondary Responsiveness

Secondary responsiveness involves substantive participation in the sense that neighborhood residents actually take part in bringing about changes in agency activities, whether through formal participatory structures or through ad hoc negotiations of various types. Instances of secondary responsiveness were classified in relation to both policy matters and program matters. The following are types of secondary responsiveness in policy matters:

Contracts are delegated to low-income resident organizations by a community decision organization.

Residents on the policy-making body of the CDO act as a bloc to accept or reject plans of the CDO.

Residents are involved in changing the CDO's hiring practices to employ residents in nonclerical, noncustodial kinds of jobs.

The CDO acts as advocate for residents vis-à-vis another CDO, or acts in concert with a residents' group vis-à-vis another CDO.

---

[e]We have attempted to use this term in an explicitly defined way (see page 55 ff.) and not as a loose, rhetorical term. The statement, however, holds for both the rhetorical use of the term and our own more specific usage.

The CDO increases the number of residents on its decision-making body or on decision-making bodies of its delegate agencies.

The CDO makes additional resources available to residents' groups (donations of space and/or equipment).

Likewise, under program matters, the following categories were included as secondary responsiveness:

Residents effect change in CDO's approach to problems within a paradigm.

Residents initiate new programs.

Residents effect or initiate change in types of programs administered by the CDO.

It should be recalled that these categories of secondary responsiveness include not only actions taken through formal or regularized channels, but actions taken in instances of ad hoc citizen action on some specific issue. Whether through regularized or ad hoc channels, the primary distinction of secondary responsiveness from gross responsiveness is that the former involves providing positions for residents where they have more than merely advisory power, or responding in tangible affirmative ways to resident requests/demands.

There is no definitional or methodological reason why the secondary responsiveness score for any CDO should be either larger or smaller than its primary responsiveness score. Any given channel of gross responsiveness might yield several instances of secondary responsiveness or none at all. It is therefore largely coincidental that the figures in Table 6-2 for secondary responsiveness are very similar to the figures for gross responsiveness. On individual CDOs within CDO types, the figures show considerable variation.

Table 6-2
Secondary Responsiveness Scores, by CDO Type[a]

Community action agency	47
Model cities agency	19
Public school system administration	16
Urban renewal agency	16
Mental health planning agency	2
Health and welfare planning council	2
Total secondary responsiveness	102

[a]The *n* for this table is 54.

The rank order of CDO types, as well as the overall scores, are markedly similar, indicating that those CDO types high in the more formal provision for participation tend to be high in the more substantive aspects of participation, as well.

Similarly, the propositions regarding the relationship between responsiveness and other variables come out approximately the same for secondary responsiveness as for gross responsiveness:

The higher the community decision organization's program/planning ratio, the higher tends to be its secondary responsiveness.[f]

The greater the diversity of professional types in a community decision organization, the higher its secondary responsiveness.[g]

Secondary responsiveness in community decision organizations varies inversely with dependence upon local organizations for financial resources.[h]

Contest interaction by a community decision organization varies directly with its extent of secondary responsiveness. (Not confirmed.)[i]

Fortunately, a more discriminating measure was available to test this last proposition, utilizing action episode data. The finding reported above was from the paired interaction analysis, which related an organization's secondary responsiveness to its *overall* degree of contest interaction (with all CDOs throughout the twenty-six month study period). But as reported in Chapter 3, the type of interaction in which a CDO engages in a specific action episode may differ from the type in which it engages in a different action episode, even when it is interacting with the same CDO. These differences are all "lost" in the overall scores, in that they represent a composite score including all action episodes and other interaction data from the narratives and from the CDO Schedules.

On the other hand, the action episode data pin a variable down to its operation in a specific episode and its relation to some other variable in that episode, for all the cases involved. In this instance, they make possible the determination of the relationship between responsiveness and contest not in general, overall CDO scores on these variables, but in the specific action episodes on which in-depth data were available. In these specific episodes, where secondary responsiveness was present, what was the nature of the interaction?

The answer to this question can be stated as follows: *There is a tendency for secondary responsiveness to be associated with contest in specific action episodes involving community decision organizations.* Table 6-3 presents the data.

Thus, though the relationship is far from invariable, most episodes where no secondary responsiveness was involved (also no primary responsiveness) were accompanied by cooperation; but most episodes where secondary responsiveness was involved were accompanied by contest. (In this analysis of action episode data, gross responsiveness is not considered. It bore so little relation to the action episodes that its tabulation would have required more operational complexities and methodological difficulties than it was worth. In practically all cases where gross responsiveness was present and pertinent to the action episode, it was because of the presence of secondary responsiveness as well.)

---

[f]The Pearsonian correlation coefficient was .35, significant at the .05 level, the same as with gross responsiveness.

[g]The Pearsonian correlation coefficient was .42, significant at the .01 level.

[h]The Pearsonian correlation coefficient was $-.42$, significant at the .01 level.

[i]The Pearsonian correlation coefficient was $-.16$, a weak *inverse* relationship, not statistically significant.

Table 6-3
Secondary Responsiveness and Nature of Interaction in Action Episodes

Responsiveness Category	Nature of Interaction		Totals
	Cooperation	Contest	
Secondary responsiveness involved	31	46	77
No secondary responsiveness involved	40	20	60
Total	71	66	137

$$X^2 = 9.5 \quad \text{d.f.} = 1 \quad p = < .01$$

Many of the organizations were reluctant to provide channels for secondary responsiveness. To the extent that they provided for citizen "input" it was purely in an advisory capacity, without any accompanying authority—hence, it constituted not secondary, but gross responsiveness. With few exceptions, this was true of all the single-field organizations: the school system administrations, the urban renewal agencies, the mental health planning agencies, and the health and welfare planning councils. Despite the fact that the Model Cities agencies at the time of the field work were only undergoing their development to full operations, they and the community action agencies together accounted for approximately twice as much secondary responsiveness as the remaining four put together.

Even so, there was some secondary responsiveness manifested by the single-field CDOs.

For example, in one city, the board of education's response to a number of boycotts and demonstrations was clearly within the secondary responsiveness category, and it set up citizen bodies whose impact has been demonstrable. Likewise, an urban renewal agency's response to one of its neighborhood rehabilitation committees was such as to delay its plans, discard some of them, and develop others in close relation to the committee, a relationship whose continuous tensions and struggles indicated that there was a genuine confrontation of conflicting interests.

The narrative data indicate that in instances of secondary responsiveness, the relation of the CDO to the participating low-income people goes beyond merely trying to provide input from its *clients*. While some of this relationship is still apparent, a new relationship begins to supersede it: the relationship to participating citizens as a *constituency* of accountability, or, in our terms, as part of the organization's input constituency. The low-income citizens were seldom recognized as the most important part of the input constituency, but nevertheless they came to be considered as a part of it.

For example, in one of the cities, the participation of citizens on the Model Cities health planning committee had a tangible impact on the nature of the mental health program. The program was largely formulated by the citizens, with the help of a professional person provided by the Model Cities agency. On several important issues they went against the advice of this professional, and their general formulation of the program prevailed.

In another instance, a Model Cities agency tried to put through its second-year action program without thorough review by the Model Cities citizens organization. The citizens organization pointed to the ordinance spelling out its review powers, forced a thorough review and renegotiation, and in the process wrested three quarters of a million dollars in projects it especially wanted.

Secondary responsiveness tended to be associated with *secondary innovation*. This is not only because the formal measures for provision of substantive participation constituted secondary innovation by definition, but also because the programs and projects and initiative developed by low-income citizens within the participatory structures were (in those cases where they represented anything new at all) of the secondary innovation type (changes in problem definition within Paradigm I; innovations in hiring practices and staffing patterns to accommodate more low-income people; providing low-income people a substantive voice in the organization's decision making, and formal efforts by a CDO to direct another agency's activities toward any of these three actions).

Secondary responsiveness also tended to be associated with *secondary contest*. Table 6-3 indicated that contest was the dominant mode of interaction in action episodes involving secondary responsiveness, while cooperation was the dominant mode in action episodes that involved either no responsiveness or only gross responsiveness. The action episodes involved interaction not only between CDOs but between a CDO and other organizations, as well (including citizens organizations). In some instances, secondary responsiveness precipitated contest between two CDOs, as where a community action agency attempted to force a school administration to increase its responsiveness to parents groups. In some instances, secondary responsiveness was associated with a contest between a community decision organization and a citizens group, as where a resident group sought to delay or change an urban renewal program. In some instances, contest with other CDOs and other organizations, including citizens organizations, occurred simultaneously.

The contest that occurred in connection with secondary responsiveness was preponderantly a part of the *blunting* process. A community decision organization sought to resist a proposal for secondary responsiveness which came either from a citizens organization or from another CDO (most often from the community action agency or the Model Cities agency).

But, parenthetically, the blunting process was not confined to contest, since in many instances it was possible for the CDO through various forms of cooptation to negotiate the assent of citizens to the reformulation of their proposals for secondary responsiveness into the gross responsiveness category. The typical case was where the low-income participants sought a policy-making prerogative which through negotiation ended up as a policy-advising prerogative.

But even where secondary responsiveness was present, the action citizens took with their newly won prerogatives rarely went beyond proposals or programs of secondary innovation, and usually were of the gross innovation type. Even in the cases where secondary innovation ensued, it basically affirmed the rationale of the community decision organization, seeking improvements in existing practices and not constituting a direct threat to the organization's stability or viability. Such proposals could be acceded to in varying degrees (although the attempt was often made, with varying success, to blunt them), customarily depending on issues of administrative convenience and the CDO's priorities and available resources.

In sum, in most cases the preventing and blunting processes operated to impede the movement of citizen action and to keep it within the constraints of citizen participation, as these were defined earlier in this chapter.

Primary Responsiveness

Primary responsiveness involves changes in the organization's activity initiated by low-income area residents, which are based on Paradigm II, that is, changes that convert program areas from those of giving services to people who need help to those of changing the pertinent aspects of the institutional structure so as to minimize or prevent the need for such services. As such, it differs qualitatively from gross and secondary innovation, which provide for varying degrees of citizen participation in the *existing* organizational structure as constrained by the existing technical, administrative, and institutional rationales of those organizations.

Primary responsiveness thus represents the successful implementation of the objective of citizen action to subordinate the established organization's rationale and viability to the wishes and needs of low-income people, as defined by them. We have already seen that most of the community decision organizations were able to ward off the citizen action movement by containing it at the gross and secondary responsiveness stages.

In one organization out of the fifty-four, citizen action penetrated to the stage of primary responsiveness: this instance provides important insight into the dynamics that occur when citizen action reaches the stage of "turning the organization around."

Before considering these dynamics, let us review the position of this single community decision organization with regard to the analytic propositions that were presented for gross and secondary responsiveness. Its history is most instructive, especially in the light of the narrative data. Since there is only one instance of primary responsiveness, we simply report what the position of that CDO was on the variables involved in the four analytic propositions.

The OEDCI, the Oakland CAA, was in fourteenth place out of an array of 45

CDOs from which the proposition regarding *program/planning ratio* was tested. It thus was quite consonant with the findings for gross and secondary responsiveness, which were supportive of the proposition of a positive association between the two.

On *professional diversity*, the Oakland CAA was somewhat above the average among the CDOs, thus conforming to the proposition regarding the positive association between the two variables.

On the inverse relationship between responsiveness and *dependence on local organizations for financial support*, the Oakland CAA was completely supportive, in that it was the most responsive and at the same time the most independent of any of the CDOs from local sources of funding.

Regarding *contest* interaction, the relationship was likewise supportive of the proposition that the greater the responsiveness, the greater the contest interaction. Indeed, on this the Oakland CDO was in a class by itself, being the only organization engaging in both primary innovation and primary contest (conflict). This relationship is especially significant, in that gross responsiveness is not associated with contest but with *cooperation*, secondary responsiveness is associated predominantly with *contest*, and primary responsiveness is associated predominantly with *conflict*.

In the case of the OEDCI, this organization came to be perceived along about the fall of 1968 as one that was under the control of low-income people and that engaged in policies and programs that broke the interorganizational consensus (i.e., were based on Paradigm II rather than Paradigm I). From this stage onward, the OEDCI found itself less and less engaged in the live-and-let-live dynamics of cooperation and secondary contest and increasingly embroiled in the qualitatively different dynamics of primary contest (conflict). On the part of the OEDCI, the conflict took the form outlined in Chapter 3 and described in greater detail in the following chapter. On the part of the local, state, regional, and federal agencies surrounding it, this conflict gained increasingly the quality of *repelling*, which in this case eventuated in the organization's demise.

Summary Analysis

The foregoing analysis has treated fairly extensively the preventing-blunting-repelling sequence as this relates to gross, secondary, and primary responsiveness, to gross, secondary, and primary innovation, and to cooperation, contest, and conflict. The relationship is not perfect, but it is statistically significant and quite in accord with our interpretation of the narrative data.

We conclude that the most important dynamic parrying the movement of citizen action toward primary responsiveness and primary innovation consisted of preventing, based on the socialization process.

Two aspects of the institutionalized thought structures described in Chapter 2 are particularly pertinent in the present context. The first is the conviction instilled in individuals through the socialization process that basically the society is sound and specifically that the professional technologies that address social problems are likewise essentially sound. They need incremental refinement, perhaps, but not total replacement. The second aspect is of equal importance: the way to bring about such improvements is through collaboration. What had been lacking was an opportunity for low-income people to take part in that collaborative process through which the common good is identified. Much of the initial struggle for "citizen control" was misnamed, being not a struggle to control, but merely the struggle for a voice in decision making, a voice that could be outweighed and outheard by other, more powerful voices, and that in the event, most often was outweighed and outheard.

An evaluative quotation from a narrative report by the project's field research associate in Newark describing the community action agency recounted a common experience:

Therefore, the most "harmonious" and "constructive" way in which to integrate the poor into the system is within a structure that carefully "balances" their interests vis-à-vis those of other competing groups. It is this concept of "balance" which accounts for the legally-mandated tripartite division of CAP trustee seats among what were apparently taken to be the three most relevant constituencies: local public officials, representatives of "the private sector" (primarily business, the unions, religious groups, and welfare organizations), and the representatives of the target population itself.

Such a distribution of power is workable only if the pluralist expectations of harmony and compromise are valid. What community activists in Newark quickly learned, however, was that their share of the vote could be rendered insignificant by the united opposition of those elements on the Board that could naturally be expected to carefully preserve and defend the status quo. *It quickly became apparent that the Board rather accurately reflected the same structure of power that it was ostensibly meant to challenge and change.*[6]

The parrying of the thrust of citizen action occurred largely with the acquiescence of the low-income citizens who participated in the channeled slots provided by the agencies. Even in Oakland, where the West Oakland Planning Committee, under strong support from the OEDCI, struggled vigorously for power and gained a large measure of power over the Model Cities program, the projects that emerged were little different from those of other cities. The data of this study support the conclusion reached quite independently by Mittenthal and Spiegel regarding citizen participation in planning the Oakland Model Cities program:

For while we must conclude that the neighborhood waged an astute contest with city hall, replete with rhetorical flourish and a kind of bombastic selfrighteousness, its power position relative to that of the Establishment did not materially change. . . . As matters stood, the concessions wrung from protracted confrontations with the city fed West Oakland's ego without putting money in its pockets or changing underlying social and physical conditions.[7]

In sum, many of those who gave vocal support to the goals of citizen action quite willingly accepted cooperation, gross innovation, and gross responsiveness within an essentially client role as appropriate steps toward accomplishing their objectives. And as we have shown, this combination clearly reinforced existing rationales, intervention strategies, and organizational maintenance needs.

Where citizen action pressed beyond such insubstantial involvement it encountered—and was usually contained by—a blunting process. The principal components of this blunting process were the exercise of various types of cooptation and the exercise of governmental authority. We have delineated four types of cooptation: technical, administrative, institutional, and the more usual "personnel" cooptation.

The other, less subtle component of the blunting process was the exercise of superordinate governmental authority. Where the city council was concerned, its actions were almost exclusively in the direction of blunting citizen action, constraining it to gross responsiveness and innovation if possible, but if not, then lopping off any perceived aspects that might go beyond secondary innovation and responsiveness.

State, regional, and federal officials utilized their authority differently in different cases. In some instances, on all these levels, they came down on the side of citizen action in moving from the gross categories to the secondary categories of innovation and responsiveness. At other times, their thrust was in the opposite direction, the direction of blunting the citizen action efforts, pushing secondary innovation or responsiveness back to its gross form, or warding off efforts to convert the secondary forms into primary innovation and primary responsiveness. Examples of the latter are the operation of the city council, the state government, and the regional and national OEO offices in the case of the Oakland OEDCI. Examples of the former were the modification of Model Cities proposals in Oakland by the federal officials, and in Boston by the local city council.

Thus, the blunting process primarily took the form of exercise of superordinate authority in the case of local, state, and federal governmental authorities, and of cooptation in the case of the CDOs.

As citizen action encountered either of these blunting processes, the reaction was that of accepting part of what had been demanded, as constituting progress in "the right direction," even if progress was not as great as had been hoped and at times demanded.

Further, there appeared to be the implicit realization that, in this study's terms, behind the blunting process lay the repelling process. As one director of a community action agency put it to his board:

Nobody who is being oppressed is going to get money from the oppressors to overthrow the oppressors; therefore, anything we do to upset the status quo like getting involved in the school issue, controversial groups, etc. will create trouble for us. . . . The Federal Government will not be liberal about our involvement in the schools.

Following his statement, a motion that had been made for the CAA board to oppose the school bond issue in an ensuing special election was tabled. The contrast with the action of the Oakland CAA on a similar issue is dramatic. (See Chapter 7.)

In most instances, the iron fist did not need to become apparent beneath the velvet glove. The agencies knew it was there, and the citizen activists knew it was there. Its very presence, however low-keyed, helped make the blunting process sufficiently effective so that the repelling process was seldom needed. For the citizen activists, there was a more familiar term than repelling—*repression.* When this was applied, as described in Chapter 7, it had the tacit support of many citizens who felt that the proper response to blunting was to settle for secondary responsiveness, for "a piece of the action," rather than pressing on to the inevitable conflict and repression.

7

The Oakland Economic Development Council, Inc.[1]

The Oakland Economic Development Council, Inc. (OEDCI) differed so striking-ly from the other fifty-three organizations of this study that its major characteristics warrant detailed attention. It differed from the others in its diagnosis of the problem of poverty in the inner city. It likewise differed from the others in its strategy and program based on this diagnosis. The difference lay principally in its emphasis on the institutional structure as the primary locus of the poverty problem, rather than on the characteristics of poor people. (Although it was largely constituted of, dominated by, and oriented toward black people, it was not exclusively so.) In our terms, it had a Paradigm II orientation. Unlike the other CDOs, the OEDCI was unsuccessful in its attempt to develop for itself a legitimated place in the interorganizational structure. This was not its first concern, in any case. Its first concern was to challenge the legitimated interorganizational structure from the standpoint of its different analytical paradigm. It engaged in programs and tactics that were perceived—correctly, we believe—as a threat to that organizational structure. Its activities, where they were well within the accepted norms of "live and let live," were responded to with cooperation or with the usual modes of essentially nonthreat-ening secondary contest. But where these activities were perceived as threaten-ing to another organization's core viability, or where they were perceived as threatening to the interorganizational structure and its supporting institutional thought structure, or where they were perceived as norm-violating, they were met with more serious resistance—at first through the blunting process and then through the repelling process. The blunting process was effective against this organization in the short run in that it prevented it from achieving its immediate objectives, but it also deepened the organization's resolve to engage in primary innovation, thus intensifying the conflict. As the OEDCI's tactics were succes-sively perceived as more and more threatening, harsher measures were brought to bear against it, measures that were part of the repelling process. Ultimately, it was destroyed.

Background

The process through which this all occurred is extremely enlightening, though difficult to disentangle conceptually. The case is not clear, or pure, for a number of reasons.

First, the OEDCI did not engage exclusively in primary innovation and primary contest, nor were the bulk of the responses by other organizations hostile. Many joint projects were undertaken with other community decision organizations which were hardly different from those of community action agencies in other cities.

Second, the conflict occasioned by the organization occurred not only between it and others, but within the organization itself, at first primarily between factions of the board of directors dominated by the mayor or by the executive director, respectively, and later by important factional splits within the staff and within the executive director's citizen constituency.

Third, the activity that took place involved a number of other organizations as well, and it is difficult to disentangle the OEDCI's activity from that of these other organizations, such as the East Oakland Fruitvale Planning Council, the West Oakland Planning Committee (the citizens organization legitimated to provide the citizen participation in the Model Cities program), and the Black Caucus.

Fourth, the organization was dominated by Percy Moore, the executive director, who all sides agree impressed his own indelible stamp upon the organization to such an extent that it became the vehicle through which his ideas were expressed and implemented. He acted as his own source of authority and was usually able to obtain organizational approval through not only the persuasiveness of his specific ideas on a given issue but also through his strong following within parts of the board, the staff, and the Oakland community.

Up until 1967, the Oakland Economic Development Council (OEDC) was a fairly typical community action agency, except that structurally it was probably more securely under the control of City Hall than many such organizations. It had developed a series of programs that were predominantly service programs of various types, in relation to numerous agencies in the community.

In 1967, two important changes occurred. The city divested itself of control over the agency, and Percy Moore was brought in from San Francisco as executive director. The circumstances leading to the OEDC incorporating as an independent agency were complex. One important aspect of the decision was that various city officials saw the growing influence of the organization as constituting a threat to their own departments. It had made a strong but unsuccessful bid for a police review board in 1966, and in 1967 it received a sizable grant of several million dollars, which the mayor had hoped would go to his own new Manpower Commission. The influence of representatives of the poor in the OEDC as a city agency was making itself felt in demands which took various forms and which were strengthened by the OEDC's official status as an agency of the municipal government. The council decided to cut it loose.

When Percy Moore became executive director in November 1967, it did not take him long to begin to change the policies of the newly incorporated OEDCI.

While not fundamentally opposed to services as such, Moore believed they were used in a way that preserved rather than corrected the inequities in the social structure, which was essentially racist and oppressive toward the poor in general and blacks in particular. Poverty funds were being used to pay the agencies to do what they should have been doing anyway—providing services to the poor—without changing the decision and control structure under which the poor had been so long neglected. Further, the poverty program, like other service programs, had the effect of fragmenting the black leadership as each leader acted as a "broker" between the poor and the establishment, having access to certain "goodies" he could deliver piecemeal to certain of the poor in exchange for their loyalty and support. In a paper written a few months after his arrival, Moore emphasized that the emerging Model Cities program should correct this situation:

Each neighborhood leader has tended to stick within his own small group and the groups have tended towards exclusion. There has been no real West Oakland community and no organization conpetent to serve a valid representational function. Each group and leader has sought favors of the establishment. . . .

One major goal of Model Cities programming must be the liberation of the masses of people living in the target area from this brokering system. . . . It is essential that this confrontation be open and honest so that the public monopolies which dominate the black community pit their technical skills against the brutal realities of people living in closed communities, where they can be victimized, exploited and dehumanized. To the community organizer, Model Cities is only important to the extent that it *builds men and women into organizations competent to take and hold power.* [2]

The need for an organization to unify and coordinate the various strands of leadership and organization within the black community was a point of great importance for Moore. Further, although gaining control over the social services provided in Oakland was important, it was not sufficient. The objective was not merely control over services, but changing the circumstances of living—quite a separate thing. A few years later, looking back on the subsequent operation of the OEDCI, and why its funds were cut off, he said, "Why was OEDCI not refunded? Probably because we were too politically aggressive. Probably because we dealt more with the interpretation of the reasons why so many Blacks are unemployed as compared to why so many whites are employed. We politicized around some of the issues so that people learned to understand that things don't just happen." [3]

Percy Moore's attitude toward service programs in relation to more fundamental changes is indicated by his emphasis on job availability as the important issue, rather than training. The following quotation illustrates the manner in which organization of the poor was predominant in his thinking:

The big thing is to break down the discrimination in these construction unions. We can expose them [the trainees in PREP, the Property Rehabilitation

Employment Program] to what it is to be involved in sheet metal work, plumbing and roofing in a training program, but if they expect to get beyond that, they'd better look around and find out who the enemy really is. Some of the cats in PREP were really getting themselves together. They are not going to be an easy group for the city to work with 'cause they gonna raise hell. . . . They want to be moved out of that training program and get into apprenticeship programs. They want to get into a trade as a journeyman and they want to make that $7 an hour.[4]

Moore was not averse to having professional people employed by the OEDCI, and indeed our study identified seven different professional types in the OEDCI in 1970, not far below the average 8.4 for CAAs. Nevertheless, he felt strongly that professionals had no mandate to speak for poor people. "No professional planner is competent to design what the nation's black community wants nor to interpret its needs and demands to the establishment. The establishment does not deserve the buffer role of the professional advocate planner in its relationship to its organized citizens."[5]

The underlying point here is that the issues are not issues for the professional to decide on some allegedly value-free basis (which was usually close to the viewpoint of city hall and the dominant agencies). They are political, having to do with the gaining and exercise of power and the preserving or changing of an oppressive institutional structure. It was in this sense—rather than in the sense of dismissing all the professionals from the OEDCI staff—that Percy Moore could remark: "We deprofessionalized OEDC over three years."[6]

Under Moore, the OEDCI played a predominant role in establishing the West Oakland Planning Committee (WOPC), the organization that was not only legitimated to provide the citizen participation input into the Model Cities program, but that also had prime responsibility for planning and operating the program. A long and bitter fight was waged for substantial degrees of control over that program, and OEDCI was in the vanguard of that fight. At one point, the regional office of the Office of Economic Opportunity became somewhat dismayed at Moore's tactics of what it called "polarizing" minority groups; Moore responded:

My problem is to recognize a polarity and move toward a bargaining situation in which the interests of parties in conflict can be negotiated. I intend that the representatives of the black community of the poor in West Oakland approach that situation with a strong bargaining position, with hat on head and not in hand. That kind of stance may be shocking to you and other powerful government officials, but it seems to me the only way in which dignity and respect of both parties can be maximized.[7]

In the late 1960s, it was not unusual to hear asserted the need for the poor, especially the black poor, to organize and "gain control." But as we have indicated, most such efforts were blunted in such a way that the control mechanisms and the specific programs that emerged did not constitute drastic change. They did not in any way undermine the continued viability of the established organizations, through whom the local Model Cities agencies were directed to operate. In Oakland, however, the movement for "neighborhood control" reached a high-water mark. The efforts were not so easily blunted.

As mentioned, the programs and activities of the OEDCI under Percy Moore did not renounce cooperation with existing agencies, but rather sought to change the power relations within which such cooperation must take place. Where this failed, the OEDCI engaged the agencies in secondary and primary contest and took back programs under its own control or set up new programs under its own control or under the control of organizations of poverty area residents.

From the many and diverse types of activity in which the OEDCI engaged, a few episodes may be briefly recounted:

A New Careers program was under negotiation in 1967. The new Concentrated Employment Program was to provide 2500 jobs for people in selected target areas. As part of this, a program to train teacher aides so that they could become full-fledged teachers was proposed to the board of education. A New Careers Development Organization was set up as a delegate agency of the OEDC to administer the Concentrated Employment Program. Because of the slow pace of negotiations with the board of education, this organization's request that the board of education take advantage of forty slots left for it was not met promptly, and so it filled the slots with other types of trainees. As a result, the program was launched with only five new careerists in education, a highly insignificant number compared with the 2500 new jobs to be developed for Oakland and the forty places orginally provided for. This represented negotiations continuing over a period of a year and a half. The negotiations had been hampered by differences between the OEDCI and the city regarding who would control the Concentrated Employment Program.

At about the time Percy Moore was coming onto the scene in the fall of 1967, the Headstart Program, financed by the federal Office of Economic Opportunity, was to become a year-round program rather than a summer program. Dissatisfaction with the Head Start Program had been growing in OEDC for some time over the expense of the program with its limited results, and over the large proportion of funds going into administration and "back-up" services, which appeared to the neighborhood leadership to be serving white professionals rather than the black community. A vote of the various neighborhood advisory committees was taken, and they approved OEDC taking it over. It was decided to leave the public schools out of the program, a decision to which the board of education objected on the basis that the parents had not been consulted. The new OEDCI delegated a number of groups to operate at various service centers around the city. The staff of the school system continued to cooperate with the program, however, and one of the higher administrators of the school system noted that because of the school system's willingness to cooperate, even though it was no longer involved in a major way, the relationships between the schools and the OEDCI had improved.

One of the most important activities of the OEDCI was the struggle to gain as large as possible a measure of local resident control over the Model Cities program. Through the West Oakland Planning Committee, which was set up for this purpose, Oakland developed one of the most protracted struggles for control and one of the most power-invested citizen participation components of all 150 Model Cities.

The early planning for Model Cities had taken place with very little participation by residents. Shortly after the designation of Oakland to receive a planning grant, in November 1967, increasing pressure by the black community leaders, along with the HUD regional office's insistence on a mutually satis-factory provision for citizen participation in the program, led the city manager to ask Percy Moore for the OEDCI to give leadership to the development of the citizen participation program. The very next night, a mass meeting was held in West Oakland, the "model neighborhood," and Percy Moore stated his position that the Model Cities program should be controlled by black people for the benefit of black people. Out of that meeting grew the West Oakland Planning Committee (WOPC). From the beginning, Moore was clear that this new committee should have independent status, rather than consisting only of the OEDCI or of its local West Oakland Target Area Advisory Committee. He urged the establishment of a new organization that would not include the City Hall appointees mandated on his own OEDCI board.

In its negotiations with the city, the WOPC insisted on a large measure of control over the Model Cities program. The negotiations were protracted and often bitter, and at one time it appeared likely that the city council would remove the program from West Oakland and try to locate it elsewhere. The WOPC's bargaining strength lay in the fact that the HUD regional office would not approve the program unless a satisfactory citizen participation program was worked out. In the bitter struggle that ensued, WOPC won an exceptionally large measure of control over the program—though not complete or exclusive control by any means; this lay by law in the hands of the city council. Nevertheless, the WOPC obtained a majority of the seats on the pivotal Model Cities Policy Committee; a veto over any proposed programs; and virtual control over the decision as to who would be the Model Cities director. Later, it demanded a similar veto not only over the supplemental funds programs within Model Cities, but over all funded programs in the model neighborhood. Although this demand received only inconclusive response from the federal and local agencies, it served to establish the WOPC as a significant and relatively powerful body in the determination of what would take place in West Oakland. These concessions, along with the wresting of a $92,000 budget for developing its own "planning" activity for Model Cities, represented a substantial movement into the area of top-level decision making, as distinguished from merely an "input" of resident opinions into decisions made elsewhere. The role of the OEDCI in establishing and giving continuous support to this organization was massive. Not only had it encouraged WOPC's establishment, but it assigned a staff member to work with the WOPC in the formulation and advocacy of its proposals. Close liaison between the two organizations was an important reality of the succeeding two years.

Meanwhile, the OEDCI was extending the idea of such local organizations to another area of black poverty in Oakland, the East Oakland Fruitvale area. It submitted a proposal to the Office of Economic Opportunity (OEO) requesting $142,000 for the establishment of the East Oakland Fruitvale Planning Council, Inc.; the funding was granted. The EOFPC was given the task of mobilizing and organizing the citizens and organizations of East Oakland around the issues of planning for their own community in the field of economic development, education, housing, environmental quality, health, and community relations (specifically, police-community relations). It got underway in October 1968. One of its first actions was to present a demand to the mayor and city manager that all city planning functions in its district henceforth be carried out by the EOFPC. It likewise made demands on the board of education for decentralized control of the schools. While neither of these efforts was successful, they served notice on the existing organizations that the EOFPC was a force to be reckoned with for more than a controlled and channeled "citizen input" into local programs.

One of the outgrowths of the efforts by the East Oakland Fruitvale Planning Council, in conjunction with the West Oakland Planning Committee, was a hard-won agreement for partnership with the Oakland public schools concerning the decision-making, administration, and implementation of the dropout prevention program. This was a program funded under Title VIII of the Elementary and Secondary Education Act. Under an agreement reached in December 1968, a board was created for the administration, management, and policy making for all project components of the dropout prevention program. The majority of the board were to be target area residents. Further, the selection of participants in the projects as well as the location of project sites was to be determined by the EOFPC and the WOPC. This constituted a definite invasion of the board of education's domain as a CDO.

The EOFPC also won a large share of decision making in the formulation of plans by the Redevelopment Agency for a Neighborhood Development Program in three target areas of East Oakland. Likewise, a working relationship was developed between the WOPC and the Redevelopment Agency in which all renewal plans were submitted to the WOPC for review and approval.

In the spring of 1969 a reaction began to set in against the new militancy of the black community. After the reelection of many of the board of education members in mid-April, the board apparently took a hardening attitude toward negotiating with the local black citizenry. At its meeting on April 29, the board repudiated the agreement on the dropout prevention program which had been made with the EOFPC and the WOPC and the OEDCI. The following week, on May 6, the board of education, having bypassed its own selection procedures for a new superintendent of schools, announced its sudden decision to engage a new superintendent from the Las Vegas school system who was at the time involved in a conflict of interest dispute. This led to a heated series of meetings and confrontations.

At a hectic board of education meeting on May 20, Percy Moore threatened to lead the OEDCI into a confrontation with the board. The board refused to rescind its action, and the chairman declared the meeting closed. Groups of protesters, who had warned that they would stay until the board rescinded its action, blocked two of the doors. A melee broke out, and police used mace and clubs to disperse the crowd, clubbing both Percy Moore and Paul Cobb, president of the Black Caucus. They arrested the president of the Oakland Federation of Teachers. The school security officer subsequently filed felony charges against Percy Moore. Misdemeanor charges were also issued against three other black leaders. The following day, the newly appointed school superintendent publicly withdrew. Looming in the background was an imminent referendum on an increase in school taxes. As the June 3 date for this vote neared, the OEDCI and the Black Caucus organized a campaign to defeat the tax increase, even though the black community had supported tax increases in the past. The campaign resulted in the tax proposal's defeat.

Incidentally, the trials of the arrested "Oakland Five" carried over an extended period of time and finally ended in acquittal or dropping of all the charges except one: blocking an aisle in a public place. The defendants pleaded "no contest" and were fined.

As a reaction to the increasingly effective organization of the black community, the Oakland City Council attempted to amend the Neighborhood Development Program proposal to take away power over the structure of citizen participation in the program from the Oakland Redevelopment Agency. As indicated above, this agency had agreements with the EOFPC and the WOPC through which they exercised a strong citizen participation function in the program. The modification was not allowed by HUD, but the move was another indication of the point-counterpoint interaction developing between City Hall on the one hand and on the other the OEDCI with its allied organizations, the East Oakland Fruitvale Planning Council, the West Oakland Planning Committee, and the Black Caucus.

The alliance formed by the OEDCI, the EOFPC, the WOPC, and the Black Caucus is of special importance. The Black Caucus was a federation which claimed membership representing over forty organizations and a constituency of over 60,000 people, slightly less than half of the black population in Oakland. The Black Caucus Steering Committee included Percy Moore, Paul Cobb (secretary, WOPC), Elijah Turner (national treasurer of CORE), Alfonso Galloway (head of the Blacks for Justice Committee), Donald McCullom (president of the NAACP), Mrs. Willie Mae Thompson (board member, OEDCI), and Laurence Joyner (acting executive director, EOFPC; vice-chairman, OEDCI). Most of these were board members of OEDCI.

From the above it can readily be seen that the OEDCI was not the only organization engaging in an aggressive struggle for black control over local community institutions; the fact that it wasn't is important, in that no single organization was depended on by the militant black leadership to press its demands to the establishment. The strategy was to set up an independent base for citizen participation, one that did not confine that participation and decision making to channels controlled by the established citywide agencies but rather negotiated with these agencies in tactics that in part abided by the generally accepted contest norms of live and let live as well as with tactics that in part violated these norms.

In sum, the OEDCI gradually came to be perceived as an organization that differed from the usual community decision organizations. While it engaged in joint programs with them on occasion, it challenged the approach to poverty problems based on the "needs of the poor" and rather defined the poverty problem in terms of inequities in the institutional structure. The OEDCI was not averse to services as such. But it sought to control them and in part to supplement or supplant them with community organization and the politicization of social problems issues which were otherwise discussed principally in professional terms and from the orientation of the powerful citywide agencies. It moved in aggressively to attempt to achieve a greater measure of citizen control wherever possible. It was not content to set up relatively powerless "advisory" committees, but struggled constantly for substantive participation in decision making. It sought to develop a base for citizen action independent of the formalized channels for "citizen participation," which were tied to specific, agency-dominated structures.

The Interorganizational Response
to the OEDCI–Blunting

It would be misleading to separate out the OEDCI's activities as the "cause" of the series of responses that led to its demise, just as it would be misleading to attribute the causation to the actions and reactions of the organizations that opposed it. The process was reciprocal, and it tended to have the characteristics of a summatory social process, which intensified with each successive response.[8]

In this reciprocal process, a series of measures were taken in order to counter the growing impact of the OEDCI. Many of this organization's efforts were controllable through the blunting process. But as the OEDCI's efforts persisted past the blunting operations, the repelling process was instituted. Although both blunting and repelling were intermixed in time, it is undoubtedly accurate to say that as time went on and the blunting proved ineffective to control the organization, the repelling process gradually eclipsed it. Rather than attempt a lengthy chronology, we give here simply some outstanding examples of these two processes, including some events already mentioned. First, some samples of blunting:

Before the OEDC incorporated independently, it proposed a police review board. The city council opposed this in various ways. It was eventually implemented after a severely compromised version, setting up a police advisory board, was worked out much later by the WOPC, the Model Cities agency, and the police chief, who thereupon took a much more supportive attitude towards the new Model Cities program.

A limited guaranteed income project was suggested by a consultant at an early task force meeting planning the Model Cities application. The Welfare Department objected strongly, stating that present programs were adequate. The idea was never implemented.

The agreement regarding control of the school dropout program, described earlier, was subsequently repudiated by the board of education.

A move by the OEDCI to set up a Housing Development Corporation was blocked by the city manager, who succeeded in blocking the use of the OEDCI's Ford Foundation money through a time-consuming and relatively unprecedented request for an audit of these funds.

The Model Cities Comprehensive Demonstration Program cleared the city council with large measures of administration and control over individual programs residing with the WOPC. In the Model Cities Administration's "Final Program Modifications," many of these responsibilities were shifted back to the city government, and WOPC's budget reduced accordingly.

These examples of blunting could be multiplied. Whether or not they are justified is not the concern at the moment. They simply illustrate the continuous process through which proposed actions that may constitute a threat to existing organizations may be stopped, changed, or molded into acceptable form from the standpoint of organizations with the power to do it. They typically involve negotiations that take the form of secondary contest. They are usually sufficient to "hold the line." In the Oakland case, however, they were not.

**The Interorganizational Response
to OEDCI—Repelling**

The OEDCI and its allied constituencies continued to engage in change strategies that became more and more threatening. Since the blunting process, though partly effective, was not sufficient to ward off the threat, the repelling process was brought into play and gradually eclipsed it.

In order to understand the sequence of the repelling behavior, it is important to keep in mind that the mayor appointed one-third of the board of the OEDCI, even after its incorporation as an independent agency. The OEDCI consequently represented from the outset a split, sometimes potential, sometimes quite real and dramatic, of the board into two main factions—those who supported the mayor and those who supported Percy Moore. This split was also a split between those who supported a services strategy along conventional lines of collaboration with other community decision organizations and their established agencies and those who supported a strategy of structural change through growing power and control over the activities in slum neighborhoods by the organized poor—mainly blacks. The repelling, largely by the municipal government and the board of education, proceeded initially in the attempt to outvote Percy Moore within the board of the OEDCI and, when this failed, to remove him from his position as executive director. These efforts at repelling from within continued right up to the end, though they were largely unsuccessful. Hence, when the leadership of the organization could not be controlled in this fashion, the strategy became one of destroying the organization itself. This strategy succeeded.

We enumerate here some of the more outstanding events in the repelling process:

In the fall of 1968, a formal attempt was made by the mayor's group to unseat Percy Moore. The attempt failed by two votes. On the basis of this key vote, Moore went ahead vigorously with his strategy of ending support for the established agencies and increasing his efforts to organize the black community.

In January 1969, the mayor wrote a long letter to Vice-President Agnew and to HEW Secretary Robert Finch stating, along with a number of other assertions, that the OEDCI was dominated "by a clique of power-oriented, anti-white, and anti-City Hall militants," and that federal grants for the antipoverty program should be made through the municipal government. By the end of August, he also began a relatively effective campaign of winning over some of the leading staff and board members of OEDCI to criticism of Moore's policies and proposing that the OEDCI return to an essentially services strategy.

In February 1969 the news was widely publicized that the OEO was conducting an investigation into an alleged shortage of over a million dollars.

In May 1969 came the arrest of Percy Moore and the others of the "Oakland Five" and the subsequent extensive efforts of the OEDCI and its allies to defeat the school tax increase.

In July 1969 the mayor announced his major campaign to achieve his objective from within the board of the OEDCI. He appointed thirteen new city representatives, thus getting rid of those who could not be trusted to go along with his policies. The mayor addressed the board meeting on July 23 emphasizing his desire for services for the poor instead of organizing the poor, and especially stressing the importance of job training and placement. However, his address came under immediate criticism by several of the board members for his policies and actions with regard to OEDCI. The OEDCI sent a delegation to Washington to challenge the mayor's new board appointees, but the OEO approved the appointments.

In August 1969 one of the board members who had formerly supported Moore made a series of charges against him which eventually led to a hearing by the OEDCI Council on October 8.

In September 1969 the mayor and the OEDCI president, who had been won over to opposition to Moore, and an additional board member met with the acting regional director of the OEO to request a probe of the antipoverty program in Oakland and of the OEDCI's administration of it. The OEO agreed to hold the probe, but indicated that it had no charges against Moore and could not intervene in the decision to discharge or retain him. Moore attributed these difficulties to City Hall's fear of an effectively organized black community and to the mayor's attempt to reorganize the board against him.

A vigorous series of actions eventuated in an October 8 meeting of the OEDCI board which, through some unsuccessful maneuvers by the opponents of Moore on the board, ended up with a bare quorum of twenty present out of the full membership of the board. But these twenty rejected the charges brought against Moore and gave him their unanimous support. This demonstrated that Moore continued to hold a majority of the total board in his support.

On October 17, the *Oakland Tribune* reported that the mayor and twenty-one other OEDCI Council members had signed a petition asking the Office of Economic Opportunity to assume control of the OEDCI.

A week or so later, Governor Reagan vetoed a grant to the East Oakland Fruitvale Planning Council and announced an investigation of the OEDCI.

Later, on January 10, 1970, Donald Rumsford, the OEO director, terminated financial support of the EOFPC. Governor Reagan's veto had followed a request from the mayor to veto the grant because the council was advocating community control of schools and police. "It is a political issue. What they were attempting to do is a political philosophy, and I did not feel that Federal funds should be used for those purposes." On the other hand, Moore asserted that the OEDCI "is demonstrating the capabilities of an organization under the strong leadership of independent black people to conduct business for a class of citizens in Oakland. That is what Mayor Reading finds intolerable."[9]

By this time (January 1970), the OEDCI's funding by OEO had been restricted to a month-to-month basis. At the beginning of February, the OEO announced its permission for OEDCI to continue through the month.

A few days later, the OEDCI was awarded a grant of $4,000,000 by the Department of Labor for the Concentrated Employment Program.

On March 9, the OEO announced its intention to conduct an on-scene review of the OEDCI.

On March 23, the state OEO began an audit of OEDCI.

In April, the mayor stated at a U.S. Senate subcommittee meeting on manpower programs, "The OEDCI's emphasis is on racism, and its attack on community problems is focussed primarily on development of political power."

On April 23 came the announcement of Governor Reagan's veto of an $80,000 grant by the OEO to the East Oakland Fruitvale Planning Council for the phasing out of its operations. This move also hit the OEDCI, since the EOFPC was in debt to it to the extent of over half of this grant.

The turmoil continued through the year 1970 and on into 1971.

At the end of February 1971 the director of the California Office of Economic Opportunity called for a "rethinking" of the OEO philosophy, asking rhetorically, "Are institutions really responsible for man's poorness?"

On March 2, 1971 the OEO regional director informed the city council of its right, if it so wished, to revoke the OEDCI's designation as the official community action agency authorized to receive OEO funds.

On March 19 it was made public that the federal government had taken the Neighborhood Youth Corps program from the OEDCI and given it over to the City of Oakland to administer.

The regional OEO director warned the OEDCI board to repudiate the actions of its executive director at its meeting on March 22, 1971. Percy Moore had allegedly broken federal rules in announcing a campaign to unseat six Oakland city council members in the coming April election. This followed on a statement by a subordinate regional OEO official two weeks earlier that Moore had not violated federal rules. Nevertheless, the regional director advised the OEDCI council that unless it repudiated Moore, its inaction would affect adversely his recommendation, to be made to the national OEO director, on whether the latter should sustain or override a governor's veto of a large grant essential to OEDCI's continuance. At the meeting, the OEDCI council "disassociated" itself from Moore's announced campaign. The regional director thereupon warned that this mild action had not been adequate and the OEDCI's future remained in "very grave doubt." The city council, which supported the Reagan veto of the grant, refused Percy Moore's request to address it on the issue or to have the OEDCI secretary address it.

On March 31 an attorney filed a suit to have the tax-exempt status of the OEDCI revoked, asserting that the OEDCI had solicited employee contributions through payroll deductions in order to engage in political activities. The complaint stated that the OEDCI "had generally and consistently used its power, prestige and position to encourage and control political activity, harass public officials, and disrupt public meetings."

On April 13 the federal director of the OEO sustained Governor Reagan's veto of the OEO grant to the OEDCI.

On April 16 the federal OEO announced an additional month's reprieve for the OEDCI, but insisted that the council not pay Moore's salary until it punished him adequately for his political activities to unseat the six city councilmen.

On April 21 the OEO notified the OEDCI that it would have until June 30 to close out its operations. The regional director stated that beginning May 1, the OEO would no longer recognize the OEDCI as the community action agency. Moore offered to resign if the governor would reverse his veto decision and the OEDCI would receive the needed funds.

On May 11, 1971, state officials refused to release funds from the $185,000 phase-out grant until alleged irregularities in the handling of OEDCI's payrolls were checked out. "We are not going to give Mr. Moore any more money to play around with until this matter is resolved," a state official declared.

On May 18, 1971, the Oakland city council took over the antipoverty program from the OEDCI.

The above account is distorted in that it is comprised of only a small selection of the successive steps in the repelling process. As mentioned at the outset, the entire sequence was characterized by an escalating interaction from both sides. That the repelling process was stimulated and restimulated by the activities of Percy Moore, the OEDCI, and allied groups is quite obvious. That much of the antagonistic action taken by the OEDCI was itself a response to frustrations encountered in seeking to negotiate in more conventional ways with the various agencies is also quite apparent. In other cities of the present study, many episodes of a similar nature occurred, but they represented only occasional outbursts of potentially lethal conflict as distinct from the more usual secondary contest which was especially marked in the community action agencies.

Why did the process escalate into repelling and destruction of the community action agency in Oakland? It was apparently because an important part of the activity of the OEDCI under Percy Moore constituted an implementation of what we have called Paradigm II. The OEDCI under Percy Moore attacked not simply this or that individual instance of injustice but the interorganizational system as a whole, and the institutional thought structure that supports it. It attacked the core legitimation of individual organizations such as the school system and some of the direct service agencies, constituting what was perceived as not merely a rhetorical threat but an actual threat, carried out in a persistent series of actions, to control or destroy these organizations. Its methods of conflict were not confined to the customary live-and-let-live tactics of interagency contest around marginal domain issues, but employed disruption, threats of reprisal, boycotts, and other methods perceived as violating proper or legal usage for the handling of disputes. It constituted an organized threat to the interorganizational structure, one that threatened to grow in power, and one that could not be "contained" by blunting tactics alone.

Central to all the statements and activities of the OEDCI was a commitment to combatting poverty through bringing changes in the institutional structure, rather than through expanding and improving "services" to the poor. Accompanying it was a similar commitment to a strategy of politicizing the black constituency to an awareness of the inequities being exercised on it and to its own potential strength through organization and through economic development. Most of all, it saw the path toward social justice lying not primarily in a collaborative planning process through which the various institutions of the city of Oakland would voluntarily change their ways, but rather through a continuous struggle in which collaboration all too often means cooptation. Such cooptation resulted from the "brokerage" system, which Percy Moore continuously admonished against, according to which a fragmented black leadership dispensed special rewards from white-dominated agencies in exchange for acquiescence to both injustice and powerlessness.

The Paradigm I Case Against the OEDCI

There is, however, an alternative explanation for the destruction of the OEDCI, which derives quite logically from Paradigm I and the institutionalized thought structure. This would be fourfold: the OEDCI under Moore made unrealistic demands; it was inept in its internal administration and in its actual task performance in terms of getting jobs and improved services; its tactics involved measures that were in the twilight zone between unconventionality and illegality; and its representation of the best interests of poor blacks, to say nothing of a sizable minority of poor Mexican-Americans, was questionable, since its policies came from a small leadership coterie consisting of Percy Moore and a limited number of faithful supporters, rather than from the broad masses of the black and Chicano community.

In the first place, it could be argued, the city council was the democratically elected government and could not abdicate its responsibilities to a community action agency, to a Model Cities agency, or to any other agency. It had to maintain control of public programs, and its right to designate the organization that should function as the community action agency implied its responsibility to see that that agency functioned in a way acceptable to the entire city.

Second, it was argued that despite its rhetoric about jobs, economic development, and the rest, the OEDCI squandered its financial and personnel resources in a vain attempt to engage the poor in essentially political action, rather than in those types of community improvement programs that might make a tangible impact on their lives. According to this argument, the poor got rhetoric and frustrating battles with the city's established agencies, rather than the additional services that the community action program might have made possible.

Again, the tactics employed by Percy Moore were alleged to include not only "irregularities" but illegalities as well. There was the vociferous disruption of public meetings; there was the school boycott; there was the hiring of personnel without the consent of the board; there was the irregularity in giving staff members terminal bonuses and then rehiring them; there was the specific activity in waging a war to unseat six city council members; there was the OEDCI's voluntary payroll deduction system to support this political activity; there were the frequent instances of failure to comply with regulations governing the receipt and dispersal of funds.

Finally, there was the serious issue of representation. It was a disputed question whether a majority of the black community of Oakland, as well as other nonblack poor people, ever gave their endorsement to the unconventional philosophy and policies of Percy Moore, or ever really had the chance to. It is certain that Percy Moore never had all the black leadership of Oakland behind him, and that as the struggle wore on, one after another of his former close supporters lost confidence and in one way or another joined the opposition. Moore was under almost constant criticism for dealing with his OEDCI board in a high-handed way, and for being more concerned with putting through his own proposals rather than listening to what his constituency had to tell him.

This fourfold explanation for the demise of Percy Moore's OEDCI is also distorted, just as was the listing of the sequence of repelling actions brought against the OEDCI. A number of allegations are implied which have never been fully checked out by anyone. For some of these questions, the answer is quite obvious. For others, the matter is much more cloudy. We simply state these matters here, without taking a position as to the justification of the charges and countercharges from the standpoint of either side. Our mode of analysis is not to adjudicate the issue, but to analyze it in terms of the two alternative paradigms and the social dynamics they engender. We have just presented two alternate accounts of what went on.

The Significance of the OEDCI Case

It is an insoluble question what proportion of the repelling sequence was engendered by the broad outlines of the OEDCI approach under Percy Moore, and what proportion was brought on by his own personal idiosyncracies. Influenced as it was by these very same personal idiosyncracies, the main outline of the sequence seems indisputable. The one organization that made a determined, persistent, and relatively coherent attempt to work for change in the general social structure of the poverty areas rather than merely in the service delivery patterns of specific agencies became engaged with other organizations in a mode of interaction that was qualitatively different from the contest strategies employed in the remaining organizations. Its persistent commitment to structured changes virtually implied a set of practices that continuously challenged the existing ways of doing things. Many of the "irregularities" alluded to above are simply a logical extension of its diagnosis of the poverty problem and the strategies needed in order to cope with it on a basic rather than a palliative level. The deflection of money from services to political organization, the "deprofessionalization," the withdrawal of contract support from existing agencies such as the health department and the school system, the building of an alliance among organizations to use political pressure to obtain social goals, the constant struggle to convince a constituency to build its political power rather than to accept small favors from existing political power structures, the concern with community control—all represent a quite different combination of elements from that which constituted the policies of the other community decision organizations. It was perceived—correctly, we believe—as a fundamental challenge and threat to the existing balance of power and organized ways of pursuing urban reform.

While nearly all the other community action agencies of the present study were able to gain legitimation as they lopped off the potentially threatening aspects of their presence as a new agency with resources in the interorganizational field, the OEDCI did the opposite.[a] It did not lop off its rough edges so as to fit and be accepted comfortably in a legitimated domain within the interorganizational field; rather it expanded its innovative approaches, increased rather than decreased its threat to other organizations, never gained, or even apparently sought, legitimation within an interorganizational domain consensus—and was destroyed.

---

[a]Significantly, one other community action agency suffered a demise during the study—that in Manchester, New Hampshire. That agency, however, did not engage in primary innovation but rather succumbed for a number of reasons, not the least of which was the persistent and effective journalistic attacks by publisher William Loeb's *Manchester Union Leader.*

8

Implications for Interorganizational Theory and Research

We have reported the findings of a study of the interaction of six community decision organizations in nine cities, with special, though not exclusive, emphasis on the manner in which their interorganizational activity is related to their efforts to address the social problems of the inner cities. The study was further centered on the variables that we call cooperation/contest, coordination, innovation, and responsiveness.

Once the study was well underway, it became apparent to us that the original research design had been based primarily on an approach to interorganizational behavior from the level of the interacting organizations, despite the fact that we had been aware, from the outset, of the importance of considering as well the inclusive field within which specific interactions take place. Part of the reason for this neglect to provide for systematic comparative data gathering on the level of the interorganizational field, we now realize, was the great difficulty presented by the need to develop a conceptualization and to operationalize it. But there is another reason why we had not confronted this difficulty at the outset: the interorganizational studies accumulated up to that time had almost invariably concerned themselves with the organizational level and had not addressed themselves seriously to the interorganizational field itself as a subject for research.

We shall develop this point further in a moment. First, a word about this chapter. The most important implications of the present study derive from the effort made to pursue the characteristics of the interorganizational field of CDO interaction. The delineation of the characteristics of this interorganizational field is useful in two major ways. It affords a useful conceptualization for understanding the dynamics of system stability and change in the area of the cities' social problems and the institutions that support and/or seek to modify them. It also provides a different and more adequate perspective on the behavior of CDOs with respect to the four outcome variables of the study. Both of these aspects have implications for the problem formulation and research methodology currently utilized in the field of interorganizational behavior. They likewise raise questions about the social context as this is related to the selection of analytical paradigms and research methodologies. This chapter explores these implications.

The Interorganizational Field Findings

The community decision organizations of this study faced great uncertainty in the turmoil that surrounded them during the intensive field study period

(1968-70). They were able to cope with this uncertainty and maintain great stability. How was this possible?

On the organizational level, we have considered the technical, administrative, and institutional components of their rationale and have indicated numerous ways in which these respective components of their organizational rationale served to afford a degree of determinateness within which they could function, even in the uncertain environment that they confronted and that sustained them. Their organizational rationale afforded them a means of defining the reality not only of routine situations but of the unique and unpredictable developments as well. Through their respective rationales they were able to ingest, as it were, this uncertainty and bring it into a supportable relationship to their own needs for regularity and predictability. In a sense, they gained the necessary degree of certainty not through their ability to predict events and make detailed plans to anticipate them, but through their continuous ability to routinize the unpredictable, to confront those aspects of events which they recognized as relevant and to deal with them in a way which they not only considered appropriate, but in which they were skilled. In their interactions with each other and with still other organizations, they also were able, with differing success, to define dissensus situations in such a way that the resolution of such situations would be essentially compatible with their continued viability. We have considered this aspect to be the essential ingredient of cooptation, which, as we have indicated, takes several forms.

On the more inclusive level, these organizations interact within a local interorganizational field which is an embodiment of the American institution-alized thought structure and which sets up both constraints and supports for their respective organizational rationales and a set of ground rules for their interaction in situations of both cooperation and contest. Viewed from this standpoint, domain is not sui generis, an organizational characteristic, as it were, but a position within the highly institutionalized network of organizations, a network, incidentally, whose counterparts exist in all nine of the cities studied and are presumably characteristic of all American cities above a certain minimum size.

In this situation, interaction around emerging issues is often not necessary, since the interorganizational domain consensus is a basis for common and similar assessment of which organization should do what, and how. Interaction does arise on occasion, however, strong interaction being occasioned more by threats than by opportunities. On closer examination, these threats reveal themselves as issues requiring minor domain adjustment at the margins, seldom constituting serious jeopardizing of the organization's viability.

Threats to the interorganizational field, as well as to individual organizations, are coped with through a succession of processes extending from preventing through blunting to repelling, with the first being the most frequently employed and the last being employed extremely seldom.

Levels of Treatment of Interorganizational Behavior

If the interorganizational field is so important in explaining the behavior of these community decision organizations, why has it been so long neglected? Perhaps the characteristics of the interorganizational field are not so important in understanding the interaction taking place between organizations that are different from community decision organizations. Or perhaps other interorganizational fields exhibit characteristics quite different from those we have found. We cannot say. Nevertheless, as one reviews the interorganizational literature, one encounters few references to the interorganizational field, let alone empirical studies of one or more such fields.

The circumstance is sufficiently important to warrant further pursuit. Three analytically distinct levels guided our own conceptualization of interorganizational behavior. We shall describe and present them briefly, giving examples from the interorganizational literature.[1]

1. A number of studies clearly focus on the individual organization and direct themselves to the ways it may articulate itself with its environment. Their focus is either explicitly or implicitly the viability of the individual organization, and its relation to its environment is considered from the standpoint of how the environment affects its viability. The term *viability* has been used in this report to refer to the organization's ability to survive and thrive. This is distinct from the notion of the organization's goal attainment, for it accommodates the situation where an organization can survive and prosper without attaining its manifest goals. In order to survive and prosper, an organization must protect or enhance its domain. Often, the attainment of its manifest goals facilitates this process, though not invariably. Conversely, an organization may survive and prosper without tangible indication of accomplishment of its manifest goals. Where there is a choice, we assume, organizations will opt for viability as against manifest goal accomplishment. The data of this study have supported this assumption.

In his "The Impact of Environment on Organizational Development," William R. Dill points out the way in which inputs from the environment "enter" the organization and decisions are made as to what, if anything, to do about them.[2] James D. Thompson's analysis of "Organizations and Output Transactions" was an important early work dealing with an organization's transactions with part or all of its environment.[3] William M. Evan developed a number of hypotheses that related a focal organization to members of its input and output set.[4] In their paper on "Organizational Goals and Environment: Goal-Setting as an Interaction Process," James D. Thompson and William J. McEwen dealt more generally with the interaction processes into which an organization may enter with one or more organizations in its environment.[5] In an interesting case study called "The Reluctant Organization and the Aggressive Environment," John Maniha and

Charles Perrow described a case where an organization's fate was largely determined by the environmental circumstance that other organizations could use it for their own purposes.[6]

2. A number of studies treat not so much the general organizational environment as interaction instances involving two or more specific organizations. Harold Guetzkow has delineated perhaps the broadest framework for analysis in this area, in his "Relations Among Organizations."[7] In an interesting but fragmentary paper called "Towards a Theory of Representation between Groups," Herman Turk and Myron J. Lefcowitz dealt with the interaction between persons in boundary spanning roles under differing circumstances regarding power and legitimation of the organizations involved.[8] Eugene Litwak has developed over a number of years an extensive theory of linkages between formal organizations.[9]

Perhaps the most widely accepted and utilized treatment of relations between specific organizations is the "exchange" concept developed by Sol Levine and Paul E. White.[10] As these investigators elaborated their theory over time, their focus remained on exchanges between specific organizations. They eventually came to consider the problem of "integration" among organizations, but they treated this problem primarily from the standpoint of the individual participating organizations rather than the characteristics of the interactional field.

3. Among the few studies that have focused primarily on the characteristics of the interorganizational field itself, as distinguished from characteristics of the separate interacting organizations, perhaps the most important is that of F.E. Emery and E.L. Trist on "The Causal Texture of Organizational Environments." They point out how organizational environments differ in their causal texture in regard to uncertainty and in many other important aspects. They delineate four different, successive types of environment, the last of which is the most interesting and pertinent to contemporary conditions. This is the "turbulent field" environment, in which "individual organizations, however large, cannot expect to adapt successfully simply through their own direct actions."[11] They give clear recognition to the importance of the interorganizational field as a subject for study in its own right, and as an indispensable part of the explanation of individual organizational behavior.

A few years after Emery and Trist, Shirley Terreberry published an article on "The Evolution of Organizational Environments," which carried their analysis further, again emphasizing the importance of the larger interorganizational system of which individual interacting organizations are a part.[12]

More typically, the interorganizational field level is approached from the standpoint of the presumed need for coordination among diverse organizations and the quest for means through which such coordination can be attained. As an example, Mayer N. Zald treats the problem of "coordination and integration" among agencies in the social services, pointing out that efforts at coordination have both costs and benefits.[13] In a somewhat different vein, Basil J.F. Mott wrote an analytical case study of an attempt by a state governor to set up a coordinating council among various departments and special agencies of the state government, and the dynamics through which the objectives of such coordination were systematically defeated by the participating agencies.[14]

In quite a different analytical vein, an article by Michael Aiken and Robert R. Alford on "Comparative Urban Research and Community Decision-Making" addressed the question of organizational interaction in relation to different types of organizational environments.[15] It is a useful analytical summary of the important multicity studies that have been made in an attempt to explore statistically the relationship between numerous city-context variables and certain "policy outputs," such as public housing programs, urban renewal, and the war on poverty.

These brief references to illustrative studies from the interorganizational literature indicate some of the ways in which interorganizational relations have been conceptualized. The emphasis has been placed primarily on the individual organizations and the circumstances in which they engage in various types of interactions with their environment generally or with specific other organizations, with little attention given to the characteristics of the interorganizational field; or as an alternative, emphasis has been placed on the presumed need for coordination for the benefit either of individual organizations, or of some larger whole. Those studies that consider the interactional field in terms of coordination tend to assume implicitly that coordination is good ipso facto. They often are not clear whether the benefit is to the participating organizations or to some larger whole, or both. They do not consider the relation of the interorganizational field to the larger society, or specify its inputs and outputs vis-à-vis the larger society, or—except in the preliminary typology of Emery and Trist—describe its systemic aspects, including its manifest and latent functions.

Implications of the Interorganizational Field Paradigm

The present study has attempted to take this concern for the interorganizational field a step farther by doing all of these things, though again not completely and not as systematically as one might hope this would be done in future studies. But even the present study, we believe, reveals a number of important implications of the hitherto largely ignored difference between an approach to interorganizational behavior from the standpoint of the individual organizations or from the standpoint of the characteristics of the interorganizational field. These implications involve the question of differences in conceptualization of certain key variables as they are seen from these alternative standpoints, and consequent differences in findings with regard to these variables; differences in methodology as these differences produce different modes of analysis and different sets of findings; different sets of possible implications of the basic concepts, methodology, and findings as these present alternative views of the nature and process of what is taking place, and the inadvertent side effects of these formulations and conclusions as related to important ideological considerations within which social reality is perceived, interpreted, and acted upon in terms of social policy.

These implications will be discussed in turn. The first major implication of the different paradigms is a global one regarding the *amount of organizational interaction*. It is the difference between an impression of great stability and one of great change and flux. On the organizational level, the appearance is of numerous new situations and adjustments, new organizations invading the domains of other organizations, new programs, new relationships, new objectives, and new technologies. Yet, when viewed from the inclusive level, the major domains, the division of labor, the legitimated technologies, the basic orientations to the social problems of the inner cities—all have shown, in their total configuration, an identifiable and specifiable stability.

Part, at least, of the discrepancy lies in the limitations of the individual organizational perspective. From that level, it is easy to conclude that these community decision organizations are indeed doing some things that are relevant to the poverty problem. It is easy to assume that if every other agency is likewise doing something relevant and effective, then great inroads on poverty must of necessity result from these aggregate efforts. But on this level there is no basis for assessing the total configuration of what is being done, in relation to the magnitude of the problem. Each organization is simply shooting its own arrow into the air, with little consideration of the aggregate outcome. It is only when one examines the inclusive effort, the configuration, that one is able to make meaningful judgments about the magnitude and direction of the total effort in relation to the nature and magnitude of the problem.

The difference becomes even more apparent in considering the *nature of the organizational interaction*. Viewed solely from the level of the interacting organizations, it is difficult if not impossible to account for the relatively little interaction encountered in this study, especially regarding new developments and new federal programs that touched more than one CDO at a time and involved possible domain conflicts. One might simply assert that domain conflicts were avoided because there existed between pairs of organizations a large degree of domain consensus, gradually worked out over time, which helped sort out new allocations of function and resources without contest, and often even without much interaction of any type.

Yet in this narrow sense, there was relatively little explicit domain consensus between pairs of organizations. Rather, there was an overall interorganizational consensus on the basis of adherence to a common institutionalized thought structure, within which new domain problems could be worked out, often tacitly, but in any case according to a common basic orientation, a common value framework, and a common set of norms governing interorganizational behavior in such domain situations.

In their article, Emery and Trist indicate what seems to them to be an emerging solution to the problem of maintaining individual organizational viability under increasingly turbulent conditions. It lies in "the emergence of *values that have overriding significance for all members of the field.*"[16] These values constitute neither strategies nor tactics, but rather rules or guidelines that channel individual action and make the actions of others less uncertain because they are all presumably guided by the same set of rules. They claim some scientific basis for the view that as such common values emerge, "the determination of policy will necessitate not only a bias towards goals that are congruent with the organization's own character, but also a selection of goal-paths that offer maximum convergence as regards the interest of other parties."[17] Precisely such a set of values is contained in the institutionalized thought structure outline in Chapter 2. A further paragraph from Emery and Trist merits extensive comment:

1. So far as effective values emerge, the character of richly joined, turbulent fields changes in a most striking fashion. 2. The relevance of large classes of events no longer has to be sought in an intricate mesh of diverging causal strands, but is given directly in the ethical code. 3. By this transformation a field is created which is no longer richly joined and turbulent but simplified and relatively static. 4. Such a transformation will be regressive, or constructively adaptive, according to how far the emergent values adequately represent the new environmental requirements.[18]

Our findings give empirical support to these theoretical statements. We have described the values alluded to in sentence 1. We have noted the way they afford stability to an otherwise turbulent field. We have identified a consensus at the level of the interorganizational field, (sentence 2), and have indicated how that consensus affords stability to interorganizational relationships and gives a cue to each organization affected by any specific new development as to how other organizations also affected can be expected to react (sentence 3). The expectations are not common in the sense of precisely similar reactions, but rather in terms of differential reactions which represent an already agreed upon division of labor on principal issues, based on a common, inclusive thought structure within which these issues are perceived. Hence, interaction on these issues is often not necessary in order for marginal domain adjustments to be made separately by the individual organizations. By the same token, a flood of events that may seem highly rapid and varied may be perceived and routinized in accordance with the organizations' differentiated but mutually compatible rationales.

Under these circumstances, organizations responding separately to specific developments that may pose threats to them or to the interorganizational field may behave—even in the absence of concerted decisions—in ways that in aggregate provide the preventing-blunting-repelling behavior through which the interorganizational field is preserved and their own viability protected. On the level of interaction between specific organizations, developments that are perceived as possible threats to individual domain and that become the subject of contest interaction between community decision organizations appear to involve vigorous contest. Yet on the level of the interorganizational field they can be seen as essentially functional for the system within which the contest takes place and eventually functional for the individual organizations as well, since they limit the nature of system adjustment or change to narrow confines that protect not only the winners of these contests, but also the losers. In contest situations, limits are set on the type of organizational action that may or may not be employed and on the area within which marginal domain questions may swing toward the one agency or the other. In aggregate, these limits assure that each agency will "get its share" of wins and losses.

In this respect, as we have pointed out, the difference between cooperation and contest within these shared norms and values is not nearly so great as between either of these processes and conflict, as we have defined and described it in Chapter 3.

To comment only briefly here on sentence 4 of the Emery and Trist quotation, note that although the authors indicate that the transformation may be regressive or constructively adaptive, they do not indicate for whom. Do they mean for the individual organizations? for the aggregate of interacting organizations under consideration? or for some such inclusive third party as customers, the community, the poor, social agency clients, etc? From the context, we conclude that they mean for the aggregate of interacting organizations, rather than for the benefit of some third party. We note at this point simply that the two are not necessarily identical—or, as we said earlier, that manifest goal achievement and individual organizational viability are not in all cases synonymous.

Thus, organizational interaction, especially along the cooperation-contest dimension, takes on a quite different appearance when viewed from the interorganizational field.

In the case of *coordination*, as well, the interorganizational paradigm both offers a more inclusive understanding of the extent of coordination and yields a more adequate and systematic analysis of what coordination is and the forms it takes. The view from the inclusive system does not confirm the assumption—apparently supported when viewed from the level of interaction between specific organizations—that the behavior of relatively autonomous organizations interacting with each other in their own respective best interests produces a largely unstructured situation characterized by organizations working at cross-purposes with each other, "cancelling each other out," as each goes its own way without reference to what the others are doing.

On the contrary, the interorganizational field paradigm reveals a highly structured field and a set of processes of concerted decision making which result in allocational decisions regarding functions and resources, only some of which processes are customarily recognized as coordinative. Not only does the interorganizational field paradigm facilitate attention to the concerted decision making that takes place outside formal structural channels on an ad hoc coalitional or mobilizational basis. It also permits a recognition that coordinative functions for the inclusive system may be performed by the relatively benign form of norm-abiding contest that takes place between these organizations within the general confines of the cooperative inclusive context of the institutionalized thought structure. The inadequacy of current conceptualizations to recognize structure and organization in this instance is reminiscent of the early article by William F. Whyte correcting the notion that slum areas are "disorganized." He found a high degree of organization in the neighborhood he studied. Likewise, Nisbet challenges the notion of social disorganization in the macrosociety. The macrosociety is highly organized, he avers, especially in large-scale organizations of various types in various sectors. The problem of disorganization, if the term is to be used at all in this connection, occurs in relationships of small groups and interpersonal relationships. Both these writers point out that the customary analytical concepts and modes neglect important aspects of the subject matter, giving a misleading interpretation of the reality under study.[19]

The paradigm difference is particularly pronounced in the consideration of *innovation*. We have seen in Chapter 5 that approaches to innovation from an organizational standpoint are characterized by ambiguity of meaning of the term and a consequent implicit assumption that innovation is desirable, even though in specific cases—which are seldom if ever conceptually differentiated from other cases—the innovations may be recognized as undesirable. In the present study, simple schedule data on innovations would have given no hint of the nature of the preventing-blunting-repelling sequence if there had not been extensive narrative data which traced through longitudinally what happened to some of these innovations and which took into consideration not only the behavior of individual organizations but their behavior as an interacting system. The question of what happened to an innovation when it arose in this interorganizational system permitted a more adequate answer than the question of what happened to an innovation when it arose in one or another of these organizations.

Perhaps more important, the system paradigm permitted a reclassification of innovations into, roughly, those which were more or less routine products of the system and which promoted system stability through minor modifications while preserving and enhancing its overall viability (gross and secondary innovations), and those which were directed at reordering the system in a qualitatively different way (primary innovations). The drastically different configurations of processes and events surrounding these different types of innovation attest to the importance of the distinction in definitions of innovation, and the importance of the inclusive paradigm.

The interorganizational paradigm likewise places a different perspective on *responsiveness*. From the standpoint of the individual organizations, such responsiveness is seen as the means by which citizen "input" is provided for, either through formal organizational channels or on an ad hoc basis. But attention to the larger field makes apparent the obvious circumstance that there is something more to citizen participation than the interaction between individual organizations and groups of citizens. To acknowledge the difference, we have called this type of participation *citizen involvement*. But beyond this type of specific interaction, there is a more inclusive entity which must be given attention. Independent of any of these community decision organizations there exists what we have called the *citizen action* movement. Much decision making regarding citizen participation takes place within the movement, relatively independently of the formal committees and councils and other channels provided by individual community decision organizations. Examples of such independent rubrics for decision making are a Black Caucus, a federation of Chicano organizations, or a loose coalition of various component parts of the citizen-action movement.

The interorganizational paradigm, looking beyond the individual organization, directs attention more readily to this citizen action movement as a different, but equally important aspect of citizen participation in community decision organizations.

The difference is at least partially illustrated by the manner in which the data on responsiveness were gathered. The initial methodology called for the administration of a rather lengthy schedule on responsiveness to the organizational executive or his delegate, to be supplemented by any narrative data gathered that dealt with this aspect of the organization's behavior. An early decision was made, however, to ask the field research associates to develop a lengthy report on the neighborhood and ethnic group movement in each city as this had developed over the preceding fifteen years.

With these data before us, we could not fail to recognize what would perhaps have escaped us if only individual agency data had been employed: the citizen action movement existed as an entity in its own right independent of (though interacting with) the specific provision for citizen participation made by each community decision organization. This consideration also led to the decision to administer the same schedule of questions regarding each CDO's responsiveness to the citizen leader of the organization that provided citizen participation for the Model Cities agency, and also to the leader of one of the independent citizen action groups. With such a data base, one could gain an understanding of the way in which specific interaction between citizens and individual organizations was both constrained and supported by the organization's grounding in the institutionalized thought structure and the citizen participants' grounding in the citizen action movement. With this perspective, the preventing-blunting-repelling process could be discerned as a process occurring not solely through the actions of a single organization, but as a characteristic of the field.

Thus, in sum, as one examines methodically the system properties of the interorganizational field, a vastly different aggregate picture of the behavior and interorganizational relations of these community decision organizations emerges. What appears to be surprisingly little interaction in the face of a turbulent and troubled period turns out to be readily understandable. What appears to be relatively intense contests between these organizations turn out to be but minor processes of adjustment of the inclusive system that sustains them. In contrast with the few instances of system conflict, the contest episodes look very much like cooperation episodes. What appears to be a relatively chaotic field of planning organizations going their own way turns out to be a highly structured field with much more coordination than is apparent with conventional conceptions based on the individual organizational paradigm. What appears as a fairly impressive level of innovation turns out to be largely of a sort that maintains the basic configurations of current practice, giving it a somewhat modified managerial organization. Citizen participation most often turns out to be a largely managed input constrained by and subordinate to organizational rationale and viability, in which in nearly all instances the preventing-blunting-repelling process assures agency viability and stability when these are counterposed by the citizen action movement's demands for first priority to be given to the needs and wishes of low-income citizens as defined by them.

One should add that not only concepts like cooperation-contest-conflict, coordination, innovation, responsiveness, and citizen participation take on new meaning, but also other concepts than these principal variables around which this report is organized. Examples are an expanded concept of organizational domain, a differentiation of constituencies into input and output constituencies, and a greatly expanded typology of different types of organizational cooptation.

The quite different implications of the two paradigms warrant further brief consideration of Kuhn's analysis of alternative paradigms in science. Interestingly, Kuhn confines his analysis to the natural sciences and mathematics, since "it remains an open question what parts of social science have yet acquired such paradigms at all." (p. 15). Yet anyone familiar with such alternative principles of data organization and analysis as the Gestalt versus the behavioristic modes (paradigms) in psychology or the social system versus symbolic interaction modes of analysis in sociology must see that they fit Kuhn's concept of the paradigm. This concept as Kuhn analyzes it does not have so much to do with the alleged degree of precision acquired within the scientific paradigm as with its function as an organizing principle for data gathering and interpretation.[20]

Kuhn points out not only that alternative paradigms present alternative ways of conceiving and investigating scientific problems, but that they entail alternative statements as to what kinds of possible information will constitute "data" and what kinds of information will be ignored; what kinds of investigative procedures will be employed and what kinds will not; what kinds of data will constitute proof or disproof, and what kinds will not. In other words, the nature of the reality to be studied and reported on is partly determined by the definition of that reality implicit in the explanatory paradigm.

Further, since all this is the case, the task of "normal science" is confined within the paradigm that directs it, so that it can not throw the paradigm itself into question, but can only confirm and support it, whatever may be the specific findings regarding any specific set of variables defined by the paradigm. Hence, paradigms are self-reinforcing. They dictate the methods by which they, themselves, will be tested. Scientific investigation, in normal scientific endeavor, does not deliberately question paradigms, but only alternative statements within paradigms.

Paradigms are brought into question, therefore, not by the scientific research they suggest is important, what Kuhn calls the "mopping up" operations of normal science, but rather they are brought into question as people begin to place importance on what the paradigm leaves out, or on various anomalies, situations at the border of the theoretical conceptualization which do not fit neatly into the paradigm and its tested relationships. Paradigms do not continuously succeed in adjusting themselves incrementally to accommodate these anomalies; or better said, such adjustment begins to eat away at the credibility of the central paradigm. Meantime, alternative paradigms may be suggested, each with its own set of problems it can solve well, but with its implicit anomalies. At a particular point, one of these alternative paradigms may appear to a growing number of investigators to make a better "fit" with reality than the paradigm in question. The adoption of one of these alternative paradigms, with its accompanying rejection of the older paradigm, constitutes the dynamics of the scientific process.

In our own case, it became apparent that we were faced with a choice of paradigms, each of which would define differently the nature of the variables to be researched (even though they were nominally the same set of variables, and the same set of organizations), the methods of investigation most likely to capture those variables adequately for the analysis to be made, and the nature of the potentially relevant data which would be ignored or made a central focus of analysis.

As indicated in Chapter 2, these alternative paradigms were the approach to interaction from the standpoint of the individual organizations, or the approach from the standpoint of the interorganizational field. These alternative paradigms involve alternative *methodological and conceptual* approaches. They are not the same as Paradigms I and II, which are alternative *substantive* explanations for the persistence of poverty and its attendant social problems.

Methodological Implications

Because of its important implications for interorganizational research in this and other studies, a further consideration of this choice of methodological paradigm is warranted. The problem of alternative paradigms can be well illustrated by considering an article on "The Comparative Study of Organizations," by Peter M. Blau.[21] Blau makes the point that the level of analysis in organizational research must determine the level at which a plurality of units of investigation must be taken. He points out that a case study approach to an organization cannot take the organization as such as its unit of investigation, but only parts of that organization which can be compared with each other.

By the same token, the study of the influence of the environment on organizations would have to employ a research design that includes organizations in a variety of different environments, and since hardly any studies do so, the complaint often heard that we know virtually nothing about the impact of the social setting on organizations is quite justified.[22]

If this logic is followed, several different substructures would need to be studied if the system level to be described is that of subsystems of an organization; many different organizations would have to be studied if the level of analysis is that of the organization itself; and many different organizational environments would have to be studied if the system level to be investigated is that of the organizational environment and its impact on the organization. Blau himself points to the paucity of comparative studies of organizations, so that even this level of analysis is poorly researched. Presumably, any study that, like ours, purports to make meaningful statements regarding a particular type of organizational environment would have to investigate not just a number of different organizations, but a number of different kinds of environments, in order to state any meaningful relationships existing within any one type of environment. Strictly speaking, Blau's implication would be that we have no basis for saying anything about the environment within which these organizations interact, since we have not made comparative studies of several different types of environment.

But, as Blau points out, the comparative basis for studying individual organizational characteristics is achieved only rarely, let alone the more inclusive basis for studying sets of environmental characteristics. Hence, the paradigm followed by Blau excludes the possibility even of addressing the area of investigation that this study claims is the most important of all, and without which we assert that findings acquired on a more fragmented basis are confusing and misleading. We have obviously demurred from being constrained by Blau's strictures on this important question.

Blau does offer an alternative, though it applies only to the level of studying organizations, not of studying environments. "One way out of this impasse is to study the major attributes of many organizations and sacrifice any detailed information on their internal structures." Thus, following Blau's methodological paradigm, comparative studies of organizations must restrict themselves to major attributes, foregoing the possibility of considering detailed information on their internal structures in the analysis, while systematic study of organizational environments, such as the interorganizational field under discussion in the present study, becomes practically, if not methodologically, impossible.

Blau's methodological paradigm has its own consistent, inherent logic. Once you accept the methodological paradigm, you must accept Blau's somewhat perfectionistic implications. In this study, we accepted neither. In renouncing Blau's perfectionistic strictures, we of course renounce the presumed scientific certainty Blau's proposed methodology implies is possible and desirable. We do this not because such certainty, if more than specious, would be anything but highly desirable, but rather because the price we would have had to pay for this particular paradigmatic certainty is the sacrifice of any consideration of the impact of the environmental context in which community decision organizations interact, and any consideration of the impact of this environmental context on the manner in which they address the perplexing and important problems with which they are charged. We do not need a comparative study of x number of different types of organizational environments in order to begin to sketch out some of the relevance of the interorganizational field to the type of thing these organizations do and the manner in which they interact with each other.

Blau's is not the only conception of the relation between the quantitative paradigm and the process of generalization regarding organizational environments. A number of investigators have approached the problem of organizational environment on the basis of large n studies which relate some particular outcome variable to the type of environmental configuration prevailing in the cities. Beginning with the noteworthy study of "Community Power and Urban Renewal Success" by Amos H. Hawley,[23] there have been a number of studies which seek to relate some variable—usually innovation—to certain configurations of variables in the cities.[24] These studies constitute an attempt to utilize the quantitative method for building up configurations of interorganizational environments. After this point, though, the resemblance to the present study ceases, for none of these studies attempts to investigate these configurations as dynamic contexts in any city. The configurations did not arise from an analysis of dynamic contexts, but of statistical associations of various independent and intermediate variables with a particular operationalized measure of an outcome variable across a large number of cities. None of these studies investigated the actual development of the interaction that produced the innovation. The method, reduced to its simplest terms, is a quantitative analysis yielding the configuration of variables associated with a particular measure of success in a number of cities that scored high on it, as contrasted with the configuration in a number of cities that scored low on that measure of success.

These studies seek to explain differences in behavior in terms of differences in interorganizational field variables. The present study emphasizes similarities in the interorganizational field across the nine cities as being much more important than dissimilarities in the interorganizational field in accounting for the characteristic behavior of community decision organizations within which both similarities and dissimilarities in outcome variables are explained.

The implications of this difference involve still a third difference between the present study and those studies that seek to base a description of the interorganizational field on a quantified analytical paradigm. They are often based on what, from the present study, appears to be a highly simplified conceptualization of the outcome variable. Success in Hawley's study over a decade ago was measured in terms of planning, execution, and completion of urban renewal programs. No question was raised as to the desirability of such programs. They were simply taken as indicators of success, and the implication to be drawn was that successful communities are those that can and do conduct such programs, thus achieving "success in any collective action affecting the welfare of the whole." Other studies have used as their "success" measure one or more of such developments as: public housing programs, urban renewal programs, school system desegregation, fluoridation of water supply, flow of federal antipoverty funds, manpower training programs, and formation of hospital councils.

Since Hawley's study, extensive debate over the apparently highly mixed results of urban renewal programs would seem to suggest caution against using such simple measures of community success, and to raise questions about whether such "innovations" are invariably beneficial for "the community" or only for certain segments of it, and if so, for which ones. In the absence of such questions, something is implicitly defined as desirable which may or may not be, according to one's group affiliation or ideological position. Hence, by some ironic consequence of methodology, the more "scientifically" objective the investigator becomes about quantitative measurement, the more naive and unwittingly value-laden become the tacit implications of the research design.

An occasional parenthetical recognition is given to the problem of validity of such "objective" measures of "success" or "innovation" in some of the later studies.[25] But the methodology is not conducive, apparently, to the kind of qualitative, theoretical, and substantive examination of the nature of the output variables that is undertaken in the present study; nor is it apparently conducive to a consideration of the concrete manifestation of whatever dynamic behavior constitutes the process through which different configurations in the city characteristics have their differential impact on the output variables.

The above paragraphs are not by way of refutation of either Blau's methodological arguments or of the more modest yet quantitatively derived path to city configurations pursued by the investigations described above, for each methodological paradigm has its advantages and disadvantages. It does some things well and other things poorly. Were this not so, it would be much easier for students of the same field to agree on appropriate, definitive methodologies. The point here is that we entered upon this study with an awareness (though hardly as clear as at present) of the different possibilities of different methodological approaches, and even, to a certain extent, of their sometimes contrary substantive results. We therefore attempted as long as we could to derive benefit from both paradigms, the one of abstraction and quantification and statistical manipulation, the other of intense study, though comparative, of actual complex situations, in all their rich multivariableness. Finally, at the point of the final analysis and exposition for purposes of reporting, we became aware of the vast differences in the substance and meaning of the findings, depending on whether they were pursued from the standpoint of "constructing" the nature of the interorganizational field from the results of the tested propositions alone, focused as they were at the organizational level, or from a theoretical interorganizational conceptualization which was holistically derived principally from the narrative data and which focused on the more inclusive interorganizational field.

Our clear conviction of the value of the latter over the former, of the serious omissions from consideration of so much that is important both theoretically and practically in the atomistic purely quantitative approach, leaves us skeptical about the value of much systematic, "objective," quantitative research in interorganizational behavior. It also leaves us highly aware of its latent function of directing attention away from meaningful questions relating to the social utility or social disutility of what the organizations are doing or the directions in which they are innovating, or the results of coordination, and so on. Since just such considerations play back upon the behavior of the organizations themselves, it is truly an unreal world which is described by those studies that ignore them.

In this connection, most of the empirical studies in the organizational and interorganizational areas confine themselves to the manifest functions being performed or proclaimed. Since our findings indicate the crucial importance of latent functions, the question arises as to why they are so systematically ignored. We believe that part of the reason is methodological, in that the considerations of organizational research are so often limited to the relation of a number of identifiable variables to some resultant variable such as organizational effectiveness, organizational innovation, etc. The pressure toward "clean," "elegant" studies pushes the investigator to consider only those variables that can be readily operationalized and easily quantified. The reduction of the analysis to such selected variables inexorably excludes the possibility of giving adequate consideration to less quantifiable variables, and the procedure of "randomization" is depended on to give some degree of assurance that whatever such "extraneous" variables may be, they will not operate to bias the specific findings.

In the present study, the organized narrative data forced us repeatedly to note and question the importance of the variables used quantitatively, and to consider other aspects of the interaction processes which those variables did not address. As already indicated, one of the principal foci around which such challenges occurred was the different implications of interaction processes when looked at from the standpoint of the inclusive system and from the standpoint of the individual organizations. But even on the level of the individual organizations, a consideration of manifest and latent functions appears equally essential if one is to understand organizational behavior in interaction.

The preceding paragraphs contain components of both methodology and substantive theory. And so they should, from our point of view. Theoretical conceptualization and methodology are inevitably intertwined. The question is whether the investigator is aware of this interrelationship, and if so, whether he recognizes that not only does theoretical conceptualization influence methodology, but that in turn methodology influences theoretical conceptualization.

Alternative Interorganizational Paradigms and the Sociology of Knowledge

Knowledge is socially derived and in turn feeds back upon the social structure. This statement is so widely accepted in contemporary sociology that it seems almost banal to state it. Yet we believe that in the light of this study's findings, it warrants further elaboration here, for it is difficult to accept both this statement and the major conclusions of this study without applying the implications to the social role and function of the social scientist in research related to social stability and social change.

One would have to be quite obtuse not to recognize the different ideological implications contained in the conceptualization, methodology, and findings based on the alternative paradigms addressed in the present research. The organizational paradigm presents a configuration that assumes the need for coordination as an important road to effectiveness, that assumes the desirability of innovation and presents a picture of widespread efforts toward innovation on the part of these organizations. It likewise presents a picture of intensive developments in the direction of citizen participation and responsiveness. Because of an ambiguous and overgeneralized conception of innovation and responsiveness, it simply accepts the decision to prefer the agency concern for viability over meeting the citizen action movement's demands for responsiveness without even an awareness that such a decision has been made.

The implications derived from findings within the organizational level paradigm are clear. Much progress is being made; agencies are seeking to improve their effectiveness through coordination; they are innovating in structure and administration as well as in policy and program, and in their relationships with other agencies. They are making widespread provision for citizen participation. Citizen participation that is unmanaged, that does not conform to the channels and processes prescribed by the agencies in keeping with their primary emphasis on viability, is disruptive.

All of these implicit assumptions or substantive findings of the organizational level paradigm have the effect of legitimating the existing interorganizational structure, of taking seriously—partly by assumption, partly on the basis of findings yielded by research within the paradigm—that the agencies are essentially on the right track, that they are striving to be more effective, that the way of progress lies in greater coordination, and that it lies within the present configuration of power and technology in the interorganizational field as this is in turn supported by the society's institutionalized thought structure.

The inclusive paradigm presents a different picture, with quite different implications. We need not repeat it here, since it has been treated extensively earlier in this chapter. We do not mean to imply that the inclusive paradigm will always lead to a more critical assessment of the behavior of individual organizations in relation to poverty, or that in contrast the organizational level paradigm will invariably lead to the relatively unexamined acceptance of current agency assumptions. We do believe that there are tendencies in this direction which we have uncovered and documented and whose dynamics we have at least partially explored.

Hence, the paradigm that fragments organizational interaction in order to investigate it with greater methodological rigor, to count those things most readily measurable, to pursue systematically and quantitatively the interrelation of variables, to avoid the subjectivity of narrative data and interpretations based on it, and most deliberately and self-consciously to avoid permitting ideological considerations to affect the methodology or the findings or conclusions, turns out to be fraught with ideological implications, of which it takes no cognizance.

It does this by apparent unawareness that there is an alternative paradigm to the organizational level paradigm which can be used with equal validity as a basis for investigating interorganizational behavior. It does it by selecting only a small number of highly abstract variables which can be operationalized and quantified, analyzing them only in abstraction from the actual context in which they are operative. It does it by taking into consideration for purposes of analysis only what is measurable. It does it by the necessity of avoiding qualitative distinctions within variables. It does it not by neglecting process but rather by attempting to construct process out of the interrelation of static variables. It does it by refraining from considering the value implication of the very methods being employed, of the very findings it is generating and of the nature in which it takes as "given" the very configuration of the interacting system whose specific aspects it is myopically inspecting. By assuming the outlines of the system as given, and by refraining from inspecting the system's more inclusive aspects, it thus has a system-maintaining impact. The choice of paradigm determines the context of scientific procedure, which in this case turns out to be one of seeking the problem in the minutiae of the system rather than in its general configuration.

In this connection, it is interesting to recall the widely held viewpoint that social system analysis is essentially conservative in character, that it cannot make adequate conceptual provision for social change, that it directs attention to equilibrium and system maintenance, that its reliance on a functionalist orientation emphasizes and corroborates the importance to the adequate functioning of the system of all the existing components in the configuration—all adding up to an implicitly conservative ideological orientation, as over against the comparative objectivity and freedom from ideological considerations presented by the quantitative researcher who sticks to measurable variables and their interrelationship.

Yet, paradoxically, it is precisely in the area of purposive social change such as the efforts attendant upon the antipoverty and Model Cities programs examined here that an analysis of the inclusive system turns out to have much more radical implications. It demonstrates the tremendous resistance to change which inheres in the system-maintaining processes, which it in fact identifies and analyzes with greater alacrity than the more fragmented, "objective" research. Social system analysis would appear to have conservative implications when it is addressed to the problem of how the system maintains stability; to have more radical implications when it is addressed to the problem of how the system defeats change. In the latter case, the view from the inclusive system is radical, as it addresses the system as a barrier to change; in the former, it is conservative, being oriented to how the system may ward off change and maintain stability through minor adaptations.

The principal point under discussion, however, is not the alternative possible orientations of social system analysis, but instead the manner in which the conventional manner of approaching social change from the standpoint of the organizational level paradigm tends inadvertently to add an additional barrier to the very change it is studying, the barrier being the side effects of the definition of the research problem, the use of concepts, the choice of methodology and the consequent orientation of the findings, all of which lend support to the basic configuration of the existing system.

Community Decision Organizations and the Structure of Urban Reform

In the light of the foregoing analysis we believe the somewhat grandiose and global title given to this book is justified. We are aware that we have not given explicit treatment to many aspects of the efforts at urban social reform, even in the somewhat focused sense of addressing the social problems attendant upon poverty in the inner cities. Nor has this been our intention. Rather, we have treated what in many respects can be considered the framework that must be activated if social reform at the community level is to make an impact on the lives of low-income people. Whatever the social reform strategy, these community decision organizations, and others not included in the study, must take such actions as to make the desired or intended difference in the lives of low-income people.

One can quite understandably raise the question why much more attention has not been given here to municipal politics. After all, many community decision organizations come into being only through action of the municipal executive and council, and they typically are sustained only with their acquiescence. Control over such formal legitimation, and in many cases control over the purse strings, places great power in the local government, and in some cases the state government, to influence the mandate and policies of many of these community decision organizations, as well as to determine what *else* will be done about the cities' social problems besides what is done by and through these CDOs. Of course, the same can be said for national-level politics, and the important role of the federal government of bringing some of these CDOs into being and, through federal policy, likewise determining the demise of whole types of CDOs across the country. We shall address the federal role later.

Local governmental and political bodies are important actors in promoting or impeding social reform, and of course they would need to be treated in any work that purports to examine all the important aspects of the process. Much the same, incidentally, can be said for a treatment of the local power and decision-making structure, comprised of networks of especially powerful persons in various institutional positions who have access to resources that give them inordinate influence—when they choose to exercise it—over the course of local decision making. Other aspects of the decision-making process pertinent to social reform efforts are likewise operative.

Nevertheless, community decision organizations play a pivotal role. This study was based on that assumption, and the findings suggest that the assumption was indeed warranted. For as indicated in Chapter 2 and as illustrated in most of the interaction that we examined, these organizations have, within their legitimated fields, inordinate power to control not only what is done about specific problems, but even more basically, how specific problems will be defined, and what choices of technology and professional expertise will be employed in addressing them and, hence, what types of measures will be considered "realistic" and appropriate possibilities for action. Further, as programs and actions are decided upon, these organizations have the power to formulate and mold the manner in which these programs will be implemented in actual operation.

This is not to imply that these CDOs have complete autonomy, that they are free of constraints from various sources that can influence their actions, or from other organizations on whom they frequently depend for various types of resources, usually in some type of reciprocal relationship within which negotiation and bargaining take place. Such other sources include the federal agencies from which many of these CDOs during the period of the study derived much of their legitimation and much of their financial support. Another source is the local government, and in the case of some CDOs not in our study, such as the public welfare department, it may be the state government. Another source is that of various interest groups that have a stake in what the CDOs do or do not do. These various sources of influence constitute the input constituencies of most community decision organizations and are typically represented on their boards, governing commissions, or in various types of open or subtle lobbying relationship to legislators, elected officials, and administrators.

It is interesting to note that such sources of influence apparently operate more effectively as constraints limiting the problem definition and programs of the CDOs than as initiators of new problem definitions and programs. The period under intensive study (1968-70) was one in which new programs, at least, were being instigated not so much through these other sources as through federal legislation. The single local source that unreservedly joined with the federal effort in terms of affording it motive power was that of low-income residents and their advocates on the local scene, who operated both outside of and within the structures for social reform efforts the federal government sponsored, and strove to become an acknowledged part of the input constituency of these organizations.

We have indicated in some detail the nature of the response of these community decision organizations to programs that at the time were considered to be powerful thrusts toward major changes in the institutional structure of poverty areas, in the agencies that presumably served them, and in the responsiveness of these agencies to the needs and wishes of low-income people. In aggregate, the response has been to make minor adaptations of existing structures and programs while at the same time setting in motion processes of organizational cooptation and the preventing-blunting-repelling sequence.

Many of the proposed changes presented few problems to the agencies, since they were well within their own conceptions of organizational domain and rationale. They were things the agencies could readily be induced to do—provided additional funding was available to them for this purpose. The changes were overwhelmingly of the type that is based on the provision of services to people who are in special need of one sort or another and hence constitute "problem populations." They were developed and implemented through largely cooperative processes.

On the other hand, proposals or developments that posed a threat to organizational rationale or viability were blunted. The blunting occurred in two principal ways: through organizational cooptation—a process whose four sub-types have been described in earlier chapters—and through contest, contest that was often resolved through modification of programs at the city council level, at the state agency level, or at the level of the regional or federal offices of a federal government agency.

Hence, significantly innovative programs were blunted through organizational cooptation or through contest in such a way that the ensuing programs were consonant with the organizational rationale of the community decision organizations, with their continued viability, and, in most cases, with their convenience. The blunting process was supported by the common adherence to what we have here called the institutionalized thought structure surrounding the problem of poverty, the way it is conceived and the steps that are considered appropriate for addressing it. The repelling process, as illustrated in the OEDCI, gives massive reinforcement to these other more moderate processes that envelop the existing interorganizational structure in a protective cocoon.

The period of the sixties and earlier seventies put forth a succession of waves of urban reform directed at the problems connected with systemic poverty in the inner cities. Those efforts have been widely perceived as ineffective. There is at present a widespread sense that they have "played themselves out," and at this writing there is widespread debate, not about this loss of innovative thrust, which is generally acknowledged, but about the fate of the existing set of supplemental services, which by this time have become lodged in the interorganizational service structure of the cities involved.

Our findings suggest a number of implications with respect to this wave of what might be called "liberal reform." The implications may also be applicable to other waves emanating from the same set of liberal assumptions in the future.

The Components of Liberal Reform

The assumptions of liberal reform are derived from the institutionalized thought structure described in Chapter 2. These assumptions are that the American institutional structure, though essentially sound, must be continually improved through waves of nationally distributed efforts, at the local level, to move people out of poverty, and to provide the services expected to facilitate this process, as well as residual services to those who because of physical or mental handicaps cannot become self-sustaining members of society. Efforts to provide such services must be made more humane, must provide for citizen input, and must be made more effective. Basically, such efforts must take place in a collaborative relationship to the service-giving or service-planning agencies, for they are the ones whose task it ultimately is to do the job. Through offering them funds and through citizen pressure and through the creativity that may be generated in cooperative efforts to attack social problems, their services to the poor will be greatly improved and the cycle of poverty will be broken for large numbers of families who would otherwise remain in poverty.

In the light of this study's findings, some overall observations concerning the embodiment of liberal reform described in this book are in order.

Let us begin with magnitude. We do not believe it needs extensive elaboration that both the Economic Opportunities program and the Model Cities program were funded with a mere pittance in relation to the problems they were to addresss. When President Johnson asked Congress for $685 million for the community action program (the program that spawned a thousand community action agencies in as many localities, including those in the nine cities of the present study), Pennsylvania Representative Daniel J. Flood commented: "What a piddling effort we are really making at the fantastic problem of poverty. I believe—you correct me—I recall it as being one-half the profits of General Motors."[1] And in the case of Model Cities, for which funds of $565 million were authorized for a number of years, it need only be pointed out that the original proposal for using the single city of Detroit as a demonstration city—out of which the Model Cities program eventually developed into a program involving 150 localities—called for a total federal outlay over a period of years of close to 3 billion dollars. The total Model Cities budget for all 150 localities was only a fraction of the amount New York City alone was spending for public assistance payments to welfare recipients each year.

Turning to the citizen participation component of the liberal reform strategy, it is well to consider this component against the background of the almost incredible process of cooling the ghettos which occurred during the time at which the economic opportunities program and the Model Cities program were at their height. As an indication, civil disorders have steadily subsided from their peak in the years 1967-69 to the present. One might say that insofar as the objective of these programs was to reduce dissent to an orderly process in which it could be dealt with in a more or less routine way within the confines of the institutionalized thought structure, the programs succeeded admirably. Was it really the tangible results these programs brought about through the changed conditions they effected or the sense of meaningful participation they provided to the poor? Or was it, on the contrary, the outcome of a policy of benign neglect, the deliberate low emphasis the Nixon administration placed on the problems and programs dealing with inner city poverty, that created a situation in which President Nixon could go before the county in early 1973 and proclaim that the urban crisis had subsided?

Perhaps both of these apparently contrary policies contributed in sequence toward easing tensions in the inner cities. In the light of our own findings, we would suggest a third alternative. In our view, the slums have quieted largely because poverty area residents have lost their sense that the existing interorganizational structure in the inner cities can be made more responsive to the needs and wishes of low-income people through the avenue of citizen participation. This disenchantment arises from the frustrations that accompanied citizen participation, frustrations attributable to interminable federal delays, to what was perceived as excessive paperwork, frustrations from dealing with agencies in heated contest in which the agencies seemed to have the greater power, and frustrations with the internal divisions and weaknesses, the evanescent level of leadership and participation within the citizen participation efforts. It also arises, we believe, from a growing realization by low-income people that the tangible results that could be obtained from such a process were minimal as levers for making much difference in the institutional and physical structure of their surroundings. Their neighborhoods remained extremely unpleasant places to live in, and the occasional neighborhood center or preschool program, though welcome, hardly made a dent. Moynihan had emphasized the "tangle of pathology" that characterized the Negro family.[2] He did not emphasize the tangle of pathology that comprised the institutional structure in which so many inner city blacks live. This tangled web of pathology in the ambience of low-income urban residents was hardly permeated either by the Economic Opportunities program or the Model Cities program.

Even in those cities where a strong measure of influence over the structure of these programs was achieved by the low-income neighborhood residents, the eventuating programs were gradually perceived as highly inadequate to make a dent in the daily living of these families. Thus, we believe, there was the gradual realization that citizen participation, even strong citizen participation, was not the answer, and in the long run seemed to make little difference. These programs did not appear to provide the leverage to move many people out of poverty or to make a substantial difference in the living conditions of people who remained in poverty.

We conclude that this growing sense of disenchantment with citizen participation as an important means of effectively addressing the problem of poverty is thoroughly appropriate, even though the primary reason why such participation is ineffective in these programs is less clearly recognized. The primary reason, in our estimation, is simply that whatever the justification for improved service programs may be, they have little relevance to the task of moving people out of poverty in any large numbers. Citizen participation does not alter this basic reality. Martin Rein has put it well:

The new reforms embodied in federal legislation to reduce delinquency, poverty, and dependency assume that it is possible to change people without changing their circumstances; that a marginal increase in resources yields a large output because the problems are at root professional, administrative, and structural; that service programs are valid in the absence of a national commitment to redistribute income and to assure full employment for selected groups; and that the new reforms represent a departure from, rather than a continuity with, earlier policies for social services. . . . If society wants to reduce poverty, dependency, and unemployment, then the social services have almost nothing to contribute. Full employment and income redistribution are the only viable strategies.[3]

But unemployment and inequities in income distribution are only in small part amenable to impact from the local level. They are products of the state of the national economy and the structure of the national society. This is perhaps the most important reason why local efforts to reduce poverty largely fail, and why in the process they become deflected to a services strategy which, however much or little it may attenuate the burdens of poverty on its victims—and control their behavior by keeping it safely this side of threateningly active dissent—has little leverage on poverty itself.

One of the lessons that must surely be derived from the liberal reform effort in the cities is that reform of the social and economic structure of the cities cannot be brought about through purely local action. National economic policy has much more to do with employment and unemployment than local manpower training programs. National policy with respect to income distribution has much more to do with income differences in the cities than do local efforts to narrow the wide chasm of privilege and "life chances" between the well-to-do and the poor.

If this is the case, it has serious implications for the strategy of revenue sharing. Local efforts partially financed by the return to localities of a share of revenues raised through federal taxes can be expected to have little direct impact on inequalities in the local social structure and on local employment and employability when national fiscal policies designed to combat inflation have the impact of slowing the economy and throwing workers out of jobs. Local public employment programs have been deemed disastrous since the experiences of the 1930s. Public provision of employment, where the profit economy is not capable of providing jobs for all those seeking work, must come from a federal commitment and cannot be expected to be generated sui generis in every American city—even if substantial funds are made available to the cities—unless they are earmarked for this purpose.

In the light of this study's findings, the notion that the localities are closer to the people and therefore more sensitive than the federal government to local needs has a particularly hollow ring. Localities are being given the option as to how to use the shared revenues, and which groups to divert them to. Both the economic opportunities program and the Model Cities program were predicated, in part at least, on the fact that the existing interorganizational structure was neither sufficiently sensitive to the needs and wishes of poor people, nor sufficiently willing to provide them even their share of social services without special prodding and inducement from the federal government and the poor themselves.

From our nine-city data, there is little to suggest that this situation has changed. Our data suggest the same resistance by these local community decision organizations which stimulated the demand for federal intervention in the thirties. Particularly on the responsiveness issue, the data form the basis for considerable dubiousness concerning local initiatives by these agencies in the absence of some outside stimulus.

In view of the prevalent American conception that local organizations are closer to the needs of local people and more responsive to them (one of the fundamental assumptions behind the idea of special revenue sharing), why should it be the organizations that are less dependent on other local organizations for financial support (as indicated in Chapter 6) that are the most responsive to the needs and wishes of poverty area residents? And similarly, in a period during which the need for greater responsiveness to poverty area residents was widely acknowledged by all these six types of community decision organizations, why should those organizations that implemented this aspiration for responsiveness be the very organizations that found themselves in the most contest with other organizations in the local community?

In short, if organizations such as these community decision organizations can so successfully ward off change under strong pressure from federal agencies, there is little reason to believe that they will voluntarily change their ways with the cessation of federal pressure for change, modest as it was. Further, with federal financial and legitimating support removed from the two CDOs that constituted the greatest stimulus to change—the community action agencies and the Model Cities agencies—the death-knell of federal initiative in this respect is, in most cases, already sounding.

But in the last analysis, even with the continuation of these agencies, and even with continued designated federal funding, and even with citizen participation, there is little to support the belief that a much greater impact would be made in the future through these programs than in the past. Citizen participation, even under the best of circumstances, was destined to be ineffective. This was so because in the actual confrontation of the two opposing forces, citizen involvement clearly prevailed against the citizen action movement and assured that citizen proposals would be for services much along the existing lines. Further, the efforts were addressed to local organizations and institutions that could not, even if they wished, provide the national-level measures required to redistribute incomes and to provide full employment.

That is not to say that citizen participation is meaningless. There are differences produced at the local level and controllable at the local level. The extent to which the various agencies of the city serving low-income areas—the schools, the police, the public welfare, the hospitals, the health services, the family agencies, the urban renewal projects, the housing projects—are perceived as essentially representatives of the dominant society, however malicious or benign may be their impact, or are seen as agencies that are essentially *for* the local residents rather than against them, can reasonably be assumed to derive from two related sources. The first source is the adaptations made to the needs and wishes of low-income people through citizen involvement, even when this involvement is controlled within the constraints of organizational rationale and viability, and even when the responsiveness is confined to the gross and secondary types. The second source is the changed orientation toward the services of these agencies based on a sense of being able in some small measure to gain concessions in the time, place, manner, or volume in which the services are delivered.

Nevertheless, for citizen participation to have its full measure of impact on agency policies and programs, an organizational base independent of the agencies is necessary; for if participation is confined to the structures provided by the agencies, it will be fragmented into chunks the respective agencies can readily manage with but a minimum of adaptation. The dynamic of organizational cooptation, particularly the technical cooptation described in Chapter 6, is a strong one, the stronger because it is often imperceptible to those who are coopted to the agency's definition of the situation. Independent citizens organizations such as neighborhood action groups, black caucuses, and various action coalitions not only provide a point of leverage independent of the formal agency structures, but also serve as a locus from which citizen participation can be seen from the standpoint of citizen action, rather than citizen involvement as described in Chapter 6.

In pursuing the implications of our findings for liberal reform, we quote at length from a book that has been received as a definitive treatment of the federal programs mounted in the cities. The passage reviews the first year of the Model Cities experience, based on observations in a number of cities made both before and during the study period of the present research:

In a sufficient number of cities to prove its potential, model cities *has* provided the means for bringing together, in a single coordinated plan, programs for physical reconstruction, economic development, and improvement of social services—a range "as broad as the life of the city." It *has* enlisted on an unprecedented scale the cooperative efforts of the public and private agencies that have talent and resources to contribute. It *has* provided a structure within which a city's elected officials can exert energetic leadership in attacking the city's ills. It *has* mobilized an extraordinary degree of resident participation in the formation and execution of plans to attack the deep-seated problems of slum neighborhoods—despite the difficulties of organizing participation in the initial year. And, at the same time that it has encouraged self-assertion by the poor—and hence confrontation with the established agencies—it *has* required the resolution of conflict as a condition to the continuance of the program; ultimately, an agreed plan must and does go forward. . . . Given such circumstances, the plans that were produced were creditably imaginative and innovative.[4]

The authors go on to urge that this achievement in coordinative effort be compared with previous coordinating processes, rather than with "a standard of perfection." On this basis, they conclude, Model Cities must be adjudged as reasonably successful and as offering great promise as a central coordinating mechanism.

Our purpose in quoting the long passage above is not to disagree with it. We assess it as a somewhat enthusiastic, but nevertheless, essentially valid description of what happened—at least in the nine cities we studied intensively. We give it as an excellent embodiment and illustration of the liberal reform movement. Here, in a very dramatic sense, were the dreams and aspirations of the liberal reform movement come true. Of course, the process was not yet perfected, but essentially the path to liberal reform in the cities had not only been discovered, but was already being followed. All the principal ingredients are explicit or implied in the quotation: comprehensive planning including physical, economic, and social aspects; a cooperative effort of both public and private agencies; central cognizance and direction from City Hall; citizen participation, and programs that eventually combine the somewhat contrary interests of the parties concerned. It was, of course, an early diagnosis, but the statement describes the Model Cities program of 1974 as validly as the Model Cities situation after only one year of operation, in 1969.

The point, of course, is that all these things were true, yet nothing much happened, other than an expansion of some types of social services for the poor. Referring to community action and Model Cities programs, John H. Strange writes:

In some cases the number of groups participating in the pluralistic contest for power and influence has been expanded, but no radical changes in the distribution of influence, power, services, rewards, or other benefits has occurred.[5]

The Ineffectiveness of Liberal Reform

Why did programs from which so much was expected deliver so little tangible results? The question has importance not only for programs like community action and Model Cities, but for the whole set of assumptions on which liberal reform is based. The first such assumption, alluded to often in this book, is that social services will reduce poverty. Many of these services can and perhaps should be justified and continued, on grounds other than their poverty-reduction potential. But the point is not the desirability of social services. It is simply that in the balance, liberal reform chooses social services as an alternative to changes in income distribution and in social structures that produce poverty, including periodic unemployment because of inability of the economy to offer jobs to all those seeking work, and the payment, in large sectors of industry, of wages that do not permit families an income above the poverty level. We do not say that adequate income is a substitute for all social services, or that the social problems connected with poverty in low-income areas of the inner cities can be solved by money alone. We simply say that they cannot be solved by services alone, unless these families have adequate income and unless they are extended a greater measure of equality in the public goods such as housing facilitation, schools, and a host of other governmental goods which go inordinately to middle- and upper-income groups.

As a part of what is implied by changes in social structure, we note the constraint that liberal reform embodies in the principle that reform efforts must take place by and with the willing assent of existing agencies. We have treated at length the manner in which existing agencies are able to divert change efforts aimed at the institutional structure into efforts aimed at service improvement which suits their own comfort and viability. Bruno Stein has made a challenging statement which, we believe, the data of the present study fully support: "If the non-poor make the rules . . . antipoverty efforts will only be made up to the point where the needs of the non-poor are satisfied, rather than the needs of the poor."[6] We would suggest that a paraphrase would be equally valid: If the agencies make the rules . . . antipoverty efforts will only be made up to the point where the needs of the agencies are satisfied, rather than the needs of the poor. Both community action and Model Cities were designed and implemented with citizen participation, yes, but with the very definite constraint that the agencies would make the rules, and with the tacit corollary that agency viability would supersede expressed needs and wishes of low-income people at all margins where the two began to conflict. Citizen participation thus became citizen involvement—the provision of a citizen voice in agency decision making within the confines of what the agency was willing to do.

Hence, liberal reform called for working with and through existing agencies, a policy that was implemented stringently after the first few years of Model Cities indicated that citizens here and there were choosing some alternative to those existing agencies. The protection of the viability of the agencies and the virtually monopolistic attribution of specific service domains to existing agencies was accepted by many citizen leaders precisely in the spirit of liberal reform. The following statement by the director of a multistate organization of local Model Cities citizen participation groups might seem paradoxical were this not the case:

Syracuse's first-year action plan basically divided the Model Cities pie among the existing agencies, each of which is supposed to use the funds to improve its services, develop more projects for the Model Neighborhood, and increase the sensitivity of the agencies' staff to the needs of the Model Neighborhood residents. The focus on institutional change in this city is so paramount that by joint agreement among all the critical actors, no funds were to be set aside to create any new institutions during the first action year.[7]

In return, the Model Neighborhood Board had a "sign-off" right on all Model Cities contracts to such agencies, each agency had to agree to have a citizens advisory input into its operation, and the Model Neighborhood Board had certain rights in respect to jobs for local residents. Nevertheless, the program is designated by the regional citizens group leader as "a classical model of HUD's commitment to institutional change through existing local agencies."

The apparent paradoxes in the above fade rapidly away with the acceptance of the essential legitimacy of existing agencies and the trust in collaborative processes of agency change sparked by inducements in the form of additional funds as an adequate strategy for providing needed change. But such a change strategy has proved inadequate in the past. There are important components of organizational theory that explain why it must be inadequate. The present study has documented some of the dynamic processes through which the change process is defeated. It would seem rather a late date for seriously considering public policy proposals for change which emanate from these assumptions and commitments of liberal reform—unless, of course, a program is to be judged in terms of its ability to "quiet things down," to remove or reduce the threat of open and organized dissent, and to accomplish this with only the most modest expenditures of tax monies and of concessions that might make it difficult for individual agencies to endure.

One other important component of liberal reform is the emphasis on coordination as a remedy for the ineffectiveness of existing service patterns. We remind the reader of the final section of Chapter 4, in which the side effects of preoccupation with coordination are pointed out, including: the assurance to existing agencies that coordinative efforts reaffirm their legitimated, virtually exclusive claim to their respective domains and to what occurs within them; the prevention of competition as in the Syracuse example cited above; and the reinforcement of the belief that what is needed is not any drastically different approach, but rather simply the more efficient articulation of existing services with each other.

More recently, the direction of liberal reform has been modified, largely as a result of the essential failure of these earlier efforts. The new efforts are focused on mechanisms that will give the local municipal government more power vis-à-vis such relatively independent community decision organizations as the boards of education and the various independent local authorities. They emphasize the need to strengthen the local chief executive's technical ability in the field of planning and service coordination, especially through such hardware as computers and through such technologies as systems analysis. They seek to bring some degree of coordination between cities and their surrounding metropolitan areas by providing for a host of metropolitan-level planning boards—in councils of government, in comprehensive health planning units, in mental health planning boards, in councils on the aging, and on through a long list. In this respect, parenthetically, it is interesting to note that already at the metropolitan level there is emerging the problem of "coordinating the coordinators," namely, the various specialized metropolitan planning bodies. This series of developments appears to be simply another new wave emanating from liberal reform, the "model for the seventies," as it were. While it hopefully will result in some economies of administration and planning, nothing in its substantive content promises more.

Beyond Liberal Reform

It may of course be said that the present analysis is unduly harsh on what is here called liberal reform. After all, the Model Cities program did, we agree, take the form that Sundquist and Davis described with enthusiasm. Not only did all the things they enumerated actually happen, but also it is irrefutable that a number of specific and highly welcome services were extended to low-income area residents with presumably some degree of greater compassion or at least in a time, place, and manner somewhat more suited to their convenience. Health clinics, day-care centers, manpower training programs—these and other types of facility made available to low-income area residents may be of great importance in their lives. We agree, even though it is also true that adequate food is preferable to treatment of dietary deficiencies, available jobs are preferable to manpower programs that do not produce job opportunities, adequate schools are preferable to remedial reading and other compensatory educational facilities, and decent and sound housing is preferable to emergency repair services.

Even so, one might say that the assessment of the fruits of these liberal reform programs is simply a matter of a glass of water that others say is half full and we say is half empty. True, these are ways of saying the same thing. But two questions occur: Half full of what? And how and with what shall the other half be filled?

The answer to the first question, as supplied by liberal reform, must be: "Half full of services," which, however desirable, have little direct impact on poverty. The cup is half full of cooperation and contest that is confined to the norms that preserve the existing organizational configuration, types of interaction that the community decision organizations can control; coordination that is much more extensive and much less productive than it is generally thought to be; gross and secondary innovation, defined and confined by agency viability considerations and by prevalent professional technologies; gross and secondary responsiveness, confined largely to issues of what services will be delivered, to whom, and how, but not including changes in the institutional structure that produces and sustains poverty; a conception of poverty area residents as agency clients and agency constituencies, but not as citizens to whom agencies are directly accountable.

The second question is more difficult to answer: How shall the other half be filled? One component of the answer probably depends on changing the pattern summarized in the preceding paragraph. Is liberal reform capable of going the rest of the way, of risking the primary contest (conflict) which attacks existing agencies at the core of their technical, administrative, and institutional rationale and threatens their viability; which likewise attacks important aspects of the institutionalized thought structure in which the viability of these organizations is rooted? Is it capable of developing and accepting effective strategies for addressing not only the services structure but other aspects of the social structure which generate and sustain poverty? Is it capable of seeking and accepting alternative organizational structures and alternative technologies for addressing the poverty problem? Is it capable of accepting modes of citizen participation which subordinate agency viability to the development of programs responsive to the expressed needs and wishes of their output constituencies, as distinguished from their input constituencies. Or, better phrased, are the agencies capable of accepting their output constituencies as the principal component of their input constituencies?

The questions themselves suggest a number of complexities and ambiguities. But generally, based on the data of the present study, one would be comparatively safe in answering each of the above questions in the negative. It is difficult to see how a positive answer could develop out of the interorganizational network as we have described it, unless it were in response to pressures much greater than those operating during the study period.

But even assuming that they occur, would such changes make much of an inroad on poverty? We are dubious, for two reasons. First, it is doubtful that those community decision organizations, however they were operated and under whomever's control, possess the kind of leverage needed to bring about the structural changes in the institutional configuration which generates and sustains both individual poverty and the poverty of social areas where the poor predominate. Second, and closely related, we have already indicated our conviction that the changes that would affect poverty are principally changes in the state or structure of the national economy, the national polity, and the national culture. These changes involve hotly disputed questions, not of improving and coordinating services, but of redistributing income and power. Such redistribution seldom has the willing support of those whose position with respect to income and power is relatively privileged. It is quite clear that these principal issues of power and income redistribution will not be accomplished by liberal reform in any series of locally or even federally sponsored programs confined to the parameters indicated in this book. In this book, we have documented the manner in which liberal reform operates in one important context, the city level. Liberal reform has proved itself capable of making the minimum adaptations necessary to keep the system intact. Since it is able to accomplish this through the processes detailed in this book, there is neither the need nor the desire to institute the more structural changes that would attack poverty as a major component of the system.

Recent years have seen a decline in the poverty population, a decline that most knowledgeable people ascribe to the state of the national economy rather than to the impact of federally sponsored local programs presumably addressed to poverty. This gradual "trickle-down" process, which places the reduction of poverty in the status of a byproduct of the national economy, rather than the object of a concerted attack, is the product not of liberal reform but of the national economy. For anything more, one can hardly look to liberal reform as exemplified in this study's fifty-four community decision organizations and their clusters of affiliated agencies.

Efforts of citizens in the direction of power or income redistribution have been dubbed political by those who oppose them. Of course they are—and must be. The nonpolitical, collaborative process to improve living conditions in slum areas should therefore be seen for what it is—a deception that gives the aura of urban reform without the substance. Social justice, as embodied in income and power redustribution and in the effective interest group organization of low-income people, will be gained, to the extent that it is gained at all, through hard-fought accomplishments for the poor which will entail losses for some of the other constituent components in American society. This statement negates the fundamental underlying tenet of liberal reform, that social justice can be brought about through a collaborative apolitical process.

Such collaborative effort has been the main thrust of liberal reform in the past years. The outcome, as this study indicates, suggests the essential fallacy of the tenet on which it is based, as well as the dynamics of the processes that make it fallacious. To the extent that this basic circumstance is understood and acted upon, the efforts of the poor and those who are their allies can be expected to switch from the nonpolitical to the political arena. If this is the case, then the question of whether the struggle takes place within the legal processes of political decision making or outside of them will presumably depend on the capacity of political institutions to respond adequately to the large number of people whose interests are at stake.

The poor have knocked on the door of liberal reform and have been turned away. They are beginning to knock on the door of political decision making. They may of course likewise be turned away. Or they may knock the door down. Or the door may open.

Appendix

Appendix: Methodology

The methodology of the study reported in this volume is characterized in part by stability, in part by change. The change has comprised a successive folding-in of broader considerations, rather than a renouncing of earlier analytic strategies. The successive folding-ins are related to the relatively increased stress placed on the interorganizational field as the study progressed. In considering the specific data-gathering processes and analytical strategies, it may help the reader to have a brief account of the modification and development of methodological emphasis in the successive stages of the study.

At the project's inception, it was planned to use narrative data almost exclusively, with care being given to the analytic design, but with little or no attempt to quantify. After all, the study was to be largely exploratory, and the nature of its findings would not hinge on the importance of a few percentage points on a number of variables, but rather on the ability to tease out theoretically significant processes and relationships.

Nevertheless, it early became apparent that, if only for purely comparative purposes, it would be desirable to have certain basic data about the organizations (their size, budgets, age, etc.) recorded in systematic fashion through use of a schedule. At that time, some of the analytic propositions had already been formulated, and others were being added. Some of the variables employed in these propositions appeared to lend themselves to assessment through schedule-type data. Hence, an attempt was made to incorporate them into the schedules, which began to grow in size. As a result, it was found possible to devise means of arriving at distributions through the use of schedule data. It thus seemed possible to test several of the propositions which it was earlier believed could not be tested in any systematically rigorous fashion, but which had been considered merely as guides for data gathering. Indeed, at one point it even seemed feasible to use schedule data exclusively for the entire analysis, and to accumulate supplementary qualitative data only as background information, and only in moderate fashion.

Two considerations kept us from going over completely to the side of making only quantitative analyses. One was that in this largely unplowed field it seemed both naïve and presumptuous to assume that we had the knowledge or ability to determine in advance the important variables, processes, structures, etc. The other was the realization that the quantifiable variables and propositions constructed from them treated organizational interaction only from the level of the individual organizations, and not from the level of the interorganizational field. Hence, provision was made for narrative reports as well as schedule data.

When the early narrative reports began to come in, it became impressively apparent that an analysis based on the statistical manipulation of schedule data exclusively would be highly fragmentary. Later in the study sequence, it was also realized that such an analysis would be not only fragmentary but also misleading, through its failure to deal with crucial considerations revealed by the narrative data and through its failure to raise what appeared to be highly important issues that dealt with how the schedule data were to be interpreted. As indicated in Chapter 2, these issues are largely subsumable under the choice of analytical paradigms—whether interaction is conceived from the analytical level of the specific interacting organizations or from the standpoint of their aggregate modes of interaction, the interorganizational field.

Later in this chapter the relation of this choice of paradigms to the question of types of data and analysis will be examined at length. As a preliminary to that, we present next the types of data and methods of data gathering.

Selection of Organizations

The community decision organizations selected for special study in this project were the urban renewal agency, the public school system administration, the mental health planning agency, the health and welfare planning council, the community action agency, and the Model Cities agency. The total number of community decision organizations fitting the conceptual definition was so great that it seemed wise not to study them all, but rather to single out a few for intensive study. There was little point to probability sampling, and so a purposive sample was made, based on a number of guiding considerations. Because of the decision to take special note of the Model Cities planning process, it was decided to select organizations likely to be involved in such a process. At the same time, these would be organizations involved in the social problems of the inner city, the broad substantive area in which we were primarily interested. We selected CDOs likely to be drawn into the Model Cities planning process.

Several other considerations governed the selection of the six CDOs. These included governmental/nongovernmental status, program/planning ratio, determinacy of organizational rationale, and purview (single-field/multi-field). The attempt was made to include a broad distribution of CDOs on each of these dimensions, so that, for example, they would not be confined only to governmental CDOs, or to CDOs with a high program/planning ratio, etc., but would be varied on these dimensions.

Thus, in governmental/nongovernmental status, the health and welfare planning councils are all nongovernmental, and the school system administrations are all governmental, while the four other organizations distribute themselves variously on this dimension, being governmental but with different types of relationship to the line authority of the municipal government, etc.

Likewise, on program/planning ratio, the school system administration has a high program component, being charged with providing regular public education for the city's children as a program, while the health and welfare planning councils are largely confined to planning and tend to shun direct program activities.

Some, like the urban renewal agencies, have a relatively determinate organizational rationale, while others, like the Model Cities agencies, have a much less determinate organizational rationale. Although at the time of sampling this difference was expressed in less sophisticated terms simply as degree of bureaucratization, the result was the same.

Finally, some of the CDOs in the sample, like the mental health planning agency, have a fairly restricted field of purview, while others extend across several fields, like the community action agency.

With a broad distribution on the above dimensions in mind, the six CDOs were purposively selected.

It should be stressed that these six CDOs are not thought of as constituting a special interaction system in themselves, but rather merely a sampling from a larger group of CDOs that interact with each other in varying degrees. Other CDOs, such as the local health department, the local welfare department, or the chamber of commerce might have been chosen, while on the other hand, such CDOs as a bridge and tunnel authority were considered more remote from the ongoing interaction around programs such as Model Cities and hence were deliberately excluded.

Selection of Cities

The rationale for the selection of the cities in the sample was somewhat similar to that for the selection of CDOs. The nine cities were likewise chosen on a purposive basis rather than on a basis of probability or random sampling. A number of constraints governed this choice. First, being essentially cowards, we simply refused to consider New York, Chicago, and Los Angeles. On the other hand, it seemed desirable to choose cities that were large enough to have a full complement of CDOs. Because of the presumed importance of the Model Cities interaction, the cities were restricted to those sixty-three cities that at the time (November 1967) had been approved for Model Cities planning grants.

It was decided to select medium-sized cities (250,000 to 750,000 population as of 1965) for seven of the nine, and to add a small city and a large one in order to explore the extent to which the size factor appeared to make an important impact on what happened. From the thirty-one approved cities that fell within the population limits indicated, seven were selected as follows: For each of the thirty-one cities, a rank order was calculated on nine different "hard data" dimensions, such as per capita income in 1965 and percent of families with incomes under $3000 in the designated Model Neighborhood Area.[a]

[a]The full list: Region of U.S.; 1965 population of SMSA; percent change in population 1950-60; percent nonwhite in total population, 1965; per capita effective buying income; percent of families under $3000 in Model Neighborhood Area, urban growth and development index, and socioeconomic status index, 1960.

In addition, the thirty-one cities were rated on four "soft data" dimensions taken from the Model Cities planning grant applications: degree of apparent commitment to the idea of resident participation; degree to which the application was oriented toward "social" rather than "bricks and mortar" programs; degree of apparent innovativeness in the proposed program; and strength of apparent commitment to mental health as an integral part of the program. Working with the lists of rank orders, the staff selected a group of seven cities, which in aggregate were broadly distributed on all thirteen dimensions.

In addition, Manchester, N.H. (1965 population 90,000) was selected as the small city, and Detroit (1965 population 1,660,000) as the large city.

Thus, in sum, seven cities of approximately the same size were chosen (actually, they varied only between 378,000 and 616,000) and one small city and one large city were added. The complete list, alphabetically: Atlanta, Boston, Columbus, Denver, Detroit, Manchester, Newark, Oakland, San Antonio.

Dimensional Sampling

The procedure for selecting sample CDOs and cities had its basis in the analytical objectives of the study, including the objective of assessing, in a sample of CDOs, the extent of association between certain variables. These presumed relationships were expressed in advance in the form of analytic propositions, which were then tested with the data of the study. Hence, in Zetterberg's terms, this part of the analysis constituted a verification study rather than a descriptive study. Zetterberg writes that the "relatively minor importance of representativeness in verification studies is in sharp contrast to the overwhelming importance of representativeness of samples in descriptive studies."[1] But he also cautions: "When using a biased sample for a verification, we must have assurance that the relationship we want to prove is not introduced into our data by selective sampling. This possibility, however, is in most cases rather unlikely."[2] With the sampling procedure used in this study, such introduction of bias seems highly unlikely, and on the other hand, the sample has the advantage of assuring broad representation on dimensions believed to be pertinent.

The procedure employed is aptly characterized as "dimensional sampling." Arnold states, "What is required to protect against bias is to lay out the dimensions along which the cases vary and then examine at least one example of each type case."[3] Rather than selecting cities and organizations to fit specific "cells" however, the procedure of this study was to assure broad distribution along the pertinent dimensions. It accords with the admonition by Glaser and Strauss: "The adequate theoretical sample is judged on the basis of how widely and diversely the analyst chose his groups for saturating categories according to the type of theory he wished to develop."[4]

The sample of the same six organizations in each of nine cities provided the basis for cross-city comparisons of types of CDOs (for instance, how the nine community action agencies compared with the nine health and welfare councils) but at the same time provided a total of fifty-four community decision organizations for purposes of testing the presumed relationship between certain variables. Thus, the study is not simply an aggregation of fifty-four different "case studies" or organizations, although it includes this component; nor is it simply an ex post facto analysis of data gathered from fifty-four organizations, although it includes this component also.

As a more tangible basis for considering the analytical strategy of the study, it is helpful for the reader to have a more specific grasp of the data-gathering process, the types of data gathered, the forms in which the data were gathered, and the field procedures.

Research Chronology

A brief tracing of the chronology of the research project follows:

Spring 1966. Preliminary interviews with executives of community decision organizations in Boston, Philadelphia, and Detroit with the aim of developing a study of community decision organizations in their interaction. Data gathering and analysis on the development of four different action projects in Boston which involved considerable organizational interaction. Preparation of two journal articles on community decision organizations. Staff work on developing a research proposal.

Spring 1967. Submission of research proposal to National Institute of Mental Health. Preliminary work on project with a view toward becoming operational with the approval of proposal.

Fall 1967. Research grant award by Metro Center of NIMH. Engaging staff and developing data-gathering instruments preparatory to commencing intensive field data collection.

July 1968 through August 1970. Field data collection by half-time field research associates in each of the nine cities. Some preliminary analysis of data, particularly narrative reports, as these became available from the field research associates.

Summer 1970. End of intensive field data collection, submission of final narrative reports and remaining schedules, final week of debriefing and staff consultations with field research associates.

Fall 1970 through summer 1971. Data reduction and analysis. Testing of analytic propositions. Preparation of substantive analysis of various topics, preparation of a number of preliminary journal articles.

Summer 1971 through spring 1973. Drafting of present book.

During the course of the study, considerable contact was maintained with the

Model Cities Administration and other federal agencies, and occasional trips to the field cities were made by members of the central staff. In all, three seminars, each lasting one week, were held at Brandeis University for central staff and field research associates.

The field research associates (FRAs) were young men and women, several of whom held masters degrees in some relevant subject, such as political science, social work, or sociology. Most of them had had work experience considered pertinent to the subject matter under investigation. Considerable effort was taken to secure comparability among these FRAs both in the more formally gathered data and in the narrative reports. Much time was spent with them in developing common procedures. Key terms were carefully defined, and specific instructions were given for the administration of each schedule or narrative report. Occasionally, clarification was requested from an FRA on some important but ambiguous point in the narrative data. Schedules were carefully edited and returned for correction if found not to conform with instructions.

Narrative Data

There follows a brief description of the types of narrative data gathered during the study period.

Narrative Reports

During the period of the field research, six specific narrative reports were secured from the field research associates in each city. These were neither simple chronologies nor completely undirected as to content. Each was based on a specific, prescribed topic, and followed a prescribed, written outline for the subtopics to be treated. Within this strict set of limitations, considerable leeway was permitted as to how the material was to be covered and as to the inclusion of material not specifically requested but thought by the field research associate to be pertinent. Two different reports covered the chronology of development of the Model Cities program, with specific emphasis on the participation of the sample CDOs in this process. One report was devoted to citizen participation and organizational responsiveness for the six CDOs in each city. Three reports were devoted to various aspects of the patterning of mental health agencies and services in the cities and the participation of mental health agencies in the Model Cities process.

Interview and Discussion Protocols

On three different occasions during the period of the field data gathering, debriefing interviews were conducted around certain key questions with each of the nine field research associates. These interviews were transcribed verbatim and added to the narrative data. Likewise, at the three seminars, round table discussions were conducted in which the field research associates exchanged information and opinions with each other and with the central staff on a number of topics of central importance. These protocols were also added to the narrative data.

Although not required to do so, the field research associates occasionally wrote special brief reports about some topic they considered sufficiently important to communicate to the central staff.

Action Episode Reports

Of special importance was a study of action episodes in which each CDO participated, preferably, though not exclusively, involving interaction with a second CDO from the study's sample. These were episodes of ad hoc interaction around some issue. Three episodes were requested for each CDO, or a total of eighteen per city, or 162 in aggregate. The actual total of usable episodes (complete on the relevant variables, and conforming to the definition and other constraints) was 141. These were added to the other narrative data, as well as forming the basis for a special study.

Central Staff Field Reports

Occasional visits to the nine cities were made by members of the central staff. Where these entailed interviews with individuals from the sample CDOs or other organizations involved in significant interaction with them, these reports were added to the narrative documents.

Newspaper Clippings and Documents

Clippings of pertinent newspaper accounts were kept throughout the study, in addition to a collection of pertinent documents including annual reports, etc. These were used for background, but not incorporated into the narrative data.

The field research associates not only spent large amounts of time in gathering the data for the schedules and narrative reports through interviews, but also spent considerable amounts of time at meetings of various sorts, especially in connection with the Model Cities program itself.

Schedule Data

There follows a brief description of the formal schedules used for gathering systematic comparative data geared to the variables of the study:

Organization Fact Sheet Schedule

Relatively "hard" data concerning each sample CDO, its age, number and types of personnel, organizational structure, and other pertinent, relatively objectively ascertainable facts that could be filled out by a delegate of the executive director.

CDO Schedule

A lengthy schedule of questions broken down into five conceptual categories or areas: Domain, input, output, interaction, and miscellaneous. The informant in each case was the CDO's executive director or a person delegated by him.

CDA Schedule

Similar to the CDO Schedule, but designed especially for the City Demonstration Agency (Model Cities Agency), which came into being during the study and required a modified schedule.

Citizen Participation Schedule

This schedule was the primary source of systematic comparable data on the "responsiveness" variable. Three copies were filled out for each CDO, the informants being respectively the executive director or his delegate, the chairman of the Model Neighborhood Board, and the leader of a "militant" minority organization.

Major Change Schedule

This was the primary source of data on innovation, although that term was not employed in the schedule. It considered major changes separately under the following categories: organizational functions and programs, organizational structure and administration, relationships with other organizations, and "other major changes." The informant was the chief executive or his delegate.

Leadership Style Schedule

This schedule presented three models of leadership style, labelled simply A, B, and C, each of which described along nine different dimensions an "ideal type" of leadership style (charismatic, bureaucratic, and collegial). Field research associates were asked to classify each of the six executive directors under one of these types or under a "don't know" category. In another part, they were asked to select from the six executives the one who best exemplified each type. The schedules were filled out after nearly two years of contact with the organization.

Affiliation Schedule

This schedule supplied data on the racial or ethnic aspects of each CDO from the standpoint of its membership, its personnel, its program orientation, and its input constituency.

Some of these schedules were both lengthy and detailed. The long CDO schedule was administered at three different points in time, the Organization Fact Sheet Schedule at two different points in time.

Data Classification

The precodable data from the schedules were punched on IBM cards. In some cases, special tabulations and classifications were made directly from the schedules or from the narrative data.

The narrative data, amounting to several thousand pages, were indexed for ready retrieval on the basis of 168 defined variables, through the use of the Key-dex system. Every page of narrative reports was coded for the appearance of any of the 168 variables. A card system then provided for the retrieval of the numbers of the pages where a particular variable appeared. In addition, it permitted the ready identification of pages where any given combination of variables appeared, so that such pages could be readily retrieved by a clerk for qualitative examination by the staff.

The large number of variables in the Key-dex is explainable in that we wanted to make as inclusive provision as possible for subsequent identification and retrieval of narrative data. The principal variables of the study are much fewer in number. They formed the basis for the analytic propositions that were systematically tested, as well as for more holistic analysis. They are as follows:

Interaction
  Nature of paired interaction (cooperation/contest/conflict)
  Nature of predominant interaction style of each CDO (cooperation/ contest)
  Frequency of interaction
  Strength of interaction
Innovation
  Gross

Secondary
Primary
Responsiveness
Gross
Secondary
Primary
Organizational decision-making context
Program/planning ratio
Leadership style of executive director
Closeness of service fields
Breadth of domain (single field/multifield)
Environmental opportunities
Environmental threats
Domain consensus
Professional diversity
Dependence upon local organizations for financial resources

These variables are defined at the point in the text chapters where they first appear.

Having described the types of data under consideration, we turn to the methods of analysis.

Qualitative and Quantitative Analysis

The types of data gathered reflect the resolution of two questions that arose as the study developed. The first was whether to study the interrelationship of a small number of variables very quantitatively across a large number of organizations, using economical and perhaps superficial operationalized measures of variables and adhering to a rigid frame of statistical analysis, or to study a broader area of concern with only a few organizations, more intensely, less quantitatively, thus gaining a more inclusive understanding of the characteristics of organizational interaction, but losing the possibility of rigorous empirical testing. The advantages and disadvantages of each approach are widely known, and we need not review them here. In the case of this study, the decision was made to combine aspects of both.

The second question was closely related: whether to confront the subject matter with a tightly preconceived design, carefully structured to answer a few questions in fairly definitive fashion, or to move in more flexibly, not forcing the data into preconceived categories but rather letting the categories of analysis develop empirically out of the experience of the study itself.

Based on our preliminary theoretical conceptualization of the relationship between community decision organizations, a program was developed for gathering qualitative data (largely in narrative form) in close relationship to careful definition of variables considered to be important, and in systematic fashion that would help assure comparability. In addition, it was anticipated that as the study progressed, new leads would develop and be exploited from preliminary analysis of the narrative data coming in. Thus, from the beginning, clear and systematic provision was made for data gathering with respect to certain variables, but at the same time provision was left for modifications, extensions, or supplementations, as these appeared promising.

The Analytic Propositions

Likewise from the beginning, a number of analytic propositions were developed, which might be considered as hypotheses derived from the theoretical formulations. We preferred to call them analytic propositions rather than hypotheses, since that ambiguous term might be confusing. We simply have tested rigorously a number of statements that were formulated in advance and report the extent to which they were supported by the data. But in addition to these analytic propositions, it was anticipated that other findings—whether qualitatively or quantitatively grounded—would emerge from the research.

Thus, we *do* have fifty-four individual case studies. But we also have analytic statements about the relation among specified variables as this was studied systematically with an *n* of fifty-four organizations.

Hence, the study has been both qualitative and quantitative, both rigorously designed and open-ended. It has maintained a close relationship between empirical data and methodology, where the nexus between the two is concept formation and the progressive exploration of the relationship of these concepts to each other within a theoretical framework which is modified in the process. The procedure embodies a point of view well stated by Zetterberg: "The progress toward validity lies in a continuous adjustment of theorizing to the techniques of research, and in a continuous adjustment of techniques of research to theorizing."[5]

The importance of the point at issue warrants further detailed consideration. Let us begin with the relation of a number of propositions to each other within some inclusive logical context. It is widely agreed that a desirable theory is comprised of a number of interrelated, mutually consistent and mutually reinforcing propositions which in turn are verifiable empirically.[6]

Weiss adapts this principle to holistic research by asserting that the latter does not aim to test a set of hypotheses, "but rather at the discovery of organization, patterning, or system in what is being studied." He then states that such holistic research generates not hypotheses but models, and that "if these models are to be tested, it must again be by means of holistic research."[7]

The present study attempts both the holistic description of the organization, patterning, or system in the interorganizational field of CDOs and modifies the initial system description on the basis of both qualitative analysis of the narrative data and the quantitative findings on the specific analytic propositions.

There is a considerable degree of commonality of this methodology with that proposed by Glaser and Strauss. It accords with their emphasis on generating hypotheses from data rather than exclusively by deduction from previous theory.[8] But the present approach differs from theirs in a number of respects.

First, we *did* enter upon the study with some preconceived notions of what was important, and of which relationships we wanted to study with special intensity. These notions came from previously existing theory, from our own exploratory studies, and from a process of examining why we thought certain variables were important—in terms of their presumed effect on other variables.

Second, Glaser and Strauss emphasize a procedure of successive selective sampling, changing the groups to be studied in accordance with the emerging findings and their indication of new theoretical leads. In the present study, rather than changing the sampling base as new questions emerged and as some earlier hypotheses appeared to be false leads, we retained the same sample, addressing new questions to it and gathering new or modified forms of data accordingly, while preserving the design with regard to the original variables that we wished to retain. Part of the reason for retaining the sample throughout is that we were more interested in establishing as firmly as possible whether or not certain relationships existed within the types of CDOs we were studying than we were in expanding the categories of organizations to which the propositions might apply.

In addition, we probably place relatively more weight than do Glaser and Strauss on verification as distinguished from hypothesis creation, or theory building. But from the beginning, we took the early theoretical formulations as tentative, subject to modification, though nevertheless valuable in constituting a better guide to finding significant relationships than as though we had entered the field "theory-less." And in effect, the initial formulation received considerable modification and transformation.

In still a different way the study's methodology approaches the procedures outlined by Glaser and Strauss, but departs from them in important details. They state:

In the beginning, one's hypotheses may seem unrelated, but as categories and properties emerge, develop in abstraction, and become related, their accumulating interrelations form an integrated central theoretical framework—*the core of the emerging theory*. The core becomes a theoretical guide to the further collection and analysis of data.[9]

But in this study, the hypotheses, or analytic propositions, were formulated in advance. What emerged was not so much a set of restated analytic propositions as a different theoretical context within which the propositions took on a different meaning. This different theoretical context did not emerge directly from an attempt to refine and order the relationships of a set of individual propositions to each other, as Glaser and Strauss suggest, but rather from a much more holistic study of the processes that were occurring and ascertainable from the standpoint of the inclusive interorganizational level.

The analytic propositions are constructed from the variables listed earlier in this chapter. They were tested in a manner similar to the testing of conventional hypotheses. Variables were defined and operationalized, and classifications or ranks or numerical values assigned, employing various statistical measures to ascertain whether the presumed relationships held. Various tests of significance were employed, in addition to measures of association wherever possible. The tests of significance assessed at least roughly the likelihood that such differences as were found could be attributable merely to sampling error rather than to systematic differences in the universes represented by the sample. To be sure, purposive samples cannot strictly speaking be assumed to be either random or representative in any definitive sense; nor do we claim that they are. But unless the actual degree of association was large enough to be significant at the .05 level, we have preferred to consider the analytic proposition to be unsupported by the data.

Those propositions that could be tested for an n of 54 were tested either with a repeated-observations, one-way ANOVA design, a technique appropriate for cases where the samples cannot be assumed to be independent, and where nominal rather than interval data are employed; or with the DATA-TEXT compute correlations option where calculation of a Pearsonian r was appropriate. In one case, a Fisher's Exact Test for contingency tables was used. In a number of cases where the analytic propositions were tested against the qualitative data of the action episodes, chi square was employed. In various multivariate analyses, depending on the nature of the variables, partial correlation, discriminate analysis, two-way analysis of variance, and analysis of covariance were utilized. The results of these analyses are not reported because they did not substantially alter the implications of the bivariate analyses reported in the testing of the analytical propositions.

Although of course not all possible relationships between the study variables formed the basis for analytic propositions, a correlation matrix was later constructed for the relationship between all possible pairs of variables, and some interesting associations were discovered which had not been hypothesized in advance. The more meaningful ones are reported in the pertinent chapters, along with the findings on the analytic propositions. Virtually all the analytic propositions are bivariate, and of course therefore the effect of extraneous variables on any given relationship must be taken into consideration. This was done through multivariate analysis and, we think more importantly, through a consideration of the more contextual narrative data and the relationships which the latter suggested. In this connection, Zetterberg's "steps in confirming a proposition" were found to be helpful.[10]

The preceding three paragraphs may give an exaggerated sense of rigor and definitiveness. We are well aware of the difficulties involved in drawing conclusions from quantitative manipulation of such relatively "soft" data as were gathered in this study. Nevertheless, it was felt that some minimal statistical rigor was appropriate.

Narrative Data Analysis

The analysis of the narrative data, on the other hand, followed no previously described course of development. It arose as a dynamic interaction process among various staff members as they perused the narrative data and also examined various completed schedules to get a sense of what these data showed by way of variable indicators. The central staff included not only the present authors but a number of students working intensively on organizing the narrative data around certain topics or questions. These efforts generated a number of questions regarding the substance of what was taking place, as did the periodic discussions with the nine field research associates. Why was it so difficult for the FRAs to find instances of ad hoc interaction between community decision organizations? What was the interaction that they did find all about? What kinds of processes seemed to be operating in relation to instances of innovation or of increased responsiveness? How did various social problems get defined by these organizations, by neighborhood groups? What different interactional styles could be adduced from the rich narrative sources on organizational interaction? What became of attempts at various kinds of coordination? What did these organizations actually contest or cooperate about? To what extent, and how, did such interaction appear to make a difference—in what?

Such questions sent the staff back for successively more refined perusal of the narrative data. They also led to extensive interactional efforts directed at conceptual clarification. They were followed by additional efforts at gathering new narrative data designed to throw further light on the puzzling questions, and to check out various hunches as to what was or was not taking place. Although most of the analytic propositions could not be tested until all the data had been gathered, it became apparent in the case of some of these propositions what the final results were likely to be. In the case of the principal variables of cooperation-contest, innovation, and responsiveness, it was gradually concluded that failure to recognize important qualitative aspects of these variables would result in a confused and misleading set of findings. The variables were therefore refined into qualitatively different subvariables, and the analytic propositions were later tested using not only the gross variables, but also the more qualitatively different distinctions within them. The qualitative analysis thus reflected back upon the quantitative methodology for testing the analytic propositions. The qualitative analysis was also influenced in part by the fragmentary early findings from the quantitative data. But these were only one small part of the qualitative considerations, and a minor one.

The qualitative analysis led us inexorably to certain kinds of questions that had been entirely neglected in the quantitative data-gathering instruments and strategy. They forced us to consider questions of the inclusive historical context, questions that had to be rigorously excluded in simpler quantitative analysis. Why, after all, did responsiveness appear to merit special study? Why was it important? What were the important issues around citizen participation? What kinds of threats did such participation pose to these organizations? And what were the ways in which they sought to protect their viability in the face of such threats? Similarly, what kinds of innovation were at issue? How did these relate to agency viability? Where did coordination fit in? Did it appear to make a noticeable difference? To whom? In what way? There were many more such questions, questions that required a qualitative understanding of the context of the interaction we were studying, and questions, incidentally, on which our analytical propositions could throw little direct light. For after all, the analytical propositions, following conventional research procedures, were quantified and abstracted in a way that blurred out everything but the particular variables as measured by the operationalized indicators. Even the testing against a number of intermediate variables, the holding of certain variables constant, etc., could not add information that is necessarily lost in the rigorous reduction process required in such quantitative strategies.

Procedures for Paired Interaction Analysis

The procedure for paired interaction analysis provided a method for judging the frequency and nature of interaction between pairs of CDOs in each of the nine cities, and rating the pairs in order to test the study's analytical propositions. There were essentially two parts to this sequence: first, combing the narrative and schedule data for instances of interaction; second, judging, ranking, and analyzing the nature of interaction.

Each CDO was paired with each of the other sample CDOs in its city (ED-CAA, ED-UR, UR-MC, etc.). No Model Cities Schedule was available for the Oakland Model Cities Agency, so in Oakland only ten, rather than fifteen pairs were judged. The overall total of pairs was thus not 135, but 130. The data on instances of interaction between each pair were aggregated and classified. A count of such interactions yielded the variable called "number of interactions." The nature of the interaction, however, required an intricate scheme for aggregation.

The initial step in the analytical process involved the summary of instances of interaction from the narrative data and from selected schedule questions taken from the Organizational Fact Sheet, the CDO Schedules, and the Model Cities

Schedules. Such data were recorded for each CDO pair on a paired interaction takeoff form.

All of the narrative data had been coded according to 168 predefined coded variables, using the Key-dex System for retrieval. Twenty-four of these variables were utilized as sources of data on interaction.

In the second part of the data takeoff procedure, three items from the Organizational Fact Sheets were used, as well as twenty-one items from the CDO Schedules and thirteen items from the Model Cities Schedules. These items were systematically scanned and the data from them were recorded on the second part of the interaction takeoff form.

The assessment of paired interaction between each pair of CDOs involved two major steps: (1) individual ratings on the interaction scale for each pair by three judges, independently, and (2) discussion of the individual ratings by all three persons, arriving at a consensus rating in the cases where they differed.

Paired interaction was classified on a five-point scale:

1. Cooperation
2. Mostly cooperation, with some contest
3. Approximately equal cooperation and contest
4. Mostly contest, with some cooperation
5. Contest.

In this scale, cooperation is defined as instances of interaction between two or more organizations in order to bring about the same desired issue outcome, and contest is defined as instances of interaction between two or more organizations in order to bring about contrary desired issue outcomes. (See page 45 ff.)

Each instance from the paired interaction takeoff forms was listed and rated by each of the three judges as to the level of cooperation and/or contest. There was also space on the form for comments by the person judging to comment on the reason for a particular rating, unusual variations in the interaction, etc. The level of cooperation and contest was judged (each separately) as high, moderate, or low. While there were no hard and clear criteria for judging the level of interaction, there were indicators that each judge took into account: intensity, amount of resources allocated to the interaction by each organization, importance or significance of the interaction to each organization. If an episode showed elements of both cooperation and contest (i.e., initial cooperation on running a program that develops into contest over a particular aspect of the program, or initial contest that is resolved and leads to cooperation) the level of both types of interaction was rated separately.

A summary judgment of all these instances of interaction for each CDO pair was then made by each judge. This summary judgement again rated the level of contest and/or cooperation as high, medium, or low. Instances of contest and instances of cooperation were given separate summary ratings.

These separate summary judgments of cooperation and contest for each CDO pair were then aggregated into one single inclusive judgment by each judge, reflecting the predominant nature of interaction over time between the two CDOs in the pair.

The three judges then reviewed their classifications together, going first through the individual instances and then comparing their summary judgments. The judgments were made by pairs of CDOs, city by city, with 130 pairs altogether. All pairs were judged before any attempt was made to aggregate the resultant rankings, thus preventing any biased feedback into the initial judgments out of which the summary judgments were to be formulated.

Notes

Notes

Chapter 1
Community Decision Organizations and Urban Reform

1. This circumstance is treated in Roland L. Warren, *The Community in America*, 2nd enlarged edition (Chicago: Rand McNally & Co., 1972), chapter 7: "Alternative Auspices for the Performance of Locality-Relevant Functions."

2. The following will serve as examples:

Herbert Gans, *The Urban Villagers* (New York: The Free Press of Glencoe, 1961).

Harold Kaplan, *Urban Renewal Politics: Slum Clearance in Newark* (New York: Columbia University Press, 1963).

Martin Meyerson and Edward C. Banfield, *Politics, Planning, and the Public Interest: The Case of Public Housing in Chicago* (Glencoe, Ill.: The Free Press of Glencoe, 1955).

Russell D. Murphy, *Political Entrepreneurs and Urban Poverty: The Strategies of Policy Innovation in New Haven's Model Anti-Poverty Project* (Lexington, Mass.: D.C. Heath Lexington Books, 1971).

David Rogers, *110 Livingston Street* (New York: Random House, 1968).

Peter H. Rossi and Robert A. Dentler, *The Politics of Urban Renewal: The Chicago Findings* (New York: The Free Press of Glencoe, 1961).

John R. Seeley, *Community Chest: A Case Study in Philanthropy* (Toronto: University of Toronto Press, 1957).

Louis A. Zurcher, Jr., *Poverty Warriors: The Human Experience of Planned Social Intervention* (Austin, Texas: University of Texas Press, 1970).

3. Among the noteworthy are:

Michael Aiken and Robert R. Alford, "Community Structure and Innovation: The Case of Urban Renewal," *American Sociological Review* 35:4, August 1970.

_____ , "Community Structure and Innovation: The Case of Public Housing," *American Political Science Review* 64:3, September 1970.

_____ , "Comparative Urban Research and Community-Decision-Making," *The New Atlantis* 1:2, Winter 1970.

Alan S. Altshuler, *The City Planning Process*, (Ithaca: Cornell University Press, 1965).

Terry N. Clark, *Community Structure and Decision-Making: Comparative Analyses* (San Francisco: Chandler Publishing Co., 1968).

_____ , "Community Structure, Decision-Making, Budget Expenditures, and Urban Renewal in 51 American Communities," *American Sociological Review* 33:4, August 1968.

Marilyn Gittell and T. Edward Hollander, *Six Urban School Districts* (New York: Frederick A. Praeger, Publishers, 1968).

Scott Greer, *Urban Renewal in American Cities: The Dilemma of Democratic Intervention* (Indianapolis: Bobbs-Merrill, 1965).

Amos Hawley, "Community Power and Urban Renewal Success," *American Journal of Sociology* 68:4, January 1964.

Ralph M. Kramer, *Participation of the Poor: Comparative Case Studies in the War on Poverty* (Englewood Cliffs, N.J.: Prentice-Hall, Inc., 1969).

Frank W. Lutz, *Politics, Power, and Policy: The Governing of Local School Districts* (Columbus, Ohio: Charles E. Merrill, 1970).

Peter Marris and Martin Rein, *The Dilemmas of Social Reform* (New York: Atherton Press, 1967).

Francine F. Rabinovitz, *City Politics and Planning* (New York: Atherton Press, 1969).

William Ryan and Ali Banuazizi, *Mental Health Planning in Metropolitan Areas* (Boston: Boston College, 1971).

Charles E. Silberman, *Crisis in the Classroom: The Remaking of American Education* (New York: Random House, 1970).

4. Roland L. Warren, "The Interaction of Community Decision Organizations: Some Basic Concepts and Needed Research," *Social Service Review* 41:3, September 1967, and "The Interorganizational Field As A Focus for Investigation," *Administrative Science Quarterly* 12:3, December 1967.

5. William Lilley III, "Urban Report/Model Cities Program Faces Uncertain Future Despite Romney Overhaul," *National Journal*, October 11, 1970. This report gives an excellent summary of developments in the program at the federal level.

Chapter 2
The Interorganizational Field

1. Thomas S. Kuhn, *The Structure of Scientific Revolutions*, 2nd enlarged ed. (Chicago: University of Chicago Press, 1970).

2. Ibid., p. 94.

3. Much of the following paragraphs has been described at greater length in Roland L. Warren, "The Sociology of Knowledge and the Problems of the Inner Cities," *Social Science Quarterly* 52:3, December 1971.

4. Theodore J. Lowi, *The Politics of Disorder* (New York: Basic Books, Inc., 1971), pp. 18, 19.

5. Sol Levine and Paul E. White, "Exchange as a Conceptual Framework for the Study of Interorganizational Relationships," *Administrative Science Quarterly* 5:4 (March 1961), p. 597.

6. *American Journal of Sociology* 64:3, November 1958. The authors acknowledge a great debt to this article.

7. Reprinted by permission of the *Journal of the American Institute of Planners* 38:3 (May 1972), p. 138.

8. Ibid., p. 137.

9. F.E. Emery and E.L. Trist, "The Causal Texture of Organizational Environments," *Human Relations* 18:1 (February 1965), p. 28.

10. *The Politics of Disorder* (New York: Basic Books, Inc., 1971), p. xiv.

11. Robert K. Merton, *Social Theory and Social Structure*, rev. ed. (London: The Free Press of Glencoe, 1957). Statements of the distinction are given especially on pages 51, 63, 66, and 68.

12. Stephen M. Rose, *The Betrayal of the Poor: The Transformation of Community Action* (Cambridge, Mass.: Schenkman Publishing Co., 1972).

13. These concepts were given preliminary formulation by J. Wayne Newton, of the project staff, in a mimeographed paper on "Cooptation in the Interaction of Community Decision Organizations," Florence Heller Graduate School for Advanced Studies in Social Welfare, Brandeis University, December 1970.

Chapter 3
Interaction Among Community Decision Organizations

1. James D. Thompson and William J. McEwen, "Organizational Goals and Environment: Goal-Setting As an Interaction Process," *American Sociological Review* 23:1 (February 1958), p. 30.

2. Demonstration Cities and Metropolitan Development Act of 1966, Title I, Sec. 101.

3. For a more extended discussion of these points, see Roland L. Warren, "The Concerting of Decisions as a Variable in Organizational Interaction," in *Truth, Love, and Social Change: and Other Essays in Community Change* (Chicago: Rand McNally Co., 1971).

4. Sol Levine and Paul E. White, "Exchange as a Conceptual Framework for the Study of Interorganizational Relationships," *Administrative Science Quarterly* 5:4 (March 1961), p. 597. See also Sol Levine, Paul E. White, and Benjamin D. Paul, "Community Interorganizational Problems in Providing Medical Care and Social Services," *American Journal of Public Health* 35:8 (August 1963), pp. 1190-91.

5. James D. Thompson, *Organizations in Action: Social Science Bases of Administrative Theory* (New York: McGraw-Hill Book Co., 1967), p. 10.

6. Philip Selznick, *TVA and the Grass Roots* (New York: Harper Torchbooks, 1966) p. 13.

7. James D. Thompson and William J. McEwen, "Organizational Goals and Environment: Goal-Setting as an Interaction Process," *American Sociological Review* 23:1 (February 1958), pp. 27, 28.

8. The following paragraphs are adapted from an earlier paper on

"Cooptation among Community Decision Organizations" by J. Wayne Newton, of the study staff. Mimeographed, April 1971.

9. Reprinted in Martin Rein, *Social Policy: Issues of Choice and Change* (New York: Random House, 1970), pp. 371-72.

10. Peter L. Berger and Thomas Luckmann, *The Social Construction of Reality: A Treatise on the Sociology of Knowledge* (Garden City, N.Y.: Doubleday Anchor, 1967), p. 115.

Chapter 4
Interorganizational Coordination

1. Julie Gustafson, of the project staff, did much of the assembling and preliminary analysis of the data for this chapter.

2. Amitai Etzioni, *The Active Society: A Theory of Societal and Political Processes* (New York: The Free Press, 1968, p. 388).

3. The process has been examined in Roland L. Warren, "Concerted Decision-making in the Community," in the *Social Welfare Forum, 1965* (New York: Columbia University Press, 1965) and in "The Concerting of Decisions as a Variable in Organizational Interaction," in Matthew Tuite et al., eds. *Interorganizational Decision Making* (Chicago: Aldine Publishing Co., 1972). Both are reprinted in Warren's *Truth, Love, and Social Change.*

4. William Graham Sumner, *The Folkways: A Study of the Sociological Importance of Usages, Manners, Customs, Mores, and Morals* (Boston: Ginn and Company, 1906), p. 16ff.

5. Georg Simmel, *Conflict* and *The Web of Group-Affiliations*, trans. by Kurt H. Wolff and Reinhard Bendix (New York: The Free Press, 1955). The quotation is from the essay on *Conflict*, p. 14.

6. By J. Wayne Newton of the project staff.

7. Mayer N. Zald, "The Structure of Society and Social Service Integration," *Social Science Quarterly* 50:3. (December 1969), p. 558. Italics in original.

8. Gideon Sjoberg, "Contradictory Functional Requirements and Social Systems," *Journal of Conflict Resolution* 4:2, June 1960.

9. Martin Landau, "Redundancy, Rationality, and the Problem of Duplication and Overlap," *Public Administration Review* 29:4, July/August 1969.

10. Shirley Terreberry, "The Evolution of Organizational Environments," *Administrative Science Quarterly* 12:4 (March 1968), p. 605.

11. Ray H. Elling, "Health Organization and the Social Environment," mimeographed, p. 20.

12. Basil J.F. Mott, "Coordination and Inter-Organizational Relations in Health," in Paul E. White and George Vlasak, eds. *Interorganizational Research in Health* published jointly by the National Center for Health Services Research and Development and the Department of Behavioral Sciences, School of Hygiene and Public Health, Johns Hopkins University, 1971, p. 67-68.

13. Robert Boguslaw, *The New Utopians: a Study of System Design and Social Change* (Englewood Cliffs, N.J.: Prentice-Hall, Inc., 1965).

14. Aaron Wildavsky, "The Political Economy of Efficiency," *The Public Interest*, no. 8, Summer 1967.

Chapter 5
Innovation

1. H.G. Barnett, *Innovation: The Basis of Cultural Change* (New York: McGraw-Hill Book Company, 1953), p. 8.

2. Herbert A. Simon, "The Decision Maker As Innovator," in Sidney Mailick and Edward H. Van Ness, eds. *Concepts and Issues in Administrative Behavior* (Englewood Cliffs, N.J.: Prentice-Hall, Inc., 1962), p. 67.

3. William J. Gore, "Decision-Making Research: Some Prospects and Limitations," Ibid. See also his *Administrative Decision Making: An Heuristic Model* (New York: John Wiley & Sons, Inc., 1964).

4. Thomas L. Whisler, "The Meaning of Innovation," *Transaction* 2:2, Special Supplement (January-February 1965), p. 29.

5. James Q. Wilson, "Innovation in Organization: Notes Toward a Theory," in James D. Thompson, *Approaches to Organizational Design* (Pittsburgh: University of Pittsburgh Press, 1966), p. 196.

6. Victor A. Thompson, "Bureaucracy and Innovation," *Administrative Science Quarterly* 10:1 (June 1965), p. 1.

7. John Friedmann, "Planning as Innovation: The Chilean Case," *Journal of the American Institute of Planners* 32:4 (July 1966), p. 195 (italics in original).

8. See Stephen M. Rose, *The Betrayal of the Poor: The Transformation of Community Action* (Cambridge, Mass.: Schenkman Publishing Co., 1972), and Roland L. Warren, "The Sociology of Knowledge and the Problems of the Inner Cities," *Social Science Quarterly* 52:3, December 1971.

9. The point about alternative scientific theories is made strongly by Kuhn in his book on scientific revolutions, to which the authors acknowledge a great debt. The present discussion of explanatory paradigms is an extension of his analysis to the analogous field of social problems. See Thomas S. Kuhn, *The Structure of Scientific Revolutions*, second edition (Chicago: University of Chicago Press, 1970).

10. These are Selznick's terms. His distinction can be summarized as the distinction between participation that is significant, in the sense of "making a difference" in the outcome of decision making, and participation that is merely superficial, providing the illusion, rather than the reality, of significant participation in decision making. See Philip Selznick, *TVA and the Grass Roots: A Study in the Sociology of Formal Organization* (New York: Harper & Row, 1966) p. 220.

11. Steven Arthur Waldhorn and Judith Lynch Waldhorn, "Model Cities:

Liberal Myths and Federal Interventionist Programs," *Urban Law Annual*, 1972 (St. Louis, Mo.: Washington University School of Law, 1972).

12. "Model Cities: A Report on Progress," special issue of the *Model Cities Service Center Bulletin* 2:9, June 1971.

13. Op. cit., pp. 50-51.

14. Victor A. Thompson, "Bureaucracy and Innovation," op. cit., p. 4.

15. Michael Aiken and Jerald Hage, in their study of joint programs of health and welfare organizations, found that one of the highest correlates of innovation as measured in that study was "the number of different types of occupations in an organization and the number of joint programs (r equals 0.87)." See their "Organizational Interdependence and Intra-organizational Structure," *American Sociological Review* 33:6 (December 1968), p. 920.

16. Martin Rein, "Organization for Social Change," *Social Work* 9:2, April 1964.

17. Sol Levine and Paul E. White, "Exchange as a Conceptual Framework for the Study of Interorganizational Relationships," *Administrative Science Quarterly* 5:4 (March 1961), p. 590.

18. Op. cit.

19. Op. cit., p. 196.

20. James G. March and Herbert A. Simon, *Organizations* (New York: John Wiley & Sons, 1959), pp. 183-84.

21. James Q. Wilson, "Necessity versus the Devil," *Transaction* 2:2 (January-February 1965), p. 37-38.

22. See also his "Innovation in Organization: Notes Toward a Theory," op. cit. In this, he clearly asserts the importance of crisis (p. 108). In the light of the present analysis, one wonders whether greater discrimination as to the direction and qualitative difference of the innovations involved might throw light on the seeming contradictions.

23. Shirley Terreberry, "The Evolution of Organizational Environments," *Administrative Science Quarterly* 12:4 (March 1968), p. 610. Terreberry hypothesizes that "organizational change is largely externally induced."

Chapter 6
Responsiveness

1. In their book on *Regulating the Poor: The Functions of Public Welfare* (New York: Pantheon Books, 1971), Frances F. Piven and Richard A. Cloward marshal evidence to indicate that the expansion of welfare services is usually a response to periods of social unrest.

2. Philip Selznick, *TVA and the Grass Roots* (New York: Harper Torch Books, 1966), p. 220 ff.

3. Spiegel has developed this point in distinguishing between citizen participation as seen by the "program manager," an agency official, and citizen

participation as seen by the "neighborhood spokesman." See Hans B.C. Spiegel, "Citizen Participation in Federal Programs: A Review," *Journal of Voluntary Action Research*, Monograph No. 1, 1971, pp. 4-31.

4. Excerpted from a document on goals and methods for achieving a workable plan for the Model Cities program of one of the cities studied, by the local health and welfare council, dated January 1967.

5. Melvin B. Mogulof, *Citizen Participation: A Review and Commentary of Federal Policies and Practices* (Washington, D.C.: The Urban Institute, January 1970), page 78.

6. Andrew Lea, *Newark: Citizen Participation and Organizational Responsiveness.* Narrative Report No. 3, Interorganizational Study Project. Italics added.

7. Stephen D. Mittenthal and Hans B.C. Spiegel, *Urban Confrontation: City Versus Neighborhood in the Model Cities Planning Process* (New York: Institute of Urban Environment, School of Architecture, Columbia University, 1970), pp. 153, 154.

Chapter 7
The Oakland Economic Development
Council, Inc.

1. The material for this chapter comes primarily from the narrative reports of Martin Lowenthal, who was the field research associate in Oakland throughout the field period from July 1968 through August 1970. In addition, the following sources were utilized: Clippings from the *Oakland Tribune*, from which many of the verbatim quotations were taken; Shirley F. Barshay, *One Meaning of "Citizen Participation": A Report on the First Year of Model Cities in Oakland, California*, multigraphed document, no date; report from the Muleskinners Democratic Club of Oakland, no title, no date; a series of reports on the demise of the OEDCI by Valerie Jo Bradley in the *California Voice* in July and August, 1971. Other publications, especially by Melvin B. Mogulof, Hans B.C. Spiegel, Stephen D. Mittenthal, and Ralph M. Kramer were also read, but were not directly utilized in compiling this chapter.

2. Percy Moore, "The Case for the Oakland Approach to Model Cities Planning," unpublished manuscript, May 1968, (italics added).

3. In an interview with Valerie Jo Bradley published in the *California Voice* July 22, 1971.

4. Ibid.

5. Percy Moore, op. cit.

6. Interview with Valery Jo Bradley, op. cit.

7. Shirley F. Barshay, op. cit., p. 33.

8. Willard Waller has made use of the concept of summatory social

processes. See his *The Family: A Dynamic Interpretation* (New York: The Dryden Press, 1938); Coleman has described the dynamics of such escalation of contest in his *Community Conflict* (Glencoe: The Free Press, 1957).

9. According to a report in *Community Development*, Organ of the National Association for Community Development 6:3, February 1970.

Chapter 8
Implications for Organizational
Theory and Research

1. It would be superfluous to attempt here a complete listing of the burgeoning literature in this field. The recent publication by White and Vlasak is a useful starting place for those who seek such a review. Their publication encompasses not only health organizations, but a much broader purview. Paul E. White and George J. Vlasak, *Inter-Organizational Research in Health: Bibliography (1960-1970)* National Center for Health Services Research and Development, DHEW Publication No. (HSM) 72-3028.

2. In Sidney Mailick and Edward H. Van Ness, eds., *Concepts and Issues in Administrative Behavior* (Englewood Cliffs, N.J.: Prentice-Hall, Inc., 1962).

3. *American Journal of Sociology* 68:3, November 1962.

4. William Evan, "The Organization-Set: Toward a Theory of Interorganizational Relations," in James D. Thompson, ed., *Approaches to Organizational Design* (Pittsburgh: University of Pittsburgh Press, 1966).

5. *American Sociological Review* 23:1, February 1958.

6. *Administrative Science Quarterly* 10:2, September 1965.

7. In Raymond V. Bowers, ed., *Studies on Behavior in Organizations* (Athens: University of Georgia Press, 1966).

8. *Social Forces* 40:4, May 1962.

9. The fullest treatment is contained in *Towards the Multi-Factor Theory and Practice of Linkages between Formal Organizations* (Washington, D.C.: Social and Rehabilitative Services, U.S. Department of Health, Education, and Welfare, 1970).

10. "Exchange as a Conceptual Framework for the Study of Interorganizational Relationships," *Administrative Science Quarterly* 5:4, March 1961.

11. *Human Relations* 18:1 (February 1965), p. 28.

12. *Administrative Science Quarterly* 12:4, March 1968.

13. Mayer N. Zald, "The Structure of Society and Social Service Integration," *Social Science Quarterly* 50:3, December 1969.

14. *The Natural History of a Coordinating Council* (Pittsburgh: University of Pittsburgh Press, 1968).

15. *The New Atlantis* 1:2, Winter 1970.

16. Op. cit., p. 28. (Italics in original.)

17. Ibid., p. 29.

18. Ibid., p. 28. The sentences have been numbered here for ready reference.

19. William F. Whyte, "Social Organization In the Slums," *American Sociological Review* 8:1, February 1943; and Robert A. Nisbet, "Moral Values and Community," *International Review of Community Development*, no. 5, 1960.

20. See Thomas S. Kuhn, *The Structure of Scientific Revolutions*, 2nd enlarged ed. (Chicago: University of Chicago Press, 1970).

21. *Industrial and Labor Relations Review* 18:3, April 1965.

22. Ibid., p. 33.

23. *American Journal of Sociology* 68:4, January 1964.

24. For example, Terry N. Clark, "Community Structure, Decision-making, Budget Expenditures, and Urban Renewal in 51 American Communities," *American Sociological Review* 33:4, August 1968; Michael Aiken and Robert R. Alford, "Community Structure and Innovation: The Case of Urban Renewal," *American Sociological Review* 35:4, August 1970 and "Community Structure and Innovation: The Case of Public Housing," *American Political Science Review* 64:3, September 1970, and "Comparative Urban Research and Community Decision-Making," *The New Atlantis* 1:2, Winter 1970; Herman Turk, "Comparative Structure from an Interorganizational Perspective," *Administrative Science Quarterly* 18:1, March 1973.

25. Subsequent to the drafting of this chapter, Robert R. Alford has published a forceful criticism of these quantitative measures. See his "Quantitative Indicators of the Quality of Life: a Critique," *Comparative Urban Research*, Number 3, Summer 1973.

Chapter 9
Community Decision Organizations and
the Structure of Urban Reform

1. Cited in James L. Sundquist and David W. Davis, *Making Federalism Work: A Study of Program Coordination at the Community Level* (Washington, D.C.: The Brookings Institution, 1969), p. 41.

2. Daniel P. Moynihan, *The Negro Family: The Case for National Action* (Washington, D.C.: U.S. Department of Labor, Office of Policy Planning and Research, 1965), p. 29 ff.

3. Martin Rein, *Social Policy: Issues of Choice and Change* (New York: Random House, 1970), pp. 346-47.

4. James L. Sundquist and David W. Davis, op. cit., pp. 118-19.

5. John H. Strange, "The Impact of Citizen Participation on Public Administration," *Public Administration Review* vol. 32, September 1972, p. 468.

6. Bruno Stein, *On Relief: The Economics of Poverty and Public Welfare* (New York: Basic Books, 1971), p. 171, cited in Herbert Gans, "The Positive Functions of Poverty," *American Journal of Sociology* 78:2, September 1972.

7. William Bethea, "Regional Citizens' Group Looks at Model Cities," in *Model Cities: A Report on Progress*, special issue of the *Model Cities Service Center Bulletin* 2:9 (June 1971), p. 12.

Appendix
Methodology

1. Hans L. Zetterberg, *On Theory and Verification in Sociology*, third enlarged ed. (Totowa, N.J.: The Bedminster Press, 1965) pp. 129-30.

2. Ibid., p. 129.

3. David C. Arnold, "Dimensional Sampling: An Approach for Studying a Small Number of Cases," *American Sociologist* 5:2 (May 1970), p. 148.

4. Barney G. Glaser and Anselm L. Strauss, *The Discovery of Grounded Theory: Strategies for Qualitative Research* (Chicago: Aldine Publishing Co., 1967) p. 63.

5. Op. cit., p. 115.

6. Meehan puts it this way: "The goal in explanation is a perfect match or fit between a complete system and a description rather than a logical fit between a single event and a general proposition, as in the deductive paradigm." See Eugene J. Meehan, *Explanation in Social Science: A System Paradigm* (Homewood, Ill.: The Dorsey Press, 1968) p. 51. And Zetterberg: "To 'test' a theory, we check how well each of its propositions conforms to data and how well several propositions in conjunction with each other account for the outcome of a given situation" (op. cit., p. 28).

7. Robert S. Weiss, "Issues in Holistic Research," in Howard Becker et al, eds. *Institutions and the Person* (Chicago: Aldine Publishing Co., 1968), p. 342-58.

8. "Generating a theory from data means that most hypotheses and concepts not only come from the data, but are systematically worked out in relation to the data during the course of the research. *Generating a theory involves a process of research*" (op. cit., p. 6). Italics original.

9. Op. cit., p. 40.

10. Op. cit., p. 104 ff.

Index

Index

About the Authors

Roland L. Warren is Professor of Community Theory at the Florence Heller Graduate School for Advanced Studies in Social Welfare, Brandeis University. He is a widely known authority in the field of community, and the author of *Studying Your Community, The Community in America, Politics and the Ghettos, Perspectives on the American Community, Truth, Love, and Social Change*, and articles in numerous professional journals. Dr. Warren is the past chairman of the Committee on Community Research and Development of the Society for the Study of Social Problems, and chairman (1972-74) of the Community Section of the American Sociological Association. He is a former Guggenheim Fellow and the recipient of a research scientist award from the National Institute of Mental Health.

Stephen M. Rose is associate professor at the School of Social Welfare, State University of New York at Stony Brook. He has had extensive experience in consulting with citizens groups, and was engaged in research with the Office of Economic Opportunity on community action programs as well as at Brandeis University, where he participated in research on both Community Action and Model Cities. Dr. Rose is the author of numerous articles and papers on citizen participation, as well as of *The Betrayal of the Poor: The Transformation of Community Action*. He has recently completed a study on the experiences of discharged mental patients.

Ann F. Bergunder is a professional social worker in a special project of the New York City Legal Aid Society. Workers in the program plan with and counsel defendants during the duration of court cases and act as their advocates. In this work, she says, "I experience daily the contradictions analyzed in this book." Before coming to the Interorganizational Study Project at Brandeis, where she supervised the data analysis, Ms. Bergunder worked with the City of Dayton Planning Board and with the Montgomery County Welfare Department.